THE BOW AND THE LYRE

THE BOW AND THE LYRE

A Platonic Reading of the Odyssey

Seth Benardete

ROWMAN & LITTLEFIELD PUBLISHERS, INC.
Lanham • Boulder • New York • London

ROWMAN & LITTLEFIELD PUBLISHERS, INC.

Published in the United States of America
by Rowman & Littlefield Publishers, Inc.
4720 Boston Way, Lanham, Maryland 20706

3 Henrietta Street
London WC2E 8LU, England

British Cataloging in Publication Information Available

Library of Congress Cataloging-in-Publication Data
Benardete, Seth.
    The bow and the lyre : a Platonic reading of the Odyssey / Seth
Benardete.
        p.   cm
    Includes bibliographical references and index.
    ISBN 0–8476–8367–2 (alk. paper)
    1. Homer. Odyssey.   2. Odysseus (Greek mythology) in literature.
3. Epic poetry, Greek—History and criticism.   4. Philosophy,
Ancient, in literature.   5. Plato.   I. Title.
PA4037.B42   1997
883'.01—dc20   96-32657
                                                                    CIP

ISBN 0–8476–8367–2 (cloth : alk. paper)

Printed in the United States of America.

The *Odyssey*: Depth of thought with a surface simplicity

Eustathius

Contents

Notice to the Reader

The text used for the *Odyssey* is Peter von der Mühll's third Teubner edition (1984). I have followed, largely, its readings and punctuation, but have not necessarily followed its indications of interpolation.

In translating passages, I have omitted words and phrases if they are not essential for the interpretation. Passages I believe are interpolated are passed over without comment.

Most citations in the text refer to either the *Odyssey* or the *Iliad*. Arabic numbers designate the books of the *Odyssey*, Roman numerals, those of the *Iliad*.

Preface

More than forty years ago, when I first studied Homer, I used something I found in Plato in order to understand the plot of the *Iliad*; and later, when I studied Aeschylus and Sophocles, the ways in which Plato laid bare the prepolitical and the political elements that constitute the structure of the city, seemed to me to be a guide for the interpretation of *Prometheus, Seven against Thebes, Oedipus Tyrannus,* and *Antigone.* In all these cases, Plato was there as a map or grid that allowed me to trace out faint trails in older authors who could not guide me, through no fault of their own, as well as Plato could. He seemed to me to have given the arguments for what Homer, Aeschylus, and Sophocles had only shown. Logos, one might say, opened the way to the understanding of paradigm. Although I was vaguely aware that it could seem forced and willful if Plato was always there ahead of me, it never bothered me very much, any more than if one is wandering in a dark wood one questions one's luck if one comes across a clearing in which one can again take one's bearings. So Plato did not have for me a history that could explain the uncanny match between map and terrain. It did not occur to me that Plato had learned from the poets, and what for me was a projection backward inverted the indebtedness of philosophy to poetry. I was still under the spell of the opposition between them, which Plato himself had established when he had Socrates speak of "the ancient quarrel between poetry and philosophy."

The poets had originally been the wise before the philosophers had denied them the title and, despite the philosophers' own protests, had had it bestowed on themselves. The poets' wisdom was vulgar wisdom, made to dazzle a crowd of thirty thousand or more but incapable of standing up to a private argument (*Symposium* 175e2–6). If, however, there had been this constant anticipation in the poets of what Plato made explicit, it seemed one would have to resort to the notion that the poets said many beautiful things but did not know what they meant (*Apology of Socrates* 22c2–3). An occasional hit can well be artless, but a pattern of success makes one suspect that the dice are loaded. If they are loaded, the simple separation of poetry from philosophy is no longer possible. In principle, the blurring of the cut could entail the intrusion of the irrational into the rational rather than the spread of the rational over what formerly looked irrational; but I saw no reason to cast doubt on philosophic thinking, and rather I thought I saw a way to redraw the line between poetry and philosophy, or better, between some poets and Plato. This way involved Socrates' "second sailing," his own term for the turnaround in his own thinking when he abandoned a direct approach to cosmology and turned instead to speeches rather than to the beings. It was this turn in which I thought the poets had preceded him, for it had always been a puzzle to me how the principle of telling lies like the truth, upon which all of Greek poetry rests, could precede the telling of the truth, for it seemed obvious to me, as it had to Socrates, that one cannot lie knowingly unless one knows the truth.

The Muses who tell Hesiod that they speak lies like the truth say they also tell the truth when they wish. If they do not separate them completely, the songs they sing should contain both lies and truth. In the nineteenth book of the *Odyssey*, Odysseus impersonates before Penelope a Cretan. He tells a story about Odysseus's stay with him when he was on his way to Troy. The story could well be completely true if Odysseus were not Odysseus. If Idomeneus had a younger brother, who did not go to Troy, and Idomeneus had left for Troy ten or eleven days before the arrival of Odysseus, then it could have happened that Odysseus stayed in Crete for twelve days and was kindly received by the Cretan Odysseus claims to be (19.171–202). Immediately after Odysseus's tale, which, Homer says, was false but like the truth, he reports that Penelope on hearing it was streaming tears, and her skin was melting, "just as when snow melts on the top of mountains; the East wind soon melts it when the West wind pours down, and the rivers are full when it melts; so her fair cheeks were melting as she poured out tears" (19.203–8). Homer juxtaposes his own lie with Odysseus's. Homer's lie is in the speech; Odysseus's is in the speaker. Homer's lie is an image that Homer declares through the simile to be an image and false. The simile gives the context for the literal meaning of "melt" after the verb has been extended to cover Penelope's tears. The tears are presented as if they were the overflow from a face in dissolution, and nothing would remain of Penelope herself except water. Homer's image sets the truth alongside the lie. The lie thus seems superfluous; the passage could be rephrased and eliminate both the lie and the proof of the lie. It is unclear, however, whether the truth in the rephrasing would be any truer than the false in the lie. Penelope would not melt, but in not melting she could not account for Odysseus's pity in his heart as he looked upon her, or for his eyes standing fast as if they were of horn or iron (19.209–12; cf. 262–4). One lie leads to another; together they make plain what the truth would not. Homer lets us look at two forms of the impossible. His own shows an impossibility that can never but be impossible; Odysseus's is conditionally impossible and could be the case if the speakers were different.

Were we to generalize from our example, the poet puts together what never happened with what never happens; but if we stick to our example, the conditionally impossible involves the strictly impossible, since it assumes that Odysseus is himself and another, and this does not differ from the strictly impossible, for it too assumes that snow and cheek are not two but one. The poet, then, divides what is necessarily one and unites what is necessarily two. He practices his own kind of dialectic in which the truth shows up in two spurious forms. These two forms do not belong exclusively to the poet. Anytime we impersonate someone else, and we do so whenever we quote another directly, we are making one two; and anytime we speak nonliterally, and we almost always do so whenever we speak, we are making two one.[1] The poet, however, does the same systematically. We call this system the plot of poetic dialectic. The plot is the disclosure of impossibilities or apparent impossibilities. Through speech and action it discovers the things that conceal either two in one or one in two. "Two" in this formula stands for any number. "It could not be," Oedipus says, "that one could be equal to many" (*OT* 845). Sophocles shows just how this impossible arithmetic computes. It is obviously a version of the riddle Oedipus himself solved, where four, three, and two were all one. Oedipus's name designates two things, knowledge and lameness. They are apparently together by accident and could be separated into Oedipus the man and Oedipus at birth; but the plot binds them together and solves the riddle Oedipus himself is. Odysseus has two names. One he gives himself; the other his grandfather gave him. Both are significant names, but they apparently signify utterly different things. The plot of the *Odyssey* connects them.

At the peak of poetic dialectic stand the gods.[2] When Athena yanks Achilles' hair as he is about to kill Agamemnon, it is easy to say that Homer has made one into two, and Achilles' second thoughts are assigned a separate being; but Homer distinguishes elsewhere between second thoughts and a god. According to Plato, at least on one occasion (in Socrates' second speech in the *Phaedrus*), the ascent to the beings always passes divergently through the fiction of the Olympian gods. The gods are the representative of lies like the truth. They seem to combine impersonation with image making. They are both the spurious other of a one and the spurious one of a two: Eros is commonly understood to be both lover and beloved. We did not know before we turned to the *Odyssey* whether the poets themselves had anticipated Plato in this regard, or if they had pointed out to him this way of understanding their own doing or making but had stopped short of it themselves. If they had stopped short, we would know why it seemed that Plato was so sure a guide to the poets, and still the ancient quarrel between poetry and philosophy would be preserved. If, however, they had not stopped short, then Plato would have recovered a way of thinking that is not on the way to philosophy but is philosophy, and the apparent tension between Plato the poet and Plato the philosopher would disappear. My teacher, the late Leo Strauss, had often spoken to me about this possibility, but I did not know then what he really meant, and I do not know now whether what I think I now understand was what he really meant. This book, in any case, was written to explore the possibility he indicated.

I am grateful to the Carl Friedrich von Siemens Stiftung for giving me a fellowship for the spring and summer of 1994 in order to write this book. To the chairman of its board, Heinz Gumin, and its director, Heinrich Meier, I am particularly grateful for making my stay so enjoyable. I also wish to thank my students with whom over the years I have studied the *Odyssey*, and to thank my friends Robert Berman, Ronna Burger, Michael Davis, Drew Keller, Martin Sitte, and Barbara Witucki for helping me to formulate these reflections.

1

The Beginnings

Theodicy

Both the *Iliad* and the *Odyssey* are about suffering. The suffering Achilles' wrath inflicted on the Achaeans is in the announcement of the theme of the *Iliad*, and the suffering Odysseus underwent at sea is equally prominent in the proem to the *Odyssey*. The partisan perspective of the *Iliad*'s beginning, as if there were no suffering on the Trojan side, alters in the course of the poem and, in ending with the funeral of Hector, stands clear finally of any bias. In the *Odyssey*, however, the suffering depicted hardly extends beyond the immediate family of Odysseus; it certainly does not include the suitors in its compassion. That the suitors are more unjust than the Trojans is not an easy position to defend; so at least at the start one should perhaps acknowledge Homer's greater support of Odysseus than of Achilles. Homer after all allows Odysseus to tell a large part of his own song, and he does not grant that privilege to any other character. The songs Achilles sang are not recorded, and they were not in any case about himself. The *Odyssey*, then, seems to be much harsher than the *Iliad*. It seems to share in Odysseus's wrath more than the *Iliad* does in Achilles'. No one in the *Iliad* dies in pain; Eurymachus, the second most prominent of the suitors, feels pain in his heart as he strikes the ground with his forehead (22.87). Even an enhancement of death as apparently slight as "Purple death covered his eyes" does not occur in the *Odyssey*. No one in the *Iliad*, for all the threatening talk about it, is eaten by either birds or dogs; but in the *Odyssey* a disloyal servant is cut up and fed to the dogs of the household (22.474–77). With apparent disregard of the incalculable effects such cruelty might have, Odysseus encouraged if he did not exactly order his son and servants to carry out this act of revenge (22.173–77). That Telemachus disobeys his father by refusing to give

1

twelve servant girls a clean death does not bode well for the future rule of this prince for whom his father did so much (22.462–64). Regardless of how these facts must be ultimately understood, they seem to be not un-connected with the beginning of the *Iliad* and underline the necessity for us to think the two poems together. Homer tells us at the start that Achilles' wrath thrust many souls of heroes into Hades, and left themselves or their bodies as a feast for dogs and birds; but the Muse declines to ac-knowledge the truth of what Homer knows. Instead, we are given in the penultimate book Achilles' experience that the soul after all is something in Hades, and in the last book the giving back of Hector's body for burial. The Muse separates the experience of the soul's existence from the divine law of burial, which does not automatically follow from that experience: Achilles has to be ordered to stop trying to disgrace Hector's corpse.[3] In the *Odyssey*, however, though Odysseus sees many Achaeans in Hades, he does not see any Trojans. Priam is not there to tell him about his death at the hands of Achilles' son.

There is, then, at least as much pity and terror in the *Odyssey* as in the *Iliad*, even if the *Iliad* consoles us more by what it hides than the *Odyssey* can with its apparently greater openness about the dark side of things.[4] Achilles and Odysseus are each given a choice. Achilles believes he can either go home and die in old age or stay at Troy and be killed with great glory; Odysseus believes he can either go home or stay with Calypso and become deathless and ageless forever. What Achilles finally chooses is shown to be as inevitable and right as what Odysseus does, and since glory seems to be a weaker version of what Odysseus rejects (cf. XII.322–28), we are allowed to infer that Achilles would have accepted Calypso's offer and Odysseus would have sailed home from Troy.[5] Indeed, Achilles seems to tell Odysseus in Hades that he made the wrong choice (11.488–91), but we are not told that Odysseus had any regrets. The power of Homer's poetry, in any case, largely consists of persuading us that the morality of either choice—of Achilles in rescuing the Achaeans from a dire situation and of Odysseus in saving the life of his son and putting a stop to Penelope's tears—is overshadowed by the fatefulness of either choice. We are forced to look at justice from a perspective beyond justice, even if neither Achilles nor Odysseus ever came to such an understanding. It is here, in the difference between Odysseus's self-understanding and Homer's understanding of that self-understanding, that Homer possibly parts company with Odysseus and recovers a point of view as much be-yond good and evil as he assumed so readily in the *Iliad*. How Achilles comes to put on his fate is shown for the most part in the events of the *Iliad*; we do not have and we do not need to have Achilles' own account.

Our access to the grounds for Odysseus's choice, which he already made before Homer picks up his story, can only come from Odysseus himself. He has to explain from the inside, as it were, what was involved in his coming home.

What Homer tells us at the outset makes Odysseus's choice a riddle.[6] Whereas the *Iliad* begins with the names of Achilles and his father, and thus singles him out and roots him in a past, the *Odyssey* begins with a man in whom anonymity is coupled with knowledge: he wandered very far, saw the cities of many men, and came to know their mind. Odysseus's own experiences and understanding of those experiences are the equivalent of Achilles' genealogy. They make him his own man and cut him loose from both his father and fatherland. Even when Odysseus's name is finally given (1.21), it is without his father's.[7] Virgil goes even further with his protagonist; Aeneas is not named until the ninety-second line of the first book. The initial namelessness of Aeneas indicates that Odysseus's namelessness is not unambiguous, for in Aeneas's case it suggests both the subordination of the man to the city he sets out to found and the ultimate vanishing of the Aeneadae into the Romans, as Juno demands, and hence the impossibility that Virgil's fiction ever be realized (12.821–28; cf. 6.893–97). Odysseus's homecoming, on the other hand, whereby Homer allows himself to call Odysseus by his father's name only once before he returns home (8.18), is shadowed by his own claim to anonymity insofar as he understands himself as nothing but mind: Odysseus's heart laughs when he realizes that "No One" (*outis*)—the name he gave to himself—and "Mind" (*mētis*) deceived the Cyclopes (9.413–14). He is the double form of "No one," *outis* and *mētis,* together. This deep-rooted pun, which represents the degree to which Odysseus accepts and agrees with Homer's starting point, is in tension with the first of Odysseus's stories after he leaves behind the aftermath of the Trojan War. He tells the Phaeacians that he came to the land of the Lotus-eaters, who though harmless had a plant that made anyone who ate of it forget all thought of returning home; and Odysseus had to use force to get his men back to their ships. Odysseus, then, begins his account by affirming the primacy of memory only to follow up that affirmation with the anonymity of mind. Odysseus's return home thus seems to be not an unqualified return. There is, on the one hand, no possibility of his ruling his people as he did before the Trojan War (his gentleness as of a father is gone forever once he is prepared to kill a large minority of the Ithacans); and, on the other hand, he must once he gets home soon depart, staying perhaps no longer than a month (cf. 14.244–45), and come once more to many cities of mortals (23.267). The *Odyssey* catches Odysseus between a return and a departure. Odysseus's choice, then, seems to point not so much to home as to mortality. Odysseus chooses to be human and remain incomplete; or he understands there to be a completeness in the incompleteness of a certain kind of human life that is preferable to either the fixity of memory or the everlastingness of divinity.

Achilles' second thoughts, which he expresses to Odysseus in Hades, are in harmony with Odysseus's choice, not so much perhaps because he would now prefer to be the lowest of the low but because he would wish to live again even though it be for a short time provided he could defend his father from violence and make those who dishonor Peleus loathe their own strength (11.494–503). In the last book, Odysseus effects a kind of reconciliation with his father whose rule he had taken over in some unknown way. The paternal rule that prevailed in Ithaca before the Trojan War and exemplified the highest possible achievement within the ancestral was gained only by a usurpation. That usurpation, which had the consequence of preventing Laertes from defending Penelope from the suitors, merely confirms the riddle in Odysseus's choice. Odysseus's former rule was only in appearance traditional; he had broken with the equation of the good with the ancestral long before he had been given the possibility of not following in the ways of the fathers. The struggle between natural and ancestral right, with which the *Iliad* begins, had already been settled in Ithaca in favor of the son, though the son, as Athena reminds Telemachus, is rarely superior to his father (2.276–77). Odysseus's return demands violence in order to reestablish a principle that had been so effortlessly acknowledged the first time. After twenty years, that first time has been largely forgotten. Perhaps one ought to say that the very effortlessness of Odysseus's first monarchy obscured the principle on which it rested; but since the terror that goes along with the restoration obscures the principle no less, one is puzzled once more about how to understand the relation between Odysseus's wisdom and Odysseus's choice. Now that Odysseus's pre-Trojan wisdom has been so radically altered as to have at its core the knowledge of nature (10.303), what was originally an accidental coincidence of power and wisdom will have to be replaced by the conscious effort to put them together; but the terrible consequences of that effort would seem to deny the desirability of their coincidence. Homer seems to have reflected on the Platonic possibility of philosopher-kings, and either condemned it in advance of its explicit formulation or confirmed the necessity that its realization remain a devout wish.

These preliminary reflections on the beginning of the *Odyssey* do not in any way exhaust it. They have been particularly deficient in regard to two not unrelated issues, the gods and human wickedness. Homer singles out for mention Odysseus's struggle to save the lives of his men for the return home, and his failure to do so, for in their reckless folly they ate the cattle of the Sun, and the Sun took away the day of their return (1.5–9). Homer puts the stress on the return of Odysseus's men and not on his own. Odysseus's choice, then, is not entirely free, and the opposition between memory and mind might be less operative than it seemed. Homer, however, has chosen an event after Odysseus's twelve ships had been reduced to one, and there is nothing in Odysseus's own account to warrant the view that everyone who lost his life was the victim of his own wickedness. Had it not been for Odysseus's use of force, those who wanted to remain with the Lotus-eaters would have survived. Homer, moreover, gives the impression that the Sun punished Odysseus's men; but we are later told that the Sun cannot punish individual men; he can withdraw his light from gods and men equally, but he needs Zeus to carry out what alone would satisfy him (12.382–83). Homer does not mention Zeus. If we may distinguish between cosmic gods like the Sun—gods whose possible existence is manifest to sight—and Olympian gods, about whom there is only hearsay,[8] then Homer begins with a cosmic god who punishes human folly, but he is at once corrected as soon as the Muse takes over and introduces Homer and us to Poseidon, Zeus, and Athena. Homer on his own suggests that Odysseus's wisdom and justice are supported by the cosmic gods, who no less exact terrible vengeance for injustice and folly. That this suggestion is not confirmed by the Muse to whom Homer hands over the story seems to imply that Odysseus, in choosing to return home, chooses the Olympian gods. It is Odysseus's men who promise if they return safely to build a temple to the Sun (12.345–47).

Homer combines his description of Odysseus with a request to the Muse to begin the story at some point or other (1.10).[9] Had the Muse taken him as literally as we have, the story would have begun with either Odysseus's ninth adventure—the island of the Sun—or, if we take the echo of Homer's words about the cities of many men in Odysseus's account to his wife about his last voyage (23.267), the *Odyssey* would have told of how Odysseus came across a people who did not know the sea and established a sacrifice to a god whom they did not know. The Muse does not take up either of these possibilities; instead, she goes farther back and makes Poseidon, for an unknown reason, responsible for Odysseus being the last of those who survived the Trojan War to return home (1.11–21). In telling about the man who wandered very far, the Muse is given much leeway.

The *Odyssey* we have does not exhaust Odysseus. In light of the precise starting point of the *Iliad*, there is nothing more to Achilles than his wrath, and with its end the poem about him is over. The burial of Achilles forms a part of the end of the *Odyssey*; it is of no importance to the *Iliad*. This apparent difference, however, between the concentrated doom of Achilles and the indeterminateness of where in his life Odysseus would best show himself—it is in any case not in the time of the Trojan War—needs to be qualified. Although Homer seems to ask the Muse in the *Iliad* to start from the plan of Zeus, the Muse starts from Apollo, whose anger at Agamemnon provoked the quarrel between Achilles and Agamemnon, and there is no indication that Zeus was behind Apollo's actions. Even in the *Iliad*, then, the causal nexus of events is complicated through the actions of independent gods. Homer's choice of the episode about the cattle of the Sun thus seems particularly felicitous, for once one goes further back, the strands of divine causality become ever more complex and ultimately dribble out into Odysseus's fate that he knew more than twenty years before the *Odyssey* begins (2.171–76). The clarity Homer gains about the connection between justice and wisdom by simplifying the story seems not only to have a narrative advantage but also to support completely Zeus's contention that men blame the gods for their own evils while in fact they alone are responsible, by their own reckless wickedness—Zeus simply repeats Homer's own phrasing (1.7, 34)—for the suffering they have beyond their fate.[10] The poem confirms the first half of Zeus's contention absolutely: there is hardly anyone who does not fault the gods and in particular Zeus. Odysseus has no sooner escaped from the Cyclops's cave than a failure of a sacrifice prompts him to assert that Zeus was then planning how all his ships and men were to perish (9.551–55). We thus have the paradox that Homer begins by vindicating Zeus without involving Zeus, and the Muse who sets out to correct Homer vindicates the human understanding of divine causality through the very admissions Zeus himself makes.[11] It would not be reasonable to expect that this initial paradox will be allowed to stand, but rather that the story we have will ultimately show Zeus to be in the right. We can also suspect that Zeus has chosen Odysseus to be his agent in a knockdown proof of Olympian theodicy. It is through Odysseus's way of disguising and revealing himself that Laertes is made to declare that the Olympian gods still exist (24.351).

Politics

The vindication of Olympian theodicy begins in a mysterious manner.[12] After we have been told about Calypso's detention of Odysseus and Poseidon's unremitting anger against him, it is strange for Zeus to recall "blameless Aegisthus" two years after his death (3.306–7), and use him to illustrate his thesis, that the gods are blameless for human evils, and all the suffering that is beyond fate is due to a man's own reckless wickedness. If the criminal was so coddled that only a warning of retribution could possibly have deterred him, why wasn't Agamemnon equally warned against him? And what kind of retribution can it be that compels the son to avenge the father by killing the mother (3.309–10)? Telemachus is reasonably puzzled by Athena's citation of Orestes as the model for his own course (1.289–300; 3.247–52):[13] no suitor has yet killed his father or seduced his mother. Zeus's self-justification also fails to absolve the gods of human suffering short of death; for when he acknowledges that Poseidon is the cause of Odysseus's wandering, he seems to believe that since Poseidon did not kill Odysseus he is not culpable (1.75; cf. 3.236–38). Odysseus, however, is fated to return home (5.286–90); so if the only evil for which a god can be held responsible is a nonfated death, Zeus's apology does not amount to much. Homer's own example, the self-willed destruction of Odysseus's men (12.348–51), seems far better chosen; but if Odysseus was fated to return home alone and lose all his men (2.171–76), Homer did not do any better than Zeus in vindicating the ways of gods to men. If, however, the gist of both vindications amounts to this, the inevitable coincidence of necessity and will, then the human complaint against the gods is really a protest against the tragedy of life, for which the gods are apparently no more responsible than they are relevant.

Athena seems to adopt a much more cheerful and vindictive view of Zeus's meditation on Aegisthus: Aegisthus, she says, lies in a wholly fitting ruin, "and may anyone else who commits crimes like his so perish." Athena has no intention, we can already surmise, of warning the suitors (cf. 16.402–6); but as the issue of punishment is thus freed from its tragic significance, the justice of the suitors' punishment becomes problematic. That they are to be killed Odysseus has known for seven years (11.119–20); indeed, he knew it four years before they came to besiege Penelope, though he did not know that his knowledge anticipated the event. A four-year stay with Calypso, then, instead of seven, would have allowed Odysseus to return prior to the suitors' arrival; and since Poseidon's anger is completely discharged after he stirs up a single storm against Odysseus (5.375–81), Poseidon cannot really be the sole obstacle to Odysseus's delayed return. The apparently empty time that Odysseus must spend with Calypso is dictated no less by the need for Telemachus to grow up and experience fully the indignity of his position than by the need for Polyphemus's curse, which provided for Odysseus to meet with sufferings at home (9.535), to be realized. Neither Zeus nor Athena mentions any of this. The only nonfated event involves Telemachus' achievement of maturity, of which Teiresias in Hades tells Odysseus nothing. It would seem, then, that the gods' causality as well as their justice concerns Telemachus, and that the so-called *Telemacheia* is not an appendage to the *Odyssey* but the other way around: the *Odyssey* serves the *Telemacheia*, at least to the extent that its primary issue is theodicy.

Had the suitors come one year after the Trojan War and Odysseus been allowed to return three years after that, everything that fate required would have been satisfied except for the twenty years that had to pass before Odysseus could return home. Without that condition, it is hard to believe that Odysseus's reappearance all by itself would not have at once scattered the suitors, who are shown to be a bunch of bumbling braggarts and scarcely a match for Odysseus. That Telemachus never has to explain to the suitors why he removed the arms and armor from the dining hall— Odysseus had prepared for him a plausible speech (19.7–13)—shows as nothing else how small a threat they are in themselves. Even if the suitors could not have been dislodged without a fight, Odysseus could certainly have dispersed them without Telemachus, whose main contribution to the killing is a mistake that added for a moment to his father's troubles (22.154–56). We are forced, then, back to the central position Telemachus occupies in the timing and character of the suitors' punishment. Telemachus represents the political problem of succession. Penelope's entire effort for twenty years has been to preserve the throne for her son, and for the last years to distract attention from the succession by dazzling the suitors with her own attractions and making it seem that the household and not the city is at stake. Telemachus knows nothing of this. When he is directly asked whether he has called an assembly for a political reason he denies it (2.30–32). Telemachus, then, is hardly less resentful of his mother than of the suitors. The real issue of his right to the succession appears to him in the spurious form of a doubt about the legitimacy of his birth (1.215–16).

In his so-called Archaeology, Thucydides speaks of the long period of upheaval, of stasis and exile, that followed the Trojan War (1.12.2–4);[14] but for all that Telemachus sees firsthand at either Nestor's or Menelaus', life goes on there as it did before the war. Except for his son, Nestor seems to have lost not one of his army (3.7–8). Only in Ithaca has the war been completely devastating. An entire generation has been wiped out, not only in Ithaca but also in the other parts of Odysseus's small empire (II.631–35). The evident usurpation within Odysseus's palace has covered over this central fact; and the suspension of all political life for twenty years—no one has called an assembly in all that time (2.26–27)—seems to have suspended time itself. Telemachus's coming of age and the death of Odysseus's dog Argus are the only measures of real time left. Odysseus's rule was so beneficent, it seems, that it could seal up Ithaca for twenty years and allow it to run for that long without a ruler. That there is no ruler shows up only in a reputed disorder within Odysseus's own household (15.376–79; 17.319–21). On his departure, Odysseus turned over the management of his house to Mentor, but he left no provision for the care of the city (2.225–27). There had once been a council of elders in Laertes' time, but with Odysseus's rule it seems to have ceased (21.21). Penelope's daily weaving and nightly unraveling of Laertes' shroud may be said to represent the uneventfulness of Odysseus's almost perfect ordering. It could not last. That gratitude could survive seventeen years—if we count the suitors' arrival as the sign of its fading from the people's memory—is miraculous enough; one cannot expect it to be transmitted from one generation to the next without hope (4.687–95): the loyal Eumaeus, who is too reverent to name his master even in his absence, still hopes for a reward (14.62–67, 145–47). The suitors, then, whose older brothers and cousins went with Odysseus to Troy (cf. 2.17–22), contain in themselves the general disaffection of the people (cf. 3.214–15). They make it possible for Odysseus to cut out surgically the most deeply infected part of the body politic (2.265–66)—we learn in the last book that he did not cut deeply enough (24.463–66; cf. 2.166–67)—and hand over the city in a sound enough condition for a Telemachus to rule it.[15] Whether the other parts of the empire would have to be left to drift away is still up in the air at the end of the *Odyssey*, but the signs are ominous (24.418–19).

The political problem Odysseus confronts reminds one of an imaginary situation Plato's Athenian Stranger presents to a Cretan and a Spartan.[16] He supposes that a single father and a single mother have many sons, most of whom are unjust, but the minority is just; and if a judge could be found for these brothers, the question he poses is who would be a better judge, one who destroyed everyone who was bad and ordered the better to rule themselves, or one who would make the good be the rulers, and the worse, whom he would allow to live, be ruled voluntarily. To this straightforward choice, the Stranger adds a third, the judge who takes over a single family at odds with itself, kills no one, and by the laying down of laws reconciles them for the future, and makes sure they are friends with one another. Odysseus seems to have pursued the first course on his own, and to have been ordered by the gods to follow it up with the third (24.541–48).

Perhaps it is true that resentment can fade as easily as gratitude, and if Odysseus's absence is as long the second time as it was the first, Odysseus may well die old at home surrounded by a happy people (11.134–37). Behind the supposed ingratitude of Odysseus's people, however, there lies a smoldering resentment, fueled not by his long absence, but by the universal recognition that if Odysseus does return he returns alone (2.174–75). The father of Antinous puts it strongly and irrefutably: "First, he went and lost his ships and his people, and then he returned and killed the best of the Cephallenians" (24.427–29). Odysseus could not possibly have returned after his ninth adventure without being torn apart and eaten alive; for had he tried out at home the tale that went over so well among the naive Phaeacians, he would have condemned himself out of his own mouth, even if there is a higher justification for everything he did and did not do. Odysseus's story is not fit for Ithacan ears. His seven-year withdrawal from the world now seems to be that which saved his life, not from Poseidon but from his own people. It may well be that public opinion forced Odysseus to go to Troy; in one of his many lies he mentions that it did so compel the Cretan he pretends to be (14.238–39); but a people who forget their gratitude are not likely to remember their responsibility. Odysseus's compulsory withdrawal, in any case, recalls the prudence of Thucydides' Demosthenes, who after a far less disastrous campaign chose to stay away from Athens until he could report a major success (3.98.5). One wonders whether the gifts Odysseus receives from the Phaeacians, which Zeus wants to be greater than what would have been his share had he returned unscathed from Troy (5.38–40), are meant to be distributed to the Ithacans and compensate them for their losses (cf. 11.355–61; 24.486).

From the strictly political point of view I have outlined, the question of the suitors' guilt, whether collectively or individually, and if there is guilt, whether the punishment fits the crime, would be largely irrelevant (cf. 17.360–64). If Odysseus is to rescue Telemachus from an intolerable position, he must do what he does, even if he could not have brought himself to carry out his fate without believing, as he says, that the suitors refused to honor any human being, whoever came to them, base no less than noble, and on account of their reckless wickedness they met their unseemly fate (22.414–16). He certainly does not believe, in any case, as Penelope does, that there never yet have been any men as obviously wicked and insolent as the suitors (17.587–88). It is another question whether Odysseus's action, being as it is that which founds the new political order, would not necessarily come to be viewed on Penelope's terms, with consequences for the understanding of morality that we are not yet in a position to calculate.

Telemachus

The two parts of Athena's plan seem to move at cross-purposes: the son is sent away from home just before the father sets out on his way home. But Athena accomplishes at least two things through the departure of Telemachus. She makes him appear to be a threat to the suitors, so they will be forced to plan his murder, and she makes Telemachus begin to care more for the father he never knew than for the property he regards as his and that he sees being consumed before his eyes.[17] Telemachus's public denunciation of the suitors, though it does not have any immediate effect (cf. 16.374–75)—a suitor closes the assembly Telemachus summoned (2.257)—when it is combined with his secret departure, seems to point to the possibility of a second expedition of the Achaeans to support once again the integrity of the household and guest-friendship against their violation (2.325–27). Just as Penelope seems to be more deserving of esteem than Helen, so the rights of the case are clearer than they ever were in the Trojan War. Although there are allusions to a widening of the conflict throughout the *Odyssey*, and the alternative of an open struggle is built into Teiresias's prophecy (11.120), Telemachus never discusses it with either Nestor or Menelaus, and they do not make the offer.[18] Odysseus mentions it only when he is lying (14.330). The possibility of a joint expedition died with Agamemnon, and if his death were not fated, one might be led to suppose that it was not entirely displeasing to Zeus and Athena. The re-isolation of cities, so that the issue of their internal order becomes more important than their foreign relations, looks as if it belongs to the wider scheme of things; and it is only an apparent paradox that the instrument for bringing it about should be the man who wandered very far.

This re-isolation, which the premise of the *Odyssey*—the illusory domestication of a political problem—most obviously expresses, is symbolized by two events, one on the level of deed, the other of speech. The immediate consequence of the Phaeacians' safe conveyance of Odysseus to his home is Alcinous's decision, after Poseidon, at Zeus's suggestion, has turned the returning ship into stone, to suspend for the future their escort service (13.180–81). There will no longer be any easy communication by sea. The second sign of what lies in store is this. While Telemachus and Athena are conversing, Phemius is singing of the sad return of the Achaeans (1.326–27). We do not get to hear this song, which by the very nature of its being one song would have had a single perspective in its narrative; instead, we get to hear three different stories about the Achaeans' return, told respectively by Nestor, Menelaus, and Odysseus, that do not form a coherent whole. Though their stories touch upon one another and are not, in broad outline, mutually inconsistent, there is no common aim that unites them. A single account of the breakup of a once coherent expedition disappears behind the individual interests and understanding of its former participants. There is no longer a central authority for either a common action or a common speech. Everyone is now to keep to himself and put his own stamp on events.

Athena comes to Ithaca in the guise of a stranger, Mentes, the leader of the Taphians (1.105). Since no one in town has ever met the son of Odysseus's friend of twenty years (1.180–81, 187–89, 206–12), Athena looks like Mentes because she says she is Mentes; she could have said she was any other stranger without changing her appearance in any way. On this occasion alone, she is anyone and someone at the same time. Telemachus spots her first because he has been imagining in his mind's eye his noble father and supposing, "What if he were to return from somewhere or other and disperse the suitors?" (1.113–17). Inasmuch as Athena is holding a spear in her hand when she arrives on the threshold of the courtyard, Telemachus's imagination and Telemachus's sight seem to merge: Athena leaves her spear behind among Odysseus's weapons when she departs as suddenly as she came (1.126–29); Telemachus tells her that she speaks as kindly as a father to his son (1.307–8). Telemachus, moreover, begins by making a mistake; as he goes across to greet Athena, a righteous indignation stirs him—a stranger had been left standing at the entrance so long (1.119–20).[19] Athena, however, had just shot down from Olympus, and no one is at fault. The private conversation Telemachus and Athena then have occurs after the suitors have dined and are listening in silence to Phemius (1.325–26); but this does not prevent Athena from telling Telemachus that the suitors seem to her as if they were hubristic in their arrogance, and any man of sound understanding would be stirred to righteous indignation were he to see their overwhelming shamelessness (1.227–28). Athena's insight into the suitors is no doubt true; but the transparency of the suitors to her, which anticipates the evidence we are given for the insight, seems to warrant and possibly encourage, on the part of men, a fusion of imagination and evidence that, in becoming a terrifying certainty, would always be triggered to condemn. When Athena later stands by Odysseus and urges him to go begging among the suitors, "in order that he may know who are righteous and who lawless," everyone proves to be in some sense righteous except Antinous, and he is universally upbraided by the suitors themselves (17.360–488). Athena may have wanted Odysseus to realize the limits of human knowledge of the human heart; but whether he took the lesson to heart is an open question. It is certain, however, that Athena did not even try to teach it to anyone else.

Before Athena/Mentes comes around to giving Telemachus a complex set of instructions,[20] she puts an account of Odysseus's visit inside her wish that Odysseus appear among the suitors as he once stood at her father's (Anchialos's) door (1.255–66). He had come to get a deadly poison for his arrows after the king of Ephyra had turned down his request: "In his righteous indignation, he was in awe of the gods who are forever" (1.263). We learn much later that Odysseus never took his bow to war (21.38–41); so even in the time when Odysseus's rule was as gentle as a father's he sought to have an edge against his domestic enemies (cf. 16.424–30): he could have taken them out in poor light, and his aim would not have to have been deadly to be deadly.[21] While Athena hints that there are ways for Telemachus to dispose of the suitors even if Odysseus is dead—the suitors know about the possibility of obtaining poison from Ephyra but not from the Taphians (2.328–330)—she uses the friendly appearance of a fully armed Odysseus on her father's doorstep as the basis for a wish that he kill the suitors. Athena implies that she saw right through Odysseus to the deadly purpose of his visit, or that at least in Odysseus's case one could not tell friend and enemy apart.[22] Athena, moreover, inserts within the martial picture of Odysseus a less noble one, and that insertion implies that one must choose human friendship over against divine nemesis: her father loved Odysseus "terribly" and gave him the poison (1.264). The blurring of the difference between friend and enemy goes along with the overthrow of any divine constraints on human action. We really are in a postheroic world: when they are at home, neither Telemachus nor Odysseus is called a hero.[23] When they are preparing for the final battle, Odysseus tells his son that he is now facing the kind of struggle where the best are judged, and he should not disgrace the race of his fathers. Telemachus assures him that he will not, and then Laertes calls the gods his friends—the only time anyone ever does so—and rejoices that son and grandson are competing about virtue.[24] But neither Telemachus nor Odysseus kills anyone in this open fight; the rejuvenated hero Laertes gets the privilege of hurling the first and last spear of the war (24.506–25; cf. 1.189, 19.144, 22.185). As the Taphian Mentes, Athena is a trader in the new metal, iron; she is bringing it to men who speak a foreign language and offer bronze in exchange (1.183–84).

Athena/Mentes says she came because she heard that Odysseus had returned (1.194–99); but the gods, she goes on to say, are baffling his way, and wild and savage men hold him prisoner on a seagirt island. It is an odd description of Calypso, who uses only speeches to make Odysseus forget Ithaca (1.56–57), but it suits the gods to whom Athena vaguely ascribes the cause of Odysseus's detention. She implies that men alone could not detain the wily Odysseus. That the gods are remote savages seems to be in accord with the human experience of the gods; but it is not clear why Athena should want to suggest anything of the sort to Telemachus. She must know that Telemachus, who comes to know in his heart that Mentes was Athena (1.420), once he learns about Calypso from Menelaus (4.556–58), will put two and two together and draw this conclusion. Is Athena planning a revolution among the gods no less than a greater independence of men from the gods (cf. 1.203–5)? Is the denigration of the gods part and parcel of checking the human impulse to attribute all their evils to the gods? To the extent that Athena distances herself from the savage gods and has given the go-ahead to the use of any means for the punishment of enemies, she has laid the groundwork for a new "religion," with herself at its head (cf. 16.260, 264–65). What form this new religion will take cannot even be imagined at this point, anymore than we now know whether she is going to succeed. But we do know that her conversation with Telemachus prevented him from hearing from Phemius how Athena enjoined a sad return on the Achaeans (1.326–27, 348–49).

While Phemius is singing about Athena as a more remote cause than any we have heard about so far, we are witnesses to how the goddess really works as a cause. We can imagine if we want that at the very moment Athena sets out Orestes as the model Telemachus is to follow, Phemius has just finished the story of Agamemnon's murder; but we know from Athena's speech to Telemachus that it is the killing of Aegisthus that grounds the killing of the suitors, and the justification for Aegisthus's death consists in the glory Orestes obtained among all men. Athena gets inside the head of Telemachus, and when Telemachus expresses the new confidence she has instilled, it comes out in three ways: he mentions the name of his father for the first time (1.355), contradicts his mother, and defends singers. "Unlike you," he tells Penelope, "I can take it when I hear the evil fate of the Danaans—Odysseus was not the only one who perished—" and, without quite being conscious of it, the hidden message is: "I want to be celebrated for the killing of the suitors—their evil fate— for I soon will be the subject of song, since men always like to hear the latest news" (cf. 1.240; 3.203–4). Telemachus learns from Athena that no glory is attached to the reacquisition of one's property. One has to think big, and that entails the wiping out of all the suitors; a simple dispersion will no longer do. That some extraordinary transformation takes hold of Telemachus is virtually certain from the way he botches Athena's instructions; what she gave as private advice (1.279), he blurts out before the suitors and tops it with the wish that they all die in his house and he not have to pay for it (1.374–80).[25] The suitors bite their lips in amazement at Telemachus's speech; and Antinous expresses the wish that Zeus not make Telemachus king in Ithaca, even though it belongs to him by paternal right. Antinous implies that only if Telemachus were king could his wish come true. Telemachus, however, does not see the implication of Antinous' remark. He says he is satisfied if he has sole possession of his estate; but we might suspect that what he is thinking is that kingship is nothing next to glory.[26]

Penelope asks Phemius to stop singing his sad song and pick another (1.337–44).[27] Penelope calls the song sad, Homer said the song was of a sad return (1.326–27), and Telemachus argues for the singer's right to give delight in whatever way his mind is inclined (1.326–27, 346–47). Men take pleasure in hearing of suffering; they take pleasure in hearing how Zeus gives what he wills to each. The singer assigns a meaning to human suffering by ordering the apparently arbitrary events of human life through the causal agency of Zeus. The opposition, then, between the nonculpability of the singer and the culpability of Zeus is not as clear-cut as Telemachus claims it is, for even if the singers are not the causes of the gods, they are responsible for making the gods responsible. Telemachus's suddenly acquired privilege, to know the agency of a god directly, does not affect the general position of men. One wonders, then, whether Zeus's meditation on Aegisthus, in which he regretted the human disposition to blame the gods, does not refer primarily to the singers, who establish the models for understanding divine agency. There is a vast difference between a Nausicaa saying, "Olympian Zeus on his own assigns prosperity to men, noble and base, however he wills to each" (6.188–89), and a singer working out the ways in which Zeus goes about doing what Nausicaa says he does. The *Odyssey* is remarkable for the light touch with which Athena guides the course of events. Without her presence between lines 123 and 320, we could easily suppose that Telemachus's dreaming of his father while he sits among the suitors, and Phemius's singing at the same time of Athena's causality in arranging the sad return of the Achaeans, would prompt his outburst against his mother and the suitors. The *Odyssey* would have been over before it started had Athena suddenly appeared in the likeness of Odysseus. Athena is and is not in the fabric of the *Odyssey*. Telemachus is the only one who Homer says knew the goddess in his heart (φρεσὶ δ' ἀθανάτην θεὴν ἔγνω, 1.420); even Odysseus ends up merely with the suspicion of her presence (22.210).

The household setting of the first book lets the political problem only be glimpsed at in the mention of kingship, but it comes to light more clearly in the second book. Before the assembly gets started, we are told about Aegyptius and his sons. One of them, Antiphus, went with Odysseus and was the last whom Polyphemus ate; another, Eurynomus, associates with the suitors, and two were occupied in their father's fields (2.17–24). Aegyptius, perhaps because he still mourns for one son, cannot control another; and if after so long a time he cannot but weep publicly in memory of Antiphus, who was, according to Odysseus, among the best but not among the very best (9.195, 334–35), what will happen when he has to mourn for Eurynomus as well, who was among the outstandingly best of the suitors after the deaths of their chiefs (22.241–45)? It may well be that there is no resentment against Odysseus mixed in with his present grief, and no satisfaction that one son is living at no expense to himself. Telemachus, however, imagines that the people of Ithaca are maliciously using the suitors to get back at Odysseus through himself for some evil Odysseus malevolently did to them, and Telemachus proposes that it would be better were they to eat up his property themselves, for then he might get compensation by earnest entreaty, "but as it is you are imposing pain upon my heart against which no action can be taken" (1.70–79). Telemachus puts forward a case against his father in which he does not for a moment believe; but if the people's resentment were not entirely with a clear conscience, they would proceed in exactly the way in which Telemachus suggests that they are. Telemachus's suggestion, moreover, gains in plausibility once Mentor rebukes the people for their silence, and remarks how easy it would be for the many to restrain the few by words alone (2.239–40). Mentor begins his speech with the wish that no scepter-wielding king be kind and gentle any longer, but be always harsh and do evil (2.230–34). He gets his wish.

2

Pattern and Will

Nestor

The third book begins and ends with a sacrifice; the opening sacrifice is the largest Homer ever records, and the closing sacrifice gets the most elaborate description Homer ever bestows. The first sacrifice is to Poseidon, the last to Athena; Poseidon does not attend the first sacrifice; Athena is present at the first and comes to the second. Athena accomplishes what Nestor prays that Poseidon accomplish (3.54–62): Athena's usurpation seems to be on the way to being realized. The frame of the book is also in some way the theme of the book. Nestor's narrative deals to a large extent with the issue of sacrifice. Nestor's palace also differs from the other palaces we come to know. It is the only one without a singer.[28] All men need gods, Nestor's son tells Athena (3.48), but not everyone, it seems, needs song. No one sheds any tears at Pylos, and there is almost a complete absence there of words for sorrow and distress.[29] Telemachus falls silent after he asks his second question of Nestor (3.240–52), and he does not recover his voice until he whispers to Nestor's son in Sparta (4.69–70). In light of the double meaning of *rhezō*, "to sacrifice" and "to do," one might say that the third book exemplifies the deeds without the experience of the deeds, or rather that the experience of things vanishes from view. At Nestor's, Telemachus is exposed to a flat understanding of things. Athena's presence is needed, apparently, to support such an understanding; she is not needed in any case at the home of Menelaus and Helen.

It turns out that Nestor knows nothing about Odysseus since they parted ten years ago; Menelaus has the latest news, and his is two years old. Athena must have had more in mind than her stated purpose. At the very least, she wants Odysseus's old comrades in arms to confirm the legitimacy of Telemachus' birth in a more authoritative way than she had done at their first encounter (1.206–9). Helen and Menelaus notice the outward resemblance of father and son (4.141–50), and Nestor sees the resemblance in his reasonable speeches (3.123–25). Nestor puts side by side two different meanings of *eoike*: the semblance of Telemachus' speeches to Odysseus's (*muthoi ge eoikotes*) and the sensibleness of his speaking (*eoikota muthēsasthai*). To be like Odysseus in speech is to speak the likely. Though it is hard to be precise about what is entailed by Nestor's pun, one can say that it has nothing to do with the possibility of lies like the truth (19.203), and that it thus denies the very principle of Greek poetry. Just before Nestor makes this remark, he tells Telemachus that not even if he stayed for five or six years would he ask about all the evils that the Achaeans suffered, and he would return home in distress before they were told (3.113–17). The narrative would be as long as the experiences, and the pain it brings would be of the same order as the experiences themselves. Penelope had called the song of a sad return sad, but Telemachus spoke of the pleasure it gives; for Nestor there is no pleasure in the telling of the tale. The only pleasure mentioned at Nestor's is of eating (3.70). The suppression of experience in Nestor's account, which a first impression of the third book had suggested, seems to involve the virtual identification of the experience of things with the experience of the speech of things, which in turn is nothing but the rationality of things. The perfect sense of things leaves no room for the experience of things. Homer's imitation of Nestor's kind of narrative is in the closing sacrifice. The cow, he says, came from the field, Telemachus' comrades came, the blacksmith came, and Athena came (3.430–36). Athena came in just the way the cow did. That the men of Pylos see the one and not the other makes no difference. The indifference was already implied in Nestor's declaring that he was amazed at seeing the resemblance of Telemachus' speech to Odysseus's.

Nestor begins his first account with a contrast between the invariable agreement of Odysseus and himself in assembly and in council as long as the war lasted and their subsequent disagreement. That single purpose (*thumos*) in mind (*noos*) and deliberation (*boulē*) persisted despite the utter difference in Odysseus's cast of mind (*mētis*)—which surpassed everyone in every kind of guile and deceit—from his own (3.118–22). A break between them occurred shortly after they had sacked Troy. Nestor prefaces his account of the break with these words: "A god scattered the Achaeans, and then Zeus was devising in his mind a sad return for the Argives, since all were not thoughtful (*noēmones*) and just." Nestor seems to imply that just as in general wisdom and justice go together—as they evidently do in the Ithacan named Noemon (2.380–87, 4.648–51; cf. 3.51)—so in particular his own superiority in both shows up no less in the ease of his own return than in the failure of Odysseus to return. Nestor understands the scattering of the Argive fleet in terms of a strict theodicy. The gods thereby separated out in the most precise manner the just from the unjust, and each got exactly what he deserved. Such an understanding has no room for tears. Whatever is, is as it ought to be, and he is wise who knows this at the time when the pattern of things is beginning to unfold. Nestor does not at all suggest that the story he tells is a retrospective interpretation of events; it was clear to him from the start what was going to happen (3.146, 166), and again there is no suggestion that he relied on oracles or diviners. The plan Zeus worked out was effected through the wrath of Athena, who caused a dispute to arise between Agamemnon and Menelaus. Since the Atreidae called a night assembly, to which the Achaeans came drunk and disorderly, neither Nestor nor Odysseus could speak to the crowd and restore their unity, for as long as the just and the unjust were together Zeus would abstain from punishment. Menelaus wanted everyone to return home; Agamemnon wanted to hold back the host until he had sacrificed to Athena in order to appease her terrible anger: "the fool, he did not know that Athena was not going to be won over, for the mind of the gods is not quickly altered."

Up to this point, Nestor and Odysseus are in agreement; they both side with Menelaus and sail with him to Tenedos—a god spreads the sea flat—where in their eagerness for home they sacrifice to the gods. The divine purpose, then, must have been to destroy the unjust half of the army that stayed behind with Agamemnon. Since the army decided when they were drunk, it could not have been the greater rationality of the Menelaus contingent that favored their survival. Random choice sorted out the just and the unjust in a perfectly ordered way. At Tenedos, however, Zeus caused another evil dispute, and some turned back under the guidance of Odysseus and paid homage to Agamemnon. We now have to slide in another part of the story from Odysseus's narrative. According to him, after he left Troy he sacked the city of the Cicones (9.37–61). This could have occurred only after he had returned to Troy from Tenedos in the company of others who had by then regretted their former decision to abandon Agamemnon. What looked to Nestor like obeisance is presented by Odysseus as greed: he or his men were not satisfied with their share of the booty from Troy. For reasons that come to light later, Odysseus fails to tell the Phaeacians that the Cicones were Trojan allies (II.846–47), and what seems to be a wanton pirate raid, for which they pay the appropriate penalty, could as easily have been presented as retaliation.[30]

Odysseus, then, deliberately starts out his story with a suppression of his possible justice, and Nestor, as deliberately, starts out with the superiority of his wisdom, to which he ascribes a justice that is self-evident in his safe return. To determine any more closely the events at Tenedos is impossible. One would get lost in fruitless speculation if, in order to reconcile Nestor and Odysseus, one were to say that Odysseus interpreted Athena's wrath as appeasable not, as Agamemnon believed, by sacrifices but by the prosecution of the war until all the guilty were punished. It is clear nonetheless that if and only if Odysseus were still loyal to Agamemnon and subject to his command would the attack on the Cicones not simply be a pirate raid.

After the further sorting out of the Argives at Tenedos, there was a slight break in the unity of those who went on to Lesbos, for Menelaus came there late; and it is not farfetched to suppose that Menelaus had hesitated at Tenedos and thought of rejoining his brother (3.277). However that may be, when a sail straight across to Euboea became an alternative to a safer route, Nestor asked for and received a sign that ordered them to take the faster way home. After their overnight run to Geraitios, they sacrificed to Poseidon. Diomedes in three days and Nestor after that came home without a scratch. Nestor then adds that he knows by hearsay of the safe return of the Myrmidons, Philoctetes, and Idomeneus, all of whom must have stayed behind with Agamemnon. The clear-cut division between the just and the unjust is now somewhat blurred. Nestor breaks off his account with a mention of Agamemnon's return and murder, and the penalty his son exacted from Aegisthus. In Nestor's account there is no accounting for the events. Every stage that he knows firsthand is arranged by the gods, and he knows what the arrangement is; but he feels no need to go deeper into the pattern. It has no meaning beyond its manifest justice and his own wisdom in detecting it.

Nestor's understanding of events apparently denies to him two not unrelated ways of storytelling: there are no speeches of others within his speech, and he does not deck out his own narrative with any similes. The closest he comes to a simile is to say in the second account that the waves Menelaus encountered were equal in size to mountains (3.290).[31] The significance of the lack of similes can perhaps be best illustrated by Horace's so-called Cleopatra ode (1.37). What starts out as a celebration of Augustus's victory at Actium ends up as a celebration of Cleopatra's refusal to be part of his triumph. The pivot of this peripety occurs in the fifth stanza, where Augustus is either a vulture or a hunter in pursuit of his prey; since the prey are either doves or a hare, the sympathy of the reader immediately turns from the victor to the victim: the just defeat of the degenerate East becomes the wanton destruction of the helpless. A simile, by negotiating between two realities, is a two-way carrier of meaning, and in unskillful hands betrays the intention of its speaker. In the fourth book, Menelaus begins a speech with a built-in Horatian meaning of which he seems to be unaware. The suitors, he says, are like a hind who settles her newborn and suckling fawns in the lair of a mighty lion while she goes out foraging, and the lion returns and kills them all (4.333–40). Menelaus has lost control of what he wanted to say, for the innocent ignorance of the hind, to say nothing of the young, undercuts the justice of Odysseus and necessarily alters the way in which we look at the suitors.

As for the other characteristic of Nestor's story—the absence of any-one else's speech—that too may be best illustrated by Horace. In the fif-teenth ode of the first book, Horace has the truthful Nereus stop Paris's ship, which is conveying him and Helen back to Troy, and predict to him the course of the war he is bringing with him. Most of the details come from the *Iliad*, and in the fourth stanza, Paris is told that Venus will not save him—"In vain you will comb your hair proud in the support of Venus, and make songs pleasing to women with a lyre not fit for war, and in vain you will avoid in the bedroom the spear"—but this very moral theodicy merely reproduces Hector's rebuke to Paris in the *Iliad* just be-fore his single combat with Menelaus, in which Aphrodite rescues him and sets him inside Helen's bedroom (III.54–55). What in Roman lyric is the certainty of morality was in Greek epic a denunciation and false prophecy.[32] The two ways poetry has of imitation, impersonation and image making, virtually preclude the possibility of poetry's adoption of a strict morality. The poet may begin by praising whatever he selects, but unless he vanishes completely and comes forward without other voices and without images, he will give to his poem a perspective beyond good and evil.

Telemachus does not comment on the whole of Nestor's account. He contrasts the retribution Orestes exacted, with its accompanying glory and song, with his own unfulfillable wish to punish the bitter transgres-sion of the suitors (3.201–9); but after he denies that the gods, even were they willing, could grant his hope, Athena, disguised as Mentor, rebukes him sharply and says a god could easily bring a man home to safety even if he were far off, and she for one would prefer to suffer and see the day of her return than to perish at home as Agamemnon did. It is in this context that Athena for the first time makes Clytaemestra as guilty as Aegisthus; and it is the mark of the new relations Athena is setting out to establish between gods and men that she speaks in disguise just after Nes-tor says that he had never seen gods so manifestly loving as Athena in her manifest support of Odysseus at Troy (3.218–22). Nestor implies that he himself did not have this kind of support, and his understanding of the divine plan behind the breakup of the Achaean fleet did not need anything more than a single sign. That understanding is now put to a severe test by Telemachus. Precisely because Nestor is outstanding in justice and thinking (3.244; cf. 1.66), the inseparability of which seemed to be the thrust no less of Homer's proem than of Nestor's first account, Telemachus wants him to "justify" the murder of Agamemnon: "How did Agamemnon die? Where was Menelaus? What kind of destruction did Aegisthus devise, since he killed someone who was his superior by far?" Once Nestor gives his answer Telemachus never says another word at Pylos.

Nestor's second account is no longer straightforwardly chronological.[33] It interweaves the story of Menelaus with the story of Agamemnon, and what dominates both strands is not sacrifice, as in the first account, but burial (3.254–312): Hades first occurs in this book (3.410).[34] This difference is accompanied by fewer allusions to the gods (269, 279, 288), who disappear altogether once Nestor gets Menelaus to the southernmost coast of the Peloponnesus. Nestor begins with a counterfactual: had Menelaus met Aegisthus alive, nothing bad, he implies, would have happened—he does not give the apodosis—anymore than Menelaus would have allowed the people to bury Aegisthus after he was dead, but dogs and birds would have devoured him far from the city, and none of the women would have wept for him, "for he (Aegisthus) devised a great deed." After this opening, Nestor goes back to the time when the Achaeans were suffering many hardships at Troy and Aegisthus was trying to seduce Clytaemestra. As long as the singer Agamemnon had put in charge was there to protect her, Clytaemestra resisted; but when Aegisthus banished him to a deserted island, where the singer could become the prey of birds without Aegisthus killing him directly, Clytaemestra was as willing as Aegisthus, who, to celebrate his unexpected triumph, made large sacrifices to the gods. Nestor then goes back to Menelaus, and picks up his first account at the point where he and Menelaus come from Euboea to Sunium. Here Apollo kills Menelaus's helmsman, and Menelaus reluctantly stays behind so that he may bury him and perform the appropriate rites. Nestor now admits that the original division with which he started, between the just and the unjust, undergoes a further division in which the gods both directly and indirectly through the divine law break off a remnant of the just to submit to a destiny to which Nestor becomes indifferent, or else is unwilling to spell out. Menelaus's fleet was scattered off Malea, and all but five ships were smashed on the coast of Crete, but their crew survived. The rest were drawn by wind and wave to the Nile River, where Menelaus gathered much gold and goods as he wandered among people who spoke a foreign language. It is unclear whether Nestor connects his own subsequent silence about the gods with the foreignness of the people among whom Menelaus wandered.

In any case, in the fifth element of his web, Nestor returns to Aegisthus, who ruled the people of Mycenae oppressively for seven years; but in the eighth year Orestes came back from Athens and killed him. Orestes thereupon gave a funeral feast for Aegisthus and his mother, for if he were not to dishonor his mother completely he had to bury Aegisthus as well; and on this very day Menelaus returned with all his acquisitions. In bringing together in reality the two strands of his story, after he had begun with their hypothetical conjunction, Nestor implies that Clytaemestra would never have been killed had Menelaus come back in time. The husband of Helen could hardly have condoned matricide as the fitting punishment for adultery and murder. It thus emerges that Nestor was in a sense right: the gods were engaged in a continual separation, not, as Nestor said, of the unjust from the just, but of Agamemnon from anyone who could possibly save him; and this isolation was brought about by men conforming to the divine laws of burial and sacrifice. Menelaus could not get home in time to save Clytaemestra and punish Aegisthus as he deserved, for his departure from Egypt was delayed three days until he had made the sacrifices he had originally forgotten to make when he left Troy with Nestor (4.356).

Nestor splits his account in two. The focus of one part is Troy, the other Mycenae. If we reintegrate the account so that events follow one another chronologically, the seduction of Clytaemestra would be coordinated with the misery of the Achaeans at Troy; the quarrels at Troy and Tenedos would come next, followed by Menelaus's sailing with Nestor to Sunium. Athough Nestor got home safely, Menelaus went off course to Egypt and Aegisthus killed Agamemnon. It then becomes apparent that the key event is neither of the quarrels, but is Menelaus's being forced by piety to tarry at Sunium and not sail home with Nestor. Nestor is aware that the gods were out to get Agamemnon; but he refuses to admit that his murder was their way of accomplishing it, since he would then have to concede that the quarrels did not sort out the guilty from the innocent, and nothing more was needed to realize the killing of Agamemnon, the burial of Aegisthus, and a son's murder of his mother than the absence of Menelaus, who was with him. Not those who stayed behind with Agamemnon but those who abandoned him sealed his fate. Although Telemachus asked Nestor to tell the truth before the first and second accounts, Nestor promised to tell the truth only the second time (3.101, 247, 254).

What Telemachus makes of Nestor's story we do not know; but his subsequent silence seems to indicate that he abandons all thought of trying to emulate Orestes. This is not to say that Orestes' story does not reverberate in Telemachus's. Confronted at home with a version of the alternative hidden in Nestor's account—kill the mother and bury the lover or feed the lover to the dogs and spare the mother—Telemachus hangs the servant girls and feeds Melanthius to the dogs. This lies in the future. At the moment, Athena takes over. She determines first that they pour a libation to Poseidon and the other gods, and then, in revealing her presence after she makes up a plausible pretext for going away without revealing her presence, she prompts Nestor to make a special sacrifice to her (3.380–85). Prior to the sacrifice, Nestor makes a prayer that now includes a mention of his wife and excludes his people, to say nothing of Odysseus and Telemachus; and after he returns to his palace, he also pours a second libation to Athena alone and prays earnestly to her (3.386–94). The national holiday, with which the book began, yields to a domestic celebration: Nestor's daughter and daughter-in-law become part of the story (3.450–52, 464–65). Athena effects in Pylos the same shift from the political to the private as had already been done as mysteriously in Ithaca. On the next day Nestor refers to Athena's vivid (*enargēs*) presence of the day before (3.420). This vividness is a far cry from the manifest (*anaphanda*) presence she displayed at Troy (3.221–22). It is halfway between her former manifestness and her subsequent presence at the sacrifice, to which she comes, on the narrative level, in just the way anyone else does. The next and last time Athena comes to Telemachus alone, she stands beside him and addresses him without Homer ever saying whether Telemachus sees her or not (15.9–43; cf. 24.516–20). She becomes a voice. Perhaps, then, Telemachus fell silent at Nestor's when he realized that she had completely deceived him.

Helen and Menelaus

The third book began with a sacrifice and a discussion about the universal need for gods; the fourth book begins with a double wedding and a discussion of the difference between mortal and immortal.[35] There are no sacrifices or libations at Menelaus's (cf. 4.590–92). Just as Nestor's elaborate sacrifice to Athena seems to make up for an omission on his part at the end of the Trojan War, so the marriage of Hermione to Achilles' son fulfills a promise Menelaus had made at Troy (4.6–7). The *Odyssey* could not be a new beginning if it did not finish off the past.[36] That that past is over is symbolized by Homer's statement at the beginning that the gods denied any further generation to Helen once she had borne Hermione, and at the end of Menelaus's account by Proteus's prediction that he and Helen are not going to die but are to live forever on the islands of the blest (4.12–14, 561–69). The end of becoming at Sparta is a fitting preface to that which is the undercurrent of the fifth book, Odysseus's choice of becoming.

The theme of the fourth book is appearance, and it is once again fitting that it should be Aphrodite who, in her first appearance, sets the standard for appearance: the lovely Hermione has the looks of golden Aphrodite (4.14).[37] Aphrodite is followed almost immediately by Zeus. Menelaus's steward reports the arrival of Telemachus and Nestor's son Peisistratus; they resemble, he says, the offspring of great Zeus (4.27). Appearances, then, come along with false and deceptive appearances: Peisistratus traces his descent from Poseidon, and Telemachus has no genealogical connection with Zeus (cf. 4.63–64, 207–10). Although Menelaus has his hands full, what with the double marriage ceremonies for his son and his daughter, he bristles at the steward's reasonable question of whether the two strangers are to be sent on to others: "You used not to be a fool, Eteoneus, but now you speak as if you were a child" (4.31–32). Telemachus and Peisistratus look with pleasure and amazement at the palace of Menelaus, for there was a gleam throughout it, Homer says, as if of the sun and moon (4.45). Telemachus, however, whispers to Peisistratus that the house of Olympian Zeus is no doubt of the same sort within (4.64). Menelaus overhears him and sharply contradicts the comparison: "No one of mortals could compete with Zeus, for his house and possessions are deathless, but among men one may or may not rival me."

This remark launches Menelaus into a longish speech at the end of which he stirs in Telemachus the desire to mourn for his father (4.113). Since Menelaus is himself assured of a serene deathlessness, there is an element of insincerity in his speech, however edifying it may be for others. If we disregard this element, which we do not yet know about, Menelaus implies that the standard set by Zeus's immortal possessions detracts from the pleasure one would otherwise take in one's own possessions. Only in Libya, where sheep are born three times a year and lambs are suddenly horned, does generation come close to duplicating the permanence the gods have. Mortal possessions carry besides a heavy price. Menelaus would be willing to have a third of what he once held if all the men who died at Troy were safely home. Menelaus comes as close to regretting the Trojan War as Achilles will later regret his choice. Menelaus goes on to say that the pleasure he takes in grieving for all the dead is quickly sated; but when he recalls Odysseus, sleep and food become loathsome to him, for in his case there is ignorance of his fate. To the transience and cost of mortal things there is the additional burden of uncertainty. Whereas Nestor had seen everything as the unfolding in time of the pre-ordained, Menelaus expresses a vague resentment against time and change that the marriage of his daughter with the son of the dead Achilles seems to have occasioned, and which the very name of his bastard son Megapenthes ("Greatly-grieving") must have reinforced. It is therefore remarkable that Menelaus does not blame Zeus on this occasion. Given that the immortal is its foil, the mortal gets as neutral a description as one could expect. It is worth remarking, however, that Homer's simile about the splendor of Menelaus's palace, though the sun and moon are the instruments of time, could not have provoked Menelaus into making the reflection he did make on Telemachus's comparison of Menelaus's palace with that of Zeus.

Whether one is to say that the entrance of Helen in the likeness of Artemis shows that appearances live up to reality is doubtful (cf. 4.145); but Helen has none of the hesitation Menelaus has to pronounce Telemachus the spitting image of his father. Once Peisistratus confirms this and identifies himself, Menelaus recalls that Zeus had thwarted his intention to resettle Odysseus and all his people next to him. He was prepared, in order to accomplish this, to lay waste to one of the cities he ruled; "and nothing else would have separated us, in friendship and delight, until the black cloud of death enveloped us; but the god himself, who denied to him alone a return, was no doubt resentful of all this" (4.178–82). The casual ruthlessness Menelaus gives voice to astonishes; but everyone who hears him must have been grateful that Zeus frustrated his will. Zeus himself could not have given a better example of how men, even when their evil plans fail, are blind to their own wickedness and label as evil the good he caused.

The frustration of Menelaus's will stirs up the desire to mourn in everyone—Helen, Telemachus, Menelaus, and Peisistratus.[38] We are told only in Peisistratus's case what caused him to weep; it was the death of his brother Antilochus at the hands of Memnon, the splendid son of shining Dawn. Peisistratus sets the measure of mourning in the context of time. Soon it will be morning, he says, and he takes no pleasure in an after-dinner grief. It is not that he begrudges anyone the right to weep, for to cut one's hair and cast a tear are the only honors wretched mortals have to bestow on whoever dies. Peisistratus implies that even this honor has been denied him, since he never saw his brother, whose excellence as a runner and fighter is known to him only as hearsay (cf. 3.111–12). Menelaus has nothing but praise for Peisistratus' sensible speech, and he proposes to put off until tomorrow his talk with Telemachus; but Helen, who not only has an eye for appearances but sees what is within, drugs their drinks. The drug takes away any grief and anger and makes one forget all evils: "Whoever should swallow it would not cast a tear for an entire day, not even if his mother and father should die, and they should slay his brother or son before him, and he should see it with his own eyes." There is perhaps in the entire *Odyssey* no single action that shows such a deep and immediate understanding of human things as Helen's drugging of everyone. She prevents them not only from going to sleep with their grief unassuaged but also from carrying a grudge against the irreversibility of time and the unfulfillability of human wishes. Helen's drug seems to be the magical counterpart to the songs of the Muses, who, according to Hesiod, in singing of gods and men of old, make men forget their malignant thoughts and sorrows.[39] Helen too knows about song: "So that we (Paris and herself) may be the subject of song for men to come," was, in the *Iliad*, her terrifying assessment of the purpose of the Trojan War (VI.358).

Helen's drug is a temporary remedy against softness. The indifference it induces mimics the genuine toughness of Odysseus, which she illustrates in a story designed to exculpate herself while it restores in her listeners a more equable temper and acceptance of the way things are (4.235–64). Telemachus gets the gist of her story as well as of the one Menelaus tells right afterwards; he denies consequently that the characteristics they both attribute to Odysseus, "even if he were to have an iron heart within," saved him (4.293). In this way, Homer first slips in an issue that becomes in the sequel of decisive importance. Telemachus's denial recalls his remark at Nestor's, that not even the gods, should they be willing, could realize his hopes (3.227–28). Neither the gods nor an iron heart can overcome what Telemachus considers the impossible; but regardless of whether he has drawn the limits of the feasible correctly, he speaks in two different settings of two different means, the gods and the heart. The *Odyssey*, one can say, combines them; but it is more revealing to treat each apart from the other, as Medon does when Penelope asks him why Telemachus left home, "I do not know, either some god urged him, or his own heart (*thumos*) desired it" (4.712–13). The very notion of appearance leads to what does not appear, and what does not appear is primarily on the level of causality, whether it be the gods or the human will. The gods show themselves only slightly more often than does the heart: "Your heart (*ho humeteros thumos*) and unseemly deeds come to light," Penelope tells Medon, although she is in fact mistaken to include him among the suitors (4.694–95). The distinction that Medon draws would collapse if the gods not only could get inside the will and direct it but also detect the unspoken thoughts of men. In the latter case, nothing in principle would be hidden from the gods, whether it be, as Athena puts it, where the earth hides (*kuthe*) Odysseus or what thought (*mētis*) Nestor has kept hidden (*kekeuthe*) in his heart (3.16–18). The omniscience of Zeus, with the assertion of whose omnipotence Helen begins her story (4.237, cf. 379; 5.170), depends in part on whether it extends as far as the human heart. The plans he devises and realizes in human life are not comprehensive if they do not include the human experience of those plans. Nestor's theodicy had implicitly excluded experience. It was enough to know the pattern of things.

Things become mysterious as soon as Helen tells one story among many of Odysseus's strength of soul. Odysseus disguised himself to look like a beggar before he slipped into Troy. He became someone else, Helen says, completely unlike the sort he was among the ships of the Achaeans; indeed, he beat himself with unseemly blows—the sort, one might add, with which he once threatened Thersites, just before he struck him across the back and shoulders (II.261–66). None of the Trojans paid any attention to him; Helen alone recognized him for who he was. Did Athena leave Telemachus at Pylos because she knew that Helen would see right through any disguise? Helen seems to share in the ability of Argus, and perhaps in the other dogs' ability as well who whimper in the presence of Athena even though Telemachus cannot see her (17.301–2; 16.160–63). However that may be, Odysseus was unable to evade Helen's questions, and once she had bathed and dressed him, and sworn a mighty oath, he took her into his confidence and imparted to her the entire plan (*noos*) of the Achaeans. In light of the story Menelaus then tells, Helen seems to have known the secret of the Trojan horse, and Odysseus put the lives of the Achaeans in her hands and made her a part of the plan to deceive the Trojans. Odysseus went out of his way to make the Trojans know that he had been in Troy, for after he had gathered much intelligence and before he left, Helen reports, he killed many Trojans. "Hereupon the Trojan women wailed and keened," she continues, "but my heart rejoiced, since my heart had turned around, to go back home, and I regretted the infatuation that Aphrodite gave when she led me away from my dear fatherland and separated me from my daughter and husband, who was inferior to no one either in wit or in looks" (4.259–64). Helen sets side by side her penetration of Odysseus's disguise with her own disguised joy: her joy at the death of Trojans, among whom she had lived for ten years, turns on her change of heart, to which no one apparently is privy except herself.

The drug she had administered no doubt made it possible for Menelaus to hear her with indifference, both when she calls herself a shameless bitch and when she implies that had Menelaus been defective in any way she might have had no regrets. Clearly, Odysseus must have reported back to the Achaeans her change of heart and been convincing, for otherwise no one would have dared to enter the horse. The provisions of the oath—not to reveal his presence before he got back to the ships—make it clear that the killing of the Trojans was meant to back up Helen's story. The Trojans, moreover, must have trusted Helen just as much as Odysseus did, for otherwise they would not have used her as a lure to test whether anyone was hiding within the horse.

This is Menelaus's story (4.266–89). When they were sitting in the horse, Helen walked around it three times, feeling it all over, and, in calling out the names of the best of the Achaeans, imitated the voices of their wives. Diomedes and Menelaus were eager either to go out of the horse or to answer her from within; but Odysseus restrained them, and when Anticlus was going to respond, Odysseus clamped his hand over his mouth and saved the Achaeans. Odysseus alone could not be enchanted by any sorcery. Helen displays not only an uncanny intuition about the heart and a gaze before which any concealment is useless, but also she can convince Anticlus, against his knowledge, that his wife is just outside in the midst of Troy. Helen seems to have all the traits of the poet, from the coolness with which Homer depicts the most terrible things to his mimetic capacity to make things appear in all their vividness and his insight into the hiddenness of things. Her only possible rival is Odysseus, he whose eyes turn to horn while he pities Penelope in his heart (19.209–12), who tells lies like the truth (19.203), and who needs no help from Eurycleia to tell which servant girls dishonor him and which are sinless (19.496–501). Helen seems to be morally more dubious than Odysseus, who at least expects from others unswerving loyalty. He himself did not have his father's scruples when it came to women (1.433). Odysseus, however, seems never to have been under the spell of Aphrodite (22.444). If one sets this possible difference aside, and asks instead whether Odysseus really differs from Helen in sharing with Nestor a sense of theodicy that Helen lacks completely, one is onto the larger question of how Homer and possibly Odysseus can put together in a coherent way what we may call in shorthand, "Helen" and "Nestor," and whether such a synthesis, if it is possible at all, admits of only one composition. Whatever the answer, Homer praises Helen by simply letting the question arise with her rather than with Nestor. Telemachus's willingness to stay at Sparta is a sign that Helen has convinced him that, if he is ever to meet his father, his father must find him and not he his father. Odysseus is too mysterious to let himself be found out against his will.

Menelaus never explains why he chose to wander for eight years with his five ships. He too seems to have been dissatisfied with his share of the booty from Troy; but one also wonders, as one does in the comparable case of Odysseus, whether Sparta needed some time to digest its rancor against Helen.[40] Eumaeus, who is utterly removed from the experience of the war, still wishes after twenty years that Helen along with her entire family had perished (14.68–69). Menelaus picks up the story at the end of his wandering, when the gods detained him on the island of Pharos off the coast of Egypt. Helen's drug is now an antidote to the sadness of memory; but what Menelaus learned in Egypt was about the sin of forgetting: gods want men always to remember their commands (4.353).[41] He tells Eidothea—"goddess of looks" or "goddess of knowledge"—who took pity on him, that it was not because he took pleasure in suffering that he stayed on the island but because, without his knowing it, he must have sinned against the gods. Eidothea then instructs him on how he can deceive her father, Proteus, and force the truth out of him. The deception consists of concealing himself and three of his crew inside the skins of seals, which the goddess kills and flays, and the force consists in holding onto Proteus as he keeps on changing into one thing after another until he returns to the shape he had when he was asleep. The god, then, who shows in himself that all of becoming is nothing but appearance, cannot himself see through appearance and mistakes the dead for the living. Becoming is an illusion that the will by itself can overcome. Proteus tells Menelaus that he and Helen are going to live forever in a place where the weather is always the same (4.566–68). Helen and Menelaus seem to complement one another. She can see through appearance; he can get to what is beyond appearance. She understands the resentment against change and time; he stops them. At the heart of both is the heart. For Helen it is her change of heart that wipes out the past; for Menelaus it is his sense of sin that the gods reward by disclosing his crime and putting an end to time.

Menelaus learns that despite the wrath of Athena, Poseidon saved Ajax at first, and Hera, Agamemnon; but Ajax lost his life when he boasted that he had escaped the sea despite the gods, and Agamemnon landed on the coast near Aegisthus, who slew him at dinner, "as if he were an ox at the manger." Menelaus does not offer any divine explanation for Agamemnon's death; he accepts the will of the gods to be as absolute as his own. The gods, however, demand an outward conformity, whether it be in the guise of a pious speech or pious deed. Menelaus seems to have realized—perhaps Proteus's simile suggested it to him—that Aegisthus had not buried Agamemnon (11.424–26). When he got to Egypt, Menelaus erected a cenotaph to Agamemnon, "in order that his glory be unquenched" (4.584). The cenotaph recalls the sealskin that fooled Proteus. Perhaps, however, in some sense Proteus was not fooled, if appearances are always illusory. Perhaps the decisive thing was that there was still life beneath the skin. Whether we think anachronistically of Pythagorean metempsychosis, which Herodotus traces back to Egypt (2.123.2),[42] or, as Herodotus also reports, of the Egyptian teaching that the gods are not what they are represented as being (2.46.2), it is clear that Menelaus has tapped into an understanding of things that involves two radical disjunctions, between being and becoming, on the one hand, and, on the other, between reality and appearance, both of which together potentially challenge the wisdom of Odysseus. That wisdom must be of a different order if Odysseus rejects the immortality Menelaus is granted.[43]

3

Odysseus's Choice

The timing of events, if not the events themselves, seems to be under the control of the gods. For Menelaus to return on the same day as the funeral of Aegisthus and Clytaemestra must have awakened in him a sense of utter helplessness that a longer interval would have dispelled.[44] Zeus decides that Odysseus's trip from Calypso's island to the Phaeacians should take twenty days; on the eighteenth day Poseidon returns from the Ethiopians. If Hermes had gone to Calypso's at the same time that Athena came to Telemachus, and everything else remained the same, then on the fifth day after that, when Telemachus was with Menelaus, Odysseus would have set out on his raft and arrived at Alcinous's on the twenty-fifth day from the beginning; but Poseidon did not return until the twenty-ninth, and Odysseus would have arrived home before Poseidon could have caused a storm or destroyed a Phaeacian ship. Zeus, then, wanted his brother to have the opportunity to inflict a double penalty that would pit Poseidon's retaliation on behalf of his son against his punishment of the Phaeacians, his own descendants. It is hard to imagine a more fitting way for Zeus to teach a god a lesson and reaffirm his own ascendancy. Zeus too is the master of the light touch.

Athena initiates the second assembly of the gods. Her speech is mainly composed of fragments from the speeches of Mentor and Proteus (2.230–34; 4.557–60). Mentor had criticized in general the people for not remembering with gratitude Odysseus's mild rule, and he had been in particular indignant that they kept silent in the face of the few suitors and did not restrain them with words. Athena does not mention the suitors. She thus gives the impression that those who desire to kill Telemachus are the Ithacans (5.18); but since Zeus knows the truth, it is better to say that she silently rejects out of hand Mentor's suggestion, which would have perpetuated the mildness of Odysseus's rule on a democratic basis. She certainly implies, by the insertion of Calypso's detention of Odysseus between the recommendation of harshness in monarchical rule and the threat against Telemachus's life, that, had the people's memory of Odysseus remained vivid, there would be no need for Odysseus now to return.[45] She suppresses any mention of her own hand in forcing the suitors to react to Telemachus's threats. Zeus is not fooled; he asks rhetorically whether this was not Athena's plan, so that Odysseus might return and punish them. Zeus too does not at first say who "they" are (5.27). That everyone in Ithaca suffers directly would be an exaggeration (cf. 2.166–67); but it is clear that terror becomes the foundation of the new order, and it affects everyone. Whether the memory of terror is longer lasting than the memory of gratitude is another question.

The action of the *Odyssey* had begun with Zeus's recollection of Aegisthus, and how he had sent Hermes to warn him. Zeus now sends Hermes to Calypso, who under protest obeys the instructions Hermes transmits. He hardly needs to remind her of the consequences of disobedience (5.146–47). It seems, then, that Zeus has decided to have dealings only with other gods, and in the future he will send only signs to men (2.146; 20.102 [cf. 121]; 24.539). There is in the present time of the *Odyssey* nothing like the storm he once arranged at the Sun's request. Perhaps Zeus can remain the father of men only if Odysseus ceases to be like a father to his people. Athena must have convinced Zeus that no oracular pronouncement, and no appeal to shame, not even a direct order, would be effective any longer.

Homer retards his account of Hermes' transmission of Zeus's message to Calypso in two ways. He makes a likeness of Hermes' passage across the surface of the sea, and he gives us a description of Calypso's island cave and its surroundings (5.51–54, 59–74). We are given a twofold account of what Odysseus has already rejected.[46] He does not want to be able to skim the waves like a gull that wets its wings in the brine as it hunts for fish, and he does not take any pleasure in a landscape that even Hermes finds delightful enough to linger gazing at before he goes into the cave. Odysseus has turned his back to it and weeps as he looks perpetually out over the sea (5.155–58). Imagine paradise, Homer says, along with the power immortality would confer; this is that to which Odysseus said "No!" even though there is, in addition, the beauty of Calypso, which, Odysseus grants, is greater than Penelope's (5.215–18).[47] Homer could not have brought out any more plainly the self-evident folly of Odysseus than by painting a picture that seems to be designed to stir in us a longing that pulls us away from the real and the possible. It is what Menelaus looks forward to with equanimity. After the fourth book, in which ap-

pearance is at a discount, Homer gives us an appearance that the experience of it utterly belies. Homer must attract us to what repels Odysseus
and make us understand his experience without the experience. To look
at paradise and to be in paradise are altogether different. Amidst the trees,
birds, flowers, and springs, with the odor of cedar and citron spread
throughout the island, and the beautiful singing of Calypso, there seems
to be no place for man.

For Hermes, the scene has nothing but an evanescent attraction; there
are no men here who offer sacrifices and choice hecatombs (5.101–2). He
seems to believe that this is only possible if there is political life. But what
of Odysseus? If the human equivalent to the honor of sacrifice is to be
honored like a god and receive great gifts—the two things Zeus guarantees
Odysseus will get from the Phaeacians (5.36–40)—do they suffice to explain Odysseus's rejection of Calypso? Odysseus never on his own puts
forward Penelope as the sole reason behind his desire to return home (cf.
9.29–36; 13.42–43).[48] It is characteristic of him that when Calypso simply
assumes that Penelope is the sole reason for his rejection of her offer,
Odysseus deflects her very phrasing into a general longing for home
(5.209–11, 219–20). It is hard to know how much weight one ought to
give to her standard epithet *periphrōn*—"outstandingly thoughtful"—
which he cites when he agrees with Calypso that, as a mortal, "outstandingly thoughtful Penelope" is her inferior in looks and stature (5.216–17;
cf. 18.248–49; 19.325–26). Antinous also claims, absurdly, that it is Penelope's mind, despite her injustice, that makes her so attractive (2.116–22).
Given the short time Odysseus lived with her before the war and the
shorter time he will stay home—certainly far less than the seven years
with Calypso—perhaps one ought to generalize and say that it was the
absence of mind in the setting of Calypso's island that had at some time
made it pall.

The puzzle of Odysseus's choice is due in large part to the order in
which his story is told. Odysseus's past, about which we do not as yet
know much, could not be placed in the proper temporal sequence if
Odysseus were to be allowed to give his own account of it. Homer's
choice of Odysseus as his own storyteller creates the puzzle. Self-reflec-
tion necessarily distorts the order of time; so unless Homer allowed
Odysseus to tell the *Odyssey* from start to finish, there had to be an edge
that was the meeting of two narrative surfaces, one arranged by Athena
to line up with the preliminary conditions for Odysseus's return, and the
other fixed en bloc between his reception among the Phaeacians and his
return. (We may note in passing that Odysseus's second exposition to
Penelope, of which we have the summary, differs in some details from his

first [23.310–41].) The immediate consequence of Homer's delegation of
his role to Odysseus is that the fifth book, in connecting Odysseus's story
with Telemachus's, must put the stress on Odysseus's punishment of the
suitors and not on his experiences that led to his choice. They are different
issues even if his choice is his fate, for Odysseus could then have expressed
regret for his choice, as Calypso predicts that he will once he leaves the
island. She turns out not to be mistaken, though not in the way she surmised. Odysseus's justice determines his release at this moment; but we
do not know whether that coincides with Odysseus's understanding of
human wisdom as something distinct from divine knowledge, to which
presumably he would have had permanent access once he took up Calypso's offer. The kind of knowledge she imparts to him just before he
leaves—it was not an ordinary storm that destroyed his last ship, and
Poseidon was not behind it (12.389–90)—Odysseus gives up forever. He
knows that his own story would have had a different ending were it not
for Calypso's secondhand knowledge.

There are at least three ways to understand Odysseus's seven years on
Calypso's island. It is just empty time that must pass if the suitors are to
come to Penelope in the fourth year and Telemachus grow up in the last.
This emptiness would be a fitting punishment for the loss of the cattle of
the Sun that Odysseus's men consumed, since the 350 cows and 350 sheep
that make up altogether the seven herds of the Sun seem to symbolize, as
Aristotle thought (fr. 157 R), the days and nights in a solar year (12.127–
31). Since they are neither born nor perish, the partial rent in time his
men effected would have to be repaired through a forced idleness on
Odysseus's part. There is besides the indispensable interval during which
any feelings the Ithacans may have harbored against Odysseus, justified
or not, must be allowed to settle down. Odysseus has to suffer something
for the loss of six-hundred men. The crisis that Telemachus's coming of
age brings to a head determines the length of the interval, but Odysseus
does not know anything about Telemachus; so experientially the time he
spends is not affected by this "natural" length.

There is, moreover, another factor. Teiresias does not tell Odysseus
when the suitors would lay siege to his wife. An element of uncertainty
is deliberately introduced into Odysseus's future; in revealing a refined
sense of torture in whoever conceived of it, it may appeal to Poseidon as
well (5.290, 379). We have to imagine that Odysseus is counting the days
until the twentieth year is up; but he did not know he would have to
spend all that time with Calypso. While he is sleeping with her, at first
with pleasure and then by compulsion, he is given over to vain imaginings
for the first four years, when the suitors have not yet come; and though

it may well be that for the last three years what he pictures to himself conforms with the reality, such a difference is unknown to Odysseus. The gods allow him time to become suspicious of everyone, no less of Penelope than of Laertes (24.239–40). The cautiousness he always had seems to undergo a radical change that we come to witness when it is complete, but not while it is in the process of formation. This is truly empty time for us. It may be experiential time for Odysseus, however, although not even he can report on it, for its effects would be gradual and imperceptible to him. We know that he has been brooding, and with all his tears and sighs has been rending his heart (5.82–83). Calypso calls him sinful (5.182; cf. 18.139–40). Is it possible that Poseidon, whose brutality is revealed in the monstrousness of his offspring, granted other gods, with a greater sense of refinement, the opportunity to create a penitentiary, a *sōphronist-ērion* as Plato calls it, that just might have worked even on Odysseus?[49] Were that the case, Poseidon's punishment of Odysseus for the blinding of the Cyclops would have been redesigned to teach him that man too should be blind and not wander to see for himself. "Calypso" (Καλυψώ) means "Concealer." It looks like an anagram of "Cyclops" (Κύκλωψ).

In their conversation, neither Hermes nor Calypso mentions Odysseus by name. For Hermes, Odysseus is distinguished by being the most miserable of all who fought at Troy, or at least Zeus says he is; and through an extreme compression he makes Athena, against whom the Achaeans sinned on their journey home, responsible for the loss of all of Odysseus's shipmates (5.105–10). If it is not just a case of narrative syncopation, Athena would have incorporated the anger of Poseidon, whom neither Hermes nor Calypso mentions, into her scheme. Did Athena begin to dry out the timber Odysseus needs for his raft seven years before (5.240)? She certainly lets Odysseus reflect on what it means to be abandoned by the gods. Odysseus believes her desertion of him occurred right after the sack of Troy, and the excuse she gives for her absence—her reluctance to contend with Poseidon—does not cover the interval between the Cicones and Polyphemus (13.316–19, 341–43). One could say, in Athena's defense, that as long as Odysseus has chosen memory and not yet come forward as mind, she does not need to protect him. However that may be, Calypso, either on instructions or for her own reasons, confirms Odysseus's sense of abandonment; for though at some point she tells him about Hermes' visit, she does not tell him that she is under orders to let him go (7.262–63). Within, then, an almost empty fate of a twenty-year absence from home, in which Odysseus suffers much and loses all his companions, there is, in ever-narrowing circles, the anger of Athena, the effects of which he shares with all the Achaeans, the anger of Poseidon, and the anger of the Sun. It is the Sun's anger that puts him at last in solitary confinement, over which presides Calypso, the goddess of occlusion, who, in hiding him from the world, puts a veil over the gods as well.

Calypso interprets Zeus's command to release Odysseus as just another example of divine jealousy when it comes to open marriages between men and goddesses (5.118–28; cf. 15.250–51). The two instances she mentions, Orion and Iasion, certainly suggest that had Odysseus accepted her offer, he would have been killed at once. It is unclear whether Odysseus knows this; but he does treat Calypso's offer as the last temptation after the cattle of the Sun. It is certainly a curious situation in which to be caught, between the withdrawal of the gods and the possibility of becoming a god oneself, and if one resists the deadly alternative, one will receive as a temporary reward, against all odds, the punishment of one's enemies. The opacity at the heart of the *Odyssey* baffles the reader.

One way of expressing that opacity is to consider the following. According to Plato's Alcibiades, one could match up Brasidas with Achilles, and Pericles with Nestor and Antenor, but in the case of Socrates there is no legendary figure like him, unless, Alcibiades adds, one resorts to Silenus and satyrs.[50] The practice to which Alcibiades alludes goes back to Homer. Athena presented Orestes as Telemachus's model; Antinous thinks that Tyro, Alcmene, and Mycene cannot match the mind of Penelope (2.116–22). He later reminds the presumably drunk Odysseus of the story of the Lapiths and Centaurs (21.293–304). Penelope twice observes a resemblance between herself and the daughters of Pandareos (19.518–24; 20.66–79); and in the present passage, Calypso sees herself as deprived as Dawn and Demeter. No one ever matches up Odysseus with anyone in the past, and he himself never cites a mythical example. When Odysseus wishes to point a moral, he makes up a story that bears traces at times of his own life (cf. 18.138–42; 19.75–84). Homer conveys the uniqueness of Odysseus by setting him in a labyrinth of dead ends, each of which seems at first to open out into freedom, but at the heart of which there is a double mystery, the missing seven years with Calypso and the second journey to a people who do not know the sea. It is these two experiences, one of which lies in the past, the other in the future, and neither of which can be expressed, that define Odysseus and the *Odyssey*.

The voyage between Ogygia and Scheria first brings to light the difference between Odysseus and Homer. Odysseus abbreviates Homer's account when he tells Arete how he came to be wearing the clothes she herself had woven (7.241–97), and thus indicates what he believes either to be important for himself to tell or for the queen to hear. The first passage he omits concerns how he guided himself by the stars (5.272–77), for Calypso told him to keep the Bear to his left; and throughout his summary Odysseus suppresses any mention of the various kinds of divine support he received. Even the fact that Poseidon caused the storm eighteen days out looks in his version conventional and not due to Ino's information (5.339). At the time, Odysseus thought Zeus was the cause (5.304). What increases the significance of Odysseus's first omission is that this is one of the few passages in which Homer tells us how he understands poetry. Odysseus kept his eyes on the Pleiades, Boötes, and the Bear, "to which they also give the name 'Wagon'; she turns in place and keeps a sharp lookout (*dokeuei*) for Orion." Homer gives a neutral and an Olympian account of the stars. The neutral account has sunk to a mere name; the Olympian account keeps both the hunter Orion and the Bear on a literal level, where *dokeuei* has its full force. Any weakening of either Orion or Bear weakens *dokeuei* as well and turns a possible truth into an image (cf. 7.93). According to Odysseus, Orion or his image is in Hades and still hunting (11.572–75). Dawn often heralds the beginning of a new day in the *Odyssey*, but only at the beginning of the fifth book does she take over from the Sun and bring light to gods and mortals (cf. 3.1–3), and only there does she rise out of her bed from the side of Tithonus (5.1–2). That Dawn is not just a manner of speaking is confirmed by the story Calypso tells about her and, at the end, by Athena checking her from yoking the horses Lampos and Phaethon, "who bring light to men," when she prolongs the night for Odysseus and Penelope (23.241–46). It is given to Athena first to stop time and then to reverse it: the *Odyssey* ends with her rejuvenation of Laertes (24.367–82).[51]

The second kind of omission Odysseus practices in the rehearsal of his voyage is to drop any reference to the occasions on which he either talked to himself or addressed a silent prayer. There are six soliloquies in the fifth book, four in all the rest of the *Odyssey*.[52] Once Homer has established the difference between outside and inside through Helen and Menelaus, he goes inside and brings out in speech what would otherwise be merely an opinion without any split between the speaker and his heart. Such a split becomes of the greatest importance for Plato's understanding of the soul, and since he borrows from Homer the old-fashioned word for "heart" (*thumos*) and cites a passage from the *Odyssey* to exemplify what he means by the "thumoeidetic," it is particularly important for us to consider what significance Homer himself attaches to this form of self-address.[53] Whereas in the *Iliad*, it is Odysseus who first talks to himself, when he is completely alone on the battlefield (XI.401–10), here it is Poseidon, who on the way back from the Ethiopians catches sight of Odysseus on the sea (5.286–90). Poseidon recognizes at once that Odysseus has almost reached the term of his suffering, and he decides to get in his last licks. Although Poseidon submits to the decision of the gods, just as Calypso had, he has the power to take out his anger on Odysseus. Men are the gods' sticks and stones whom they can kick when they cannot get their way. Frustration of the will prompts self-address. It first occurs in the *Odyssey* after it seemed from Menelaus's account that there was nothing but the will.

Odysseus had assured Calypso that he could take whatever the gods dish out; his great experience of war and waves gave him this certain knowledge (5.221–24). When, however, the storm is gathering and before his raft has been touched, he says:

> Oh my! I am wretched. What will become of me at last? I am afraid that the goddess spoke the complete truth. She said I would get my fill of sufferings at sea before returning to my country. . . . Destruction is now certain for me. Thrice and four times blessed are the Danaans, who then perished at Troy, bringing favor to the Atreidae. How I wish I had died and met my fate on that day when the greatest number of Trojans hurled their spears at me in a fight over the dead Achilles. Then I would have got my share of funeral honors, and the Achaeans would be celebrating my glory; but as it is, it was fated for me to be caught in a miserable death. (5.299–312)[54]

Poseidon wrings out of Odysseus a confession of utter failure. He does not regret his rejection of Calypso's offer; he gives up his whole life, that which makes him interesting, for the sake of dying in a cause not his own while fighting over the nothingness of a corpse, and all that in order that the Achaeans may bury him.[55] Odysseus conceives of the emptiest day of his life in the emptiest time of his life, and says it is preferable to a death at sea. Telemachus too had said he would have preferred it had Odysseus died at Troy, for then the Achaeans would have erected a tomb for the father and the son would have had the glory (1.236–40); but Odysseus has been to Hades and knows from Achilles that it is as nothing compared to the meanest life. Odysseus faces a contingency for which neither his artful construction of the raft nor the deliberate choice of his life had prepared him. He rejected Calypso, but he did not know and could not know that he was accepting the possibility of nonanticipatable experiences, experiences that could not be extrapolated on the basis of any set of past experiences. In choosing the uncertainty of mortality, Odysseus chooses self-opacity. In the implied opposition between god and will, which characterizes the difference between "Nestor" and "Menelaus," there is complete certainty in either case—neither spoke of fear—and hence at Nestor's there was the suppression of experience and at Menelaus's the cancellation of time.[56] Both now come back with a rush.

Odysseus now knows something about himself he did not know before. We do not know whether the gods also gain this knowledge about him. It would seem to be especially important for them to know because Odysseus's wish puts the divine law of burial at the center of his choice. Odysseus does not choose the human as such; he chooses the human that does not exist at all if there are not gods. The issue of burial, which had permeated Nestor's second account and had merged with the issue of sacrifice at the end of Menelaus's story, is chosen by Odysseus himself to be the core of his choice.[57] His choice is not of an indeterminate future but of a completed past that would at least have made him a somebody, under divine auspices, and not the nothing, without the gods, he believes he is fated to become. Since Odysseus's counterfactual wish involves his own survival, it must take the form of a split between himself and himself, so that he can picture to himself what happens after his death (cf. 24.87–94). We thus have a revision, subsequent to his choice, of everything that went into making his choice, which he will expound to the Phaeacians. Homer, then, implies that Odysseus's life cannot be completely the subject of his self-told story; and what is not subject to his control is not just an accretion or modification of the story he does get to tell but also stands as its annihilation. One can say that Odysseus's expression of an unfulfillable wish is just an aberration and proves no more than that Odysseus does not have an iron heart; but if one considers all the other regrets he could have expressed—"My wife will not close my eyes," "I shall never see my son grown-up," "Laertes will pine away as did Anticleia" (11.424–32)—none of which would have canceled his life or inserted the gods inside it, there seems to be more to it than a simple lapse. Odysseus, after all, has greater assurances about his future than anyone else who rejects immortality could expect.

Between Odysseus's first and second speeches to himself, there is the intervention of Ino (5.333–53). She was once a mortal and became a goddess. Odysseus does not know this, for she does not tell Odysseus even her name. As the pity Homer ascribes to her seems to be due to her former humanity, the very first inference we can draw from Odysseus's rejection of immortality is his rejection of compassion.[58] Odysseus does not want to do anyone a favor ever again. Indeed, though he pleads for pity as long as he is away from Ithaca (5.340; 6.175, 327), he never does so once he returns home, though he is supposed to be playing the part of a beggar. That the suitors pity him does not count in their favor (17.367). Odysseus rejects the principle of those who went out of their way to help him. The harshness of the justice he metes out seems to preclude it. Even the one-time pity he felt for Penelope does not show (19.209–12); it does not lead him to reveal to her who he is and take her into the conspiracy. The suspiciousness, which goes along with his understanding of justice, never abates. Despite the desperate situation Ino finds him in, he reacts very cautiously to her information and advice. He does not accept as yet that Poseidon is the cause, but he acknowledges the possibility that Scheria is his refuge because he has seen it for himself (5.359). Ino's advice, however, that he should swim for it and abandon the raft, he believes might be a trick; he decides instead to wait and see whether the raft gets completely smashed before trying for shore. Odysseus does not mention in his self-address the *krēdemnon*, or "water-wings," she urged him to put on, though he knows he must strip off his clothes, since they weighed him down when he was thrown off the raft earlier (5.321). Once Poseidon does break up the raft, he follows Ino's advice, even though he must give up riding a beam, a practice that once saved him after a previous shipwreck (5.371; 12.422–25, 444; cf. 14.310–13).[59] It is unclear what convinces him to rely completely on an untested divine support and not wait until the beam is smashed as well; but the next time he speaks to himself he accepts the settled enmity of Poseidon (5.424), while we know that Poseidon has already left the scene and no longer has any interest in harming Odysseus. Poseidon, it seems, must have been satisfied as soon as he saw that Odysseus was no longer going to rely on any contrivance of his own (cf. 4.499–510). In any case, it is now enough for Poseidon to imagine Odysseus's future misery; he does not have to arrange or witness it (cf. 7.330–31). Poseidon's second speech to himself is addressed to Odysseus: "Go on wandering in just this way across the sea, with much suffering, until you meet with divinely-supported men, but, though I now abstain once you are fated to escape the sea, you will not find fault with your misery" (5.377–79). Poseidon does not get inside Odysseus; he pulls Odysseus inside of himself and lets Odysseus interpret his experiences on his own.

In Odysseus's third speech to himself (5.408–23), he formulates precisely two contingencies: if he approaches the shore, a wave may smash him against the rocks, and if he swims away, either a storm may seize him again or a sea monster attack him. It is at this point that Athena takes over. According to Homer, she suggested that Odysseus first cling to the rock and then swim out and look for a safe landing somewhere else (5.426–40). Odysseus is aware on his own of the two dangers he faces; but Athena puts into his head the proper sequence of responses. Odysseus does not know this, either at the moment or in the future; and as Homer presents it, he has hardly any choice in either case, for a wave pushed him against the rocks and on its return drove him away. Homer seems to imply that, without Athena's hidden counsel, Odysseus would have fought against the direction of the wave on both occasions. One wonders, however, whether Homer does not give us a double version, one from the inside and one from the outside—either heart or god—and the presentation of Athena's two suggestions are due to the opacity of Odysseus's silent deliberations. This possibility is certainly compatible with Odysseus's own narration (7.278–82), but his silent prayer seems to put it out of court. He addresses an unknown river, mentions Poseidon's threats, and claims the protection that anyone who comes as a wandering suppliant deserves even from the gods (5.445–50). The river stops its flow at once. Nothing, then, would be unknown to the gods, unless one should say that silent prayer and silent thoughts are fundamentally different; but it would be safer to infer that Odysseus's choice, which involves a partial self-opacity, entails the possibility that the gods can be at work within that self-opacity. Zeus's arrangement, which allowed Poseidon to catch Odysseus at sea, would then have had the further purpose of wringing out of Odysseus his confession, that in rejecting immortality he did not reject the divine along with it.

Once Odysseus gets on dry land, he holds another deliberation with himself; and this time Athena does not make up his mind (5.465–73). His choice is between staying on the beach with the attendant risk, in his weakened state, of succumbing to the frost and dew, and, in seeking shelter inland, becoming the prey of beasts. Odysseus chooses the latter; he chooses, if worst comes to worst, to be eaten. This is the only one of Odysseus's self-addresses so far that does not mention the gods; and his choice is in accordance with their absence. Having begun with a rejection of the Odyssean element of his life and an acceptance of the divine law of burial as of central importance, he ends up with an acceptance of what most horrified the warriors at Troy and defined Achilles' inhumanity. It is again unclear whether we are to take Odysseus's last decision as his final decision, or whether Homer means to show us that, within Odysseus's choice of the apparently human, there is only the divine and the bestial, and however significant it may be for the future that Odysseus, once he leaves the sea, goes with the beasts, the truth of the human itself consists in the two extreme choices together. There is no third.[60]

Odysseus hears from Ino for the first time a pun on his name (5.340), though we knew of it almost from the start (1.62). Ino asks Odysseus why Poseidon conceived such conspicuous anger (*ōdusato*) against him, and Odysseus picks up the verb later when he speaks to himself of Poseidon's settled anger against him (*odōdustai*, 5.423; cf. 19.275). **Odussomai* is a verb that Homer uses only of divine anger, with the exception of

Autolycus's naming his grandson Odysseus, "because," he says, "I have come here *odussamenos* against many men and women" (19.407–8).[61] If *odussamenos* is translated as a middle, it should mean "I who have conceived anger against," but it seems that Autolycus might want it to be taken passively, "against whom many have conceived an anger." However this may be, and allowing that "Odysseus" may be both the embodiment of anger and the universal object of anger, it is striking that Odysseus shares an unexpected trait with Achilles. The word *mēnis* (anger), with which the *Iliad* opens, is applied solely to divine wrath when it is not said of Achilles; but whereas Achilles' anger is not built into his name and, just as it is assumed, can be cast off or allayed, the anger of Odysseus, whether "of Odysseus" be an objective or subjective genitive, is inseparable from who he is. The verb is closer to the truth of Odysseus than the noun is to the truth of Achilles. Homer makes Odysseus's name into a riddle by his failure to explain why he linked up the account of how Odysseus received his name with the account of how Odysseus received his scar (19.392–466). The scar was inflicted by a wild boar, which suddenly attacked him out of its lair, "which the wet force of winds could not blow through, the sun could not penetrate with its rays, and the rain could not get in all the way" (19.440–42). Homer uses the same lines to describe the thicket into which Odysseus now creeps (5.476–82). After choosing to be eaten by beasts, he enters the possible lair of a beast. The fifth book thus ends with a choice that ties in Odysseus's future with Odysseus's past, and whatever Odysseus may now believe he knows about his choice, we know that he does not remember his past. It is not just Odysseus who is caught off guard when Eurycleia begins to wash his feet, but Athena as well: although she had disguised him well enough to be unrecognizable, she had not known or did not remember that he bore a scar.

4

Among the Phaeacians

Shame

The two days Odysseus spends among the Phaeacians seem to be too short to justify the length of Homer's narrative. One has the impression before Odysseus meets Nausicaa that they are a free and easy people, who would not resist Odysseus's request for help, but would just send him on his way as they always have done in the past for anyone who came to them (8.31–33). Athena's elaborate scheme thus seems superfluous. Why must Odysseus get to Alcinous through Nausicaa? He does need clothes, it is true, so he can make a decent entrance; but for all we know the *krēdemnon* Ino gave him served no purpose. It seems to have been a device to strip him naked once he got to shore and make him appear totally helpless and exposed.[62] Without our quite understanding it, however, Athena tells Odysseus that the Phaeacians are an unfriendly people (7.32–33); and she makes Odysseus invisible to them until he suddenly shows up at the knees of Arete (7.142–45). There is, then, a mystery at Scheria that is fateful for Odysseus; and it cannot be the possible marriage with Nausicaa that she wishes and Alcinous offers him, for Odysseus does not even refuse (6.244–45; 7.311–15). One comes closer to the mystery and its solution if one observes that it takes two books after Odysseus has deftly parried Arete's question before anyone thinks of asking Odysseus again for his name (8.550).[63] Odysseus has to weep openly before Alcinous's curiosity gets the better of him (8.521–22, 531–34).

We know more about the Phaeacians than Odysseus ever finds out. Despite the information Athena imparts to him, he is working somewhat in the dark. What we know and Odysseus does not is that the city he comes to is less than one generation old. Prior to their removal to a remote island, its people were neighbors of the Cyclopes, who being stronger injured them continuously (6.1–12). Odysseus learns that they are not a martial people, but he does not know that they have lost their fighting spirit almost overnight. Alcinous's father built a wall with stakes around the city when he laid it out; but there are no guards on the wall, and Nausicaa tells her servants not to be afraid of Odysseus: "There is no mortal man nor will there ever be who comes bringing hostility, for we are very dear to the immortals, and we live very far apart, and no one has dealings with us" (6.200–205). She may need Athena's encouragement to lose her maidenly fear, but she did not need it in order to overcome a suspicion of strangers. Alcinous thought nothing of sending her out of the city without bodyguards. Odysseus, then, comes to an unarmed and disarmed city in which the possibility of war has vanished along with, apparently, its memory.

Scheria was thought in antiquity to be Corcyra, and Thucydides makes the transition from his Archaeology, in which Homer is one of his main witnesses, to the alleged causes of the Peloponnesian War through his account of the Corcyraean-Corinthian conflict; in the course of it, he mentions that the people of Corcyra, which was one of the richest cities at the time and powerfully prepared for war, occasionally took pride in their fleet in light of the former occupation of Corcyra by the Phaeacians whose navy was so famous (1.25.4).[64] In its struggle against Corinth, Corcyra found itself at a disadvantage. It had made no alliances, either offensive or defensive, with other cities, and as the Corcyraeans put it at Athens, "Our seeming moderation, not to run risks in a foreign alliance at the judgment of another, has veered around to the opposite quarter and now appears as weakness and lack of planning" (1.32.4). The Corcyraeans seem to claim that they maintain the Phaeacian tradition in more than just naval glory. Indeed, the countercharge of the Corinthians, that the Corcyraeans' moderation is a smokescreen, "which they practice for criminal ends and not for virtue, wanting to have no ally for their injustice, let alone a witness" (1.37.2), has its counterpart among the Phaeacians, who at least once carried out a pirate raid in Alcinous's lifetime (7.7–11). Arete implies that once they are away from home the Phaeacians are thievish (8.443–45).[65] Nausicaa herself says that the people are arrogant (*huperphialoi*), an adjective applied in the *Odyssey* repeatedly to the suitors and once to the lawless Cyclopes (6.274; 9.106). If we now go back to Athena's advice to Odysseus, "Do not look at anyone or ask questions; the people here do not put up well with strangers, and they are not friendly to whoever comes from elsewhere, confident as they are in their fast ships" (7.321–26), we realize that the Phaeacians have no reciprocal relations with anyone, for their ships can complete the longest journey in the course of a single day (7.321–26).[66]

The Phaeacians have never been strangers or out of place. Their ships know every place and never go off course (8.559–63). They are without error or suffering. In having no need of anyone, except the gods, they do not have to establish credit that their debtors will be expected to repay (cf. 24.283–86). As far as we know, they have never given a gift to anyone who came to them before they are forced to appease Odysseus and thus treat him as if he were a god. The length of the Phaeacian narrative is primarily due to the task Zeus has set for Odysseus, to turn the Phaeacians away from their reliance on the gods to concern for another human being. That reliance is finally broken when Alcinous, while admitting that Odysseus may very well be the stranger who his father predicted would occasion the loss of a ship and the envelopment of the city in a mountain range, dismisses the prediction and chooses, in light of the uncertainty of the future, to go along the path Odysseus has chosen for himself (8.564–71). Odysseus single-handedly converts the Phaeacians to the human.[67] It is a conversion that seems to be against their own good.

Odysseus's first encounter with another human being after seven years involves shame. Shame, too, belongs to his choice, but it does not appear to be choiceworthy. The ravenous lion, to which Homer likens Odysseus when he comes face to face with Nausicaa, would not even try to enter a sheepfold; but need compels the lion to overcome his fear and not, like Odysseus, his shame: Odysseus covers his genitals with a branch (6.127–36). He is a lion with a loincloth. Immediately after, then, the stark division of the human into the divine and the bestial, the human in itself shows up as the defective. The defective shows itself in hiding itself. Shame is a transparent concealment. Athena shows her understanding of shame in sending a dream to Nausicaa, in which her contemporary speaks of her coming marriage and urges her to wash her own wedding dress as well as the clothes of those who are going to give her away (6.22–40). Out of shame, Nausicaa does not mention marriage to her father; instead, she speaks of the fresh clothes he and her unmarried brothers need, but Alcinous understands her perfectly. Athena decides to work indirectly; she knows that Nausicaa will conceal the truth and Alcinous will detect it. Neither will realize that the spurious cover Nausicaa gives to her motives contains the real reason: Nausicaa must bring the clothes of men to the washingplace. Two human beings talk to one another, and one can translate the words of the other back into the other's hidden desires; but this seeing through the surface of things masks the intention of Athena, which is solely on the surface and has nothing to do with what she exploits. The divine plan lies hidden in plain sight.

We begin with the coincidence between human shame and Athena's plan to clothe Odysseus. At line 12 of the sixth book, *mēdea* means understanding and at line 219, it means genitals.[68] Alcinous's understanding, which comes from the gods, saw through Nausicaa's shame; Odysseus could not bring himself to show himself as he is. The defectiveness Odysseus accepts both in himself and his wife does not just carry with it the choice of exposure to things outside oneself over which one has no control, which the storm at sea represents, but it is a defectiveness that carries with it the demand that it be covered. Something has to make up for one's incompleteness without making for completeness. That something seems to be, as Herodotus suggests, the law.[69] The law does not afford the kind of protection Odysseus has when he creeps into his lair, but the kind of veil Nausicaa puts over her desire. It comes out as if by nature from within man's own understanding of his defectiveness. It thus goes along with the possible withdrawal of the gods, inasmuch as their disappearance can now be at one with the veil itself and not a pattern imposed on it. Alcinous wonders whether Odysseus is not a god in disguise, and if he is whether that means that the gods, who used to come as they are—φαίνονται ἐναργεῖς ("with all the vividness of daylight")—whether collectively to sit among them at sacrifices or singly, are not devising some other relation to them, even though the Phaeacians are as near to the gods as the Cyclopes and Giants (7.199–206). That Alcinous is mistaken about Odysseus does not entail that he is mistaken about the gods' revision. Odysseus does not say he is not a god; he says he does not look like the gods (7.208–9; cf. 16.187). Later, at the moment Homer draws a veil over the Phaeacians' future, they have just prepared a sacrifice of twelve bulls to Poseidon, and Alcinous evidently does not expect him to attend (13.181–87).

The occlusion of the gods, toward which the *Odyssey* is working, puts the poet through the Muse in the position of being the sole authority about the gods. Homer likens Nausicaa, as she plays ball with her maidservants, to Artemis playing with the Nymphs (6.102–9). While Homer is putting the unknown alongside the unknown, he pretends that we have seen Artemis on Taygetus or Erymanthus, and Nausicaa will thereby become vivid to us. When Odysseus likens her to Artemis (if she is a goddess [6.150–52]), he implies that he has not seen Artemis, but Artemis must be like Nausicaa. He supplies no details; but if she is mortal, she resembles a palmtree he once saw at Delos, the island dedicated to Artemis's brother. In this case, Odysseus is as circumstantial as Homer had been about Artemis (6.160–63). Homer, then, calls our attention to the peculiarity of the Olympian gods, that though they are always invisible, they partake of visibility through speech. In speech they are in sight: Demodocus is blind (8.64). On account of the subsequent development of painting and sculpture, this distinctive trait of the Olympian gods ceases to be as wonderful as it is. One forgets the power of Homer's image-making in light of the visible copies of his speech.[70] He tells us at the end of the sixth book that, though Athena heard Odysseus's prayer, she did not yet appear (*phaineto*) before him, for she was ashamed before her uncle (6.328–31). Athena's nonappearance took the form of appearing before him in the likeness of a young girl with a pitcher (7.19–20). Odysseus knew that it was she (13.322–23), but Poseidon apparently does not. He can no more see through appearances than Proteus.

Paradise

Athena's manipulation of human shame and desire allows her to lead Nausicaa into making a mistake. Although Nausicaa has already promised to show Odysseus the way to the city (6.194), Athena decides to enhance his appearance, so that Nausicaa concludes, not unreasonably, that he has come not without the will of the gods. Since he now looks like a god, whereas before she thought him uncomely, she connects her dream with this sudden transformation and wishes that he stay and become her husband (6.239–46). Nausicaa believes that she has found a matchup between dream and reality, particularly since Odysseus had already spoken so persuasively of the special understanding that accrues to a husband and wife who think as one (6.180–85). It would be another illustration of the special providence with which the Phaeacians have hitherto been favored. Nausicaa, however, misinterprets the sequence of events, and possibly Alcinous does too, for he hopes that Odysseus will stay and be his son-in-law, even though he does not yet know his name (7.311–15). His easy reading of Nausicaa's shame would have readily led the way to this wish. Nausicaa, at any rate, traces out a plausible pattern in things that does not correspond to the truth. At first glance, it seems to be a piece of gratuitous cruelty on Athena's part; but it is through Nausicaa's misreading that she informs Odysseus about the true character of her people. To the extent that modesty permits, Nausicaa proposes marriage to Odysseus. She conceals her proposal by assigning the suggestion to the Phaeacians, who will resentfully infer, if they see Odysseus with her, that Odysseus, whether he be a stranger or a god, will be her husband, since she finds none of the Phaeacians good enough for her (6.273–86).[71] Odysseus is thus told, even before Athena confirms it, that they do not like foreigners. Nausicaa implies that he would have less trouble were they warriors or hunters and not sailors (6.27–72). The very wish Nausicaa has conceived of forces her to conceal it and at the same time reveal something that she otherwise would not have revealed. Odysseus understands the import of Nausicaa's speech; he prays to Athena that the Phaeacians be friendly and compassionate in his case (6.327). The secret hostility of the Phaeacians reminds us of the Ithacans. Athena, it seems, grants Odysseus the opportunity to make a practice run.

Athena informs Odysseus that Nausithous, the founder of the Phaeacians, was the grandson on his mother's side of the last king of the Giants, who destroyed his wicked people and perished himself (7.56–60). Nausithous had in turn two sons, Alcinous and Rhexenor, or if one translates crudely their names, "Brains" and "Brawn." The death of Rhexenor seems to have led to an imbalance in the principles of Alcinous's rule—too much moderation and not enough courage, if one may speak Platonically—that was reinforced by his marriage to Rhexenor's daughter, Arete. Alcinous honors Arete as no other woman is honored anywhere else: her rank is far higher than Penelope's. The people also honor her; they look upon her as if she were a goddess, for she knows how to resolve quarrels among those she favors (7.63–77). There is still hostility in paradise. Odysseus is told twice that he must win the favor of the queen if he is to get back home. That he gains his entrance through the daughter and his exit through the mother suggests that the female is the weak spot in the Phaeacian defenses against intruders. Odysseus has to beat down the male opposition to him and seduce the female. He must be both soft and hard.

The second paradise Odysseus enters is characterized in two different ways. On the one hand, gold and silver dogs guard the entrance to Alcinous's palace; Hephaestus made them and endowed them with understanding, "deathless and ageless for all the days"; and, on the other, there is a garden in which various fruits are always flourishing, and at no time of the year does it lie fallow (7.84–132). After Odysseus has made his choice and experienced something of what the choice entails, he confronts two ways in which what he rejected can be understood: deathlessness means either intelligent artifacts or perpetual becoming without decay (cf. XVIII.417–20). Odysseus chose becoming and passing away within the seasons of the solar year, and he rejected knowledge without error. One might say that Odysseus chose the empty time he passed with Calypso insofar as that interval, in which Telemachus grows up, can be understood as a time, like winter, of hidden processes, when nothing apparently happens, but without which nothing would happen. Is Odysseus directed toward Scheria so that he can see what he accepted and thus really accept the largish dose of "noise" he was forced to endure? At one point in

Plato's *Sophist*, the Eleatic Stranger approves of Theaetetus's natural incli-
nation to accept the view that not nature but the rational thought of a
demiurge brought everything corporeal into being; but he omits the argument for the opinion to which he knows Theaetetus's nature will on its
own go, "for otherwise," he says, "time would be superfluous."[72] Odysseus, then, is put in a sequence that is apparently preposterous, for he is
given the evidence he needs for his choice after he has made his choice,
but in fact it is the right sequence, for there cannot be any understanding
ahead of time.

This consideration makes one wonder whether Odysseus's version of
his experiences at sea, in which he relates Poseidon's enmity but suppresses every occasion except one in which he received divine support
(7.286), does not represent his now deeper understanding of the tendency
of his choice. The very sequence of self-addresses suggested that Odysseus while at sea reflected a degree of penitence that his long stay with
Calypso had induced him to undergo unwittingly, and that on being restored to land, he reverted to what he had come to understand through
his post-Trojan adventures. We first overheard perhaps the gradually
dying echoes of his change of heart and finally the single and decisive
overcoming of his despair. Odysseus's second journey is all but necessary
if the gods are to break him once and for all. However that may be, at the
moment, insofar as the neediness of his circumstances forces Odysseus
not to boast of divine support and thus highlight divine enmity, his choice
of the human not only comes out more plainly, but he prepares the
Phaeacians for the withdrawal of the gods from them. His "humanized"
narrative symbolizes their future. One has to balance this possibility,
however, against the plain fact that Odysseus now tells a lie like the truth
and, in doing so, repairs the split in the human that his conversations with
himself, particularly the first and the last, opened up. Did the discovery
of shame, with the accompanying realization that the in-betweenness of
the human does not exhaust the human, help him to repair the split?

As soon as Odysseus finishes his account, Alcinous finds fault with
Nausicaa—she should have brought Odysseus straight to the house—and
Odysseus has to tell a lie to cover up Nausicaa's shame. In order to
ground what he pretends was his own fear and shame, Odysseus puts
forward a claim about "us" (7.302–7). It is the only time in either the
Iliad or the *Odyssey* that anyone ever speaks of "we human beings." "We
human beings," Odysseus says, "are very resentful and censorious" (*dus-
zēloi*). We are angry for no reason and are terrible fault-finders; we do not
accept mistakes and readily believe in the injustice of others. Odysseus
generalizes what Nausicaa had said was characteristic of the Phaeacians;

and he has to lie about the facts of the case so that Alcinous will back down and deny that he is like that: "All things that are just and equitable are better" (7.310). Alcinous becomes friendly toward Odysseus and just toward his daughter through a lie. He is shamed into being what he claims to be. Only shame and fear, or rather the pretense to them, can avoid the self-righteousness and hostility of men. That Alcinous has to offer to make Odysseus his son-in-law in order to disprove Odysseus's characterization of men, only goes to show that had Nausicaa brought Odysseus with her, he would have taken the opposite tack. Odysseus's maxim or verdict certainly fits Telemachus, who reacted in just this way when he saw Athena at the threshold (1.119); and Odysseus too has to be measured against it (cf. 13.209–14); but it is perhaps more important to stress at the moment that Odysseus comes as close as possible to asserting that his own name in its meaning is applicable to everyone.[73] Every man is and is not Odysseus.

Pride

Once Alcinous has given his word that Odysseus will be sent home, Odysseus is delighted: "Zeus father! Would that Alcinous accomplish everything he said! Then just as unquenchable glory would be his over the face of the earth, so I would come to my homeland" (6.331–33). The Phaeacians are famous for their ships (6.22), hecatombs (7.202), houses (7.3), gifts (8.417), clothes (6.58), and singer (8.83), but no one has ever heard of them. Odysseus, of whom they have heard, implies that should he get home Alcinous will be assured of glory, and the adjectives Homer assigned his people would cease to be ornamental. Odysseus tempts Alcinous with glory. He offers the same bait the men at Troy had welcomed once they realized that they were alone, and the gods had withdrawn their support from either side (VI.1). On their realization of their mortality, they turned to the beguiling image of true immortality, immortal glory. The impending doom that Alcinous senses Odysseus's arrival has triggered, combined as it is with the possible occlusion of the gods on whom they had arrogantly relied, turns Odysseus into their last conduit to the outside world. Without him they are a vanished people (cf. 8.101–3).

The thread that runs through the eighth book is song. Demodocus sings three songs in the course of the action. We are given only the outline of the first and last songs; the second song is complete: it is told mostly through speeches, and there is one simile (8.280). Odysseus weeps at the first and tries to conceal it, shares in the pleasure of the Phaeacians in the second, and weeps openly at the third. The first and second songs are sung at the whim of the Muse or Demodocus; Odysseus, by having Demodocus finish off the Trojan War in the third song, prepares the way for his own story, but he lets us realize that, among the Phaeacians, he is the Trojan horse.[74] By the time Demodocus sings his last song of the day, Odysseus has smashed all their illusions and constituted the stranger as a permanent threat. He spreads unease. At the beginning of the eighth book, Homer applies a new epithet to Odysseus. He calls him for the first time "sacker of cities" (8.3).[75] At the same time, Athena puts into practice the new relation in which the Phaeacians, just as Alcinous suspected, are going to stand to the gods. In the guise of Alcinous's herald, she summons individually the Phaeacians to attend the assembly, so that they can learn of the stranger who has recently come and is "like in stature to the immortals" (8.7–14). Man and god become confounded in the image. Athena then beautifies Odysseus and pours over his head and shoulders a divine charm, "so that he may become a friend [dear] to all the Phaeacians . . . an object of fear and of awe" (*deinos t' aidoios te*, 8.22). The day before, Odysseus had pretended to feel fear and shame before Alcinous in order to defend Nausicaa and win over Alcinous; now the tables are turned, and the friendliness of the Phaeacians is going to be gained through terror and respect. If the seventh book is about the necessity of concealment, the eighth book is about the resentment the necessity for concealment creates. It points directly to Odysseus's actions at home.

The day begins pleasantly enough. Alcinous arranges that a ship be got ready to convey the unknown stranger home; and he invites the princes of the realm to his home, "so that we may love [show our friendliness toward] the stranger" (8.42). This friendliness seems to consist entirely of the song or songs Demodocus is to sing. Alcinous has no intention of entertaining Odysseus with anything more substantial. Demodocus's first song is, like the third, a fragment from a series of stories about the Trojan War (8.74, 499–500).[76] It is given to us in the form of a single-speaker narrative that recounts the start of the suffering of Trojans and Danaans alike "on account of the plan of great Zeus." It could not differ more from the *Iliad*, which neither starts at the beginning nor admits at the start the suffering of the Trojans, let alone that Zeus is solely in charge.[77] The obscure relation that obtains in the *Iliad* between Apollo's wrath and Zeus's plan is replaced, in Demodocus's song, by the strict subordination of Apollo's prophecy to Zeus's plan. That we are meant to think of the *Iliad* is confirmed by Demodocus singing of a quarrel between the best of the Achaeans, Achilles and Odysseus—between brains and brawn, as Eustathius says—just as the *Iliad* starts with the quarrel between Aga-

memnon and Achilles, between ancestral and natural right.[78] Homer splits
Achilles and Odysseus apart and assigns to each his own poem. Demodocus sets them at loggerheads so that Agamemnon can presumably take
pleasure, without showing it, in their leaving him the ascendancy. Odysseus had covered his head while Demodocus was singing, "for he was
ashamed of weeping before the Phaeacians" (8.86); but when Demodocus
stopped, he wiped away his tears, uncovered his head, and poured libations to the gods. No one apparently noticed any of this; only when Demodocus began to sing once more, did Alcinous hear Odysseus groan.
The Phaeacians experience nothing but the pleasure of the song and are
too enchanted to see what is right before their eyes; but we do not know
why Odysseus weeps. He implies later that he did not catch Demodocus
out in any falsehoods (8.489–91); but in his praise of the singer, he drops
any mention of the Trojans, and it is only the fate of the Danaans, their
sufferings, their toils, and their actions, that he singles out for praise. Just
as whatever occasioned the dispute between Odysseus and Achilles was
not as significant as its being the signal for the start of a conflict in conformity with a divine plan, so the conflict itself was drained of its justice.
Alcinous understands the Trojan War solely on the basis of Demodocus's
songs, and he interprets its divine purpose to have been nothing else than
to be the subject of song (8.577–80). The Phaeacians are the sole benefi-
ciaries of ten years of fighting. Odysseus's tears, then, would be at the
sheer waste of his life. He is famous no doubt; but the price is higher than
he could have expected. It is as if his momentary wish in the face of the
storm to have died for nothing had been the truth of the war, and the
consolation of burial, with its attendant glory, which he had then pictured
for himself, was its end.

Odysseus listens to a song in which he cannot recognize himself. The
blindness of Demodocus does not just preclude his unmasking before its
time, but poses the question whether, had Demodocus not been blind, he
would have recognized in Odysseus the Odysseus he celebrated.[79] In
order to distract Odysseus, Alcinous proposes that instead of listening
to Demodocus they demonstrate their superiority in boxing, wrestling,
jumping, and running; but Demodocus is taken along with everyone else.
More names of Phaeacians are thus known to us than are the names of
Odysseus's companions. No prizes are awarded at Phaeacian contests.
The competition is pure. Alcinous's son Laodamas suggests that they ask
Odysseus whether he knows any sport; he notes the appearance of great
strength in Odysseus, but he suspects an inner collapse, for the sea he
believes ruins a man as no other evil does. Laodamas knows nothing of
war, not even at secondhand through Demodocus's songs. Euryalus, to

whom we were introduced as "equal to mortal-destroying Ares" (8.115), seconds him. Laodamas then urges Odysseus rather condescendingly to compete, "for there is no greater glory of a man as long as he lives" than what accrues to him through his legs and his arms. Perhaps Demodocus was brought along to celebrate the victors. Odysseus in any case declines, and Euryalus in raillery catches Odysseus perfectly: "I do not liken you at all, stranger, to a man who knows contests, but to a seafarer, a captain of sailors and traders, mindful of freight, guardian of merchandise and of alluring profits, and you do not at all look like a competitor in games" (8.159–64). It may be just a lucky hit on Euryalus' part, but it is in partial agreement with Athena's description of Odysseus (13.291–95). It even fits the false tale Odysseus tells Eumaeus about himself (14.192–359), to say nothing of his self-portrayal to Penelope (19.283–86).

Odysseus reacts to Euryalus' speech as if Euryalus should have known who he is. That he is as unknown as if he were in disguise makes no difference. He introduces the issue of insult, or the attack on a man's dignity, as at the heart of injustice. Insult establishes the absolute measure of wrong, for just as whoever is insulted experiences the total reduction of himself to nothingness, so the retaliation he devises admits of no limits. Whatever shame Odysseus had appears to vanish in the face of Euryalus's "heart-biting speech" (8.185). He matches Euryalus's last words—"You do not at all look like a competitor in games"—with a phrase of his own: "You look like a recklessly wicked man" (8.166). Where others would see youthful indiscretion, Odysseus detects sin. His speech after this becomes difficult. One expects him to say that the gods do not grant all goods together; but instead he says that the gods do not grant the elements of grace or charm to everyone, whether it be looks, brains, or eloquence: "Just as in the case of one man, though he is inferior in looks (*eidos*), a god puts beauty (*morphē*) on his words, and others take pleasure at looking at him with reverence while he speaks unfalteringly, and he is conspicuous in the gathering; and they look upon him like a god as he comes and goes; but another, though he is like the gods in looks (*eidos*), still charm does not crown his words, so in your case your looks (*eidos*) are conspicuous, and not even a god would make them otherwise, but you are empty and vain in point of mind" (8.169–77). Euryalus is the proof that some men lack charm, for charm consists solely in speech, since speech can compensate entirely for inferiority in looks, and though one may look like a god, if there is no charm in one's words, no one takes pleasure in this dead likeness or treats one as if one were a god. Odysseus's anger may make him exaggerate the power of speech—perhaps we are meant to think of Homer's power to conjure up beauty through speech—but he does not exaggerate its effectiveness among the Phaeacians. Alcinous says there is upon him the beauty (*morphē*) of words (11.367).

Odysseus inserts a new kind of contest among the games of the Phaeacians. It is more serious than anything they have ever experienced, and whoever wins wins big. Odysseus's eloquence, it is true, has to be backed up by a deed, but only by one and not the many Athena had planned for him to win (8.22–23). All he now has to do is to challenge the Phaeacians and without entering the lists force them to appease him. His willingness to compete is enough to show his virtue (8.237; cf. XXIII.884–97). Odysseus is their model for the angry gods, with whom they have not yet become acquainted, and who put a demand on men to discount the appearances they themselves have devised. Odysseus all but admits that Euryalus's graceless speech was the truth; he does not look much like the competitor he once was (8.179–83; cf. 4.341–45). Indeed, had Athena not beefed him up, perhaps he would have done worse. Odysseus takes care not to expose his true bulk when he throws the discus (8.187). Euryalus's insult is not to be excused because the man he sees before him has a hidden ally in Athena. Odysseus puts forward a claim to a worth that is not entirely his own and insists that the counterfeit pass as the truth. In a lighter mood, he tells the Phaeacians that at Troy he was second to Philoctetes in the bow, and no one could match him with the spear (8.215–29). He tells them as plainly as he can that were he armed he could kill them all. The terror and the awe that Odysseus's speech must have aroused among the Phaeacians, whom he has reduced to silence, have to be inferred from the effort Alcinous now makes to soothe him. Alcinous acknowledges that Odysseus's speech was not without charm, and he takes back the boasts he had just made about Phaeacian prowess in boxing and wrestling. Since he has just heard that Odysseus may not be as good as he once was in running, he covers the disgrace of the Phaeacians with that small scrap of dignity, and now says that besides being outstanding in yachting they excel in dancing, feasting, constant changes of clothing, hot baths, and dalliance (8.246–49; cf. 6.286–88).[80] The song of Ares and Aphrodite follows soon afterward.

We know that Athena has a perfect understanding of shame, for as a perfect being it would not be difficult to understand what it means to be defective and to sense oneself to be defective, even apart from the shame she has before Poseidon; but it would seem that she does not understand what it means to experience the disparagement of one's self-esteem, for how could one insult either a god or a being as radically defective as man? Athena can certainly understand the boast that denies the need of the gods (4.499–510), and Odysseus is careful to limit his superiority in the bow to contemporaries (8.223–28); but can she understand simply human pride that does not challenge the gods? The question is important because Zeus had planned for Odysseus to receive gifts from the Phaeacians, and it seems that Odysseus manages to extract them on his own. His gracious praise of Alcinous's perfect execution of his boast seems to have inspired Alcinous to follow the example of Poseidon, in the story of Ares and Aphrodite, and placate Odysseus with gifts (8.389), just as Hephaestus was appeased for the insult to his dignity. Aphrodite, he says, despised him for his defectiveness (8.308–11). So, after all, there is among the gods the same experience.[81] If, then, Athena figured out how Odysseus was to open up the Phaeacians, she must have known that Demodocus would sing a song that would make Odysseus weep, that Alcinous would propose contests, that someone would challenge Odysseus and another insult him, and that finally the appeasement of Odysseus would require a song geared specifically to suggest gifts to Alcinous. The invisible web in which Hephaestus caught Ares and Aphrodite would not be more subtle than Athena's plan (cf. 13.302–5). Man, then, would be completely porous for the gods. The gods, or at least Athena, can get in anywhere, and there is no place to hide. The human is split, on the one hand, between the bestial and the divine, and on the other, between shame and pride. Odysseus himself may have chosen self-opacity, but he is an open book to Athena.[82]

The first present Odysseus receives is a handsome sword from Euryalus. He expresses the hope that Euryalus will not need it later. Odysseus then puts on the sword, and the other gifts pour in. After Arete has filled a chest with fine clothes, she urges Odysseus to tie it up with a knot, and Odysseus uses a complex one Circe taught him (8.443–48). Either distrust has suddenly spread among the Phaeacians, and Arete believes, as she says, the sailors may rob Odysseus on the journey home, or else she knows from Odysseus's behavior that he does not trust anyone, and it is better to cater to his suspiciousness. Odysseus neither now nor later thanks the Phaeacians for their gifts, though he admits on leaving that he had wanted them (13.40–41). He does thank Nausicaa after she reminds him of what he owes her; but it is unclear how he would go about fulfilling his promise, if he should get home, "I would pray to you even there as to a goddess all my days" (8.467–68). Now that he is completely secure and has gained the upper-hand over the Phaeacians, he asks Demodocus to sing of the wooden horse, "which Epeius made with the help of Athena, and Odysseus brought the trick into the acropolis, once he had filled it with men who sacked Troy" (8.493–95). His self-assurance is shown in weeping openly during the song; he no longer has any shame before the Phaeacians.[83] He seems to want "sacker of cities" no longer to

be to them, like Euryalus's "equal to mortal-destroying Ares," a decora-
tive epithet. Whether he succeeds or not is unclear; the Phaeacians apparently listen to the story with the same pleasure he had listened to the
story of Ares and Aphrodite, and as they had to the story of his quarrel
with Achilles. Its obvious effect is to make Alcinous curious about him:
how is it possible to weep at a song? So there are, after all, sad things in
the world. If the Phaeacians are to cope with the future, they must be
disenchanted.

Homer goes out of his way not to tell us the reason for Odysseus's
tears. He replaces the reason or reasons with a simile, which would have
to be translated in order to be applicable to Odysseus: "Just as a wife in
tears falls around her husband, whoever falls in front of his city and people, in warding off the pitiless day from his town and children, and she
sees him dying and gasping for breath, and in a heap keens shrilly over
him, and the enemy strike her back and shoulders with spears as they
bring her into slavery, to have toil and woe, and her cheeks waste away
in the most piteous grief, so Odysseus shed piteous tears" (8.523–31).
Demodocus seems to have complied with Odysseus's request in one important respect; he did not include the suffering of the Trojans in his song,
for had they been included, Homer's simile would have been superfluous
and Alcinous's puzzlement unintelligible.[84] Homer's simile is about any
city that is captured, any husband who dies for his country, and any wife
who faces enslavement. It fits the city of the Cicones, which Odysseus
sacked and whose women his men led away, no less than it does Troy
(9.39–42). The simile calls into question the apparent triumph of right
that the fall of Troy represents. It does not vindicate the Trojans; but it
casts Odysseus in a lurid light. According to Demodocus, he was going,
"just like Ares," with Menelaus toward the house of Deiphobus, who,
according to tradition, became Helen's husband after the death of Paris.
Odysseus is now on his way home to Penelope. The hollowness of past
and future right, when they are measured against all he has lost, makes
him experience the equivalent of Andromache's fate. He has beaten everything and everyone, but for what?

The arrangement of Demodocus's three songs makes one overlook the
middle one. It is as if a comedy had been sandwiched in between the first
and last scenes of a single tragedy. The union of Ares and Aphrodite,
however, whether it be voluntarily assumed or artfully perpetuated, seems
to symbolize the *Iliad*.[85] Aphrodite's adultery is matched by Helen's, and
the vindication of a husband's right by Hephaestus fits no less well Menelaus' claim to and exaction of his right. The casual way Aphrodite darts
off to Paphos reminds us of Helen's domesticity at Sparta. Hephaestus

outsmarts Ares, just as Odysseus outsmarted the Trojans, who had condoned adultery. But is there any equivalent among the gods to Odysseus's tears for the consequences of right? The gods laugh twice, first when they see that evil deeds do not succeed, and art compensates Hephaestus for his slowness and allows him to catch the swiftest of the gods, and second when Hermes, in answer to Apollo's question, says he would be willing to be bound thrice as tight as Ares and Aphrodite are, and have all the gods and goddesses look on, provided he could sleep beside golden Aphrodite. The gods first laugh at the success of right against might and then laugh again when they express their indifference to right. What do Odysseus's tears say? Are they a resounding "No!", and he would not go through it again? Or are his tears really parallel to Hermes' wish, and he would say "Yes!" even now to Troy's destruction? Insofar as Ares and Aphrodite "naturally" belong together, as Hephaestus admits, the song is about the triumph of legal right over natural right, and the gods' second burst of laughter acknowledges at once the natural right of antinomian Eros and the absurdity of anyone but Ares laying claim to Aphrodite. Odysseus's tears, then, could equally be for his vindication of Menelaus' legal right and rejection of Paris's "natural" claim to Helen. The old men at Troy, when they see Helen on the wall after nine years of fighting, accept at first the rightness of the war for both sides; but they have second thoughts (III.156–60).[86]

Odysseus is in two songs. In Demodocus's song, he is like Ares, and in Homer's, he is like a woman; but in the poem in which he is like a woman, he is illustrating Demodocus's second song in another way. Euryalus, who looked like Ares, insulted Odysseus as if he were the lame Hephaestus; but Odysseus vindicated the beautification of speeches over against empty good looks and thus confirmed his resemblance to Hephaestus. He then proved that he was really like Ares, and Demodocus again confirmed it in his third song. Are we then to conclude that Odysseus is both Ares and Hephaestus, and the tension of the *Iliad* is resolved in the *Odyssey*? If there is anything to this bloody resolution of the tension between natural and legal right, one has also to admit that it has no place for Aphrodite. Perhaps Odysseus already knows it.

The complete separation of the second song from the first and third seems to testify to the radical difference between laughter and the tears of things, or between distance and involvement; but Hephaestus, whose art allows the gods to laugh twice, believes it to be no laughing matter. He says, in so many words, "I wish I had never been born" (8.311–12). He makes Zeus and Hera solely responsible for his misery. The artful triumph of right does not conceal Hephaestus's wish not to exist, for if he were as good-looking as his brother, he would not have had to make right triumph, nor, we might add, would he have had the art to do so: Demodocus is blind. The funny and the unfunny thus coexist in the same story; and they can coexist because there is more than one speaker, the spectator-gods and the suffering Hephaestus. Things would cease to be funny if and only if there were not experiences that compel their patient to wish retroactively for his own annihilation. We are at the moment spectators of something equally funny and terrifying. The Phaeacians are doing the right thing in sending Odysseus home, but they are doing it at the possible price of their own destruction. Only if they were not who they are could they avoid their fate. It would be only natural, in the circumstances, if Alcinous wishes to know whether Odysseus is worth it.

The second song puts a cosmic god in relation to an Olympian god. The Sun first informs Hephaestus about Aphrodite's adultery, and later about Ares' visit, so that he can return and spring the trap. It is not said that the Sun was present or laughed at the denouement. We therefore do not know whether there was any moral purpose behind the Sun's first report; but though he was perhaps indifferent to looking at punishment, his second report seems to suggest that he was not indifferent to morality.[87] Alcinous's curiosity about Odysseus appears at first to be unmotivated. He admits that his ships, which can read men's minds (8.559), could take Odysseus home even if he remained anonymous, "for they know the cities of all men."[88] Even if the ship can read only the minds of the Phaeacians, Odysseus's name does not have to be known; but this restriction on the ship's knowledge is implausible, since "she" lands Odysseus on a remote part of Ithaca without her being told. Alcinous, then, has his own interest in Odysseus. He wants to find out about other human beings, their piety and friendliness to strangers, or their harshness and injustice (8.575–76). The Phaeacians now belong to the human race; and Alcinous wants to know what other men are like. He may have to have dealings with them. Even if his ships have this kind of knowledge, it was never of any concern to him before. The end to innocence, if it does not spell the ruin of the Phaeacians, demands a reacquaintance with the world. The stranger, who brings about the fall, must also make up for it in the form of knowledge.[89]

Alcinous wants to know the stranger's name: "Give your name, whatever it is which your mother and father used to call you at home, and everyone else did who dwelt in town or the neighborhood: no human being whatsoever is nameless, not the base, let alone the noble, as soon as he is born, but parents give names to all whenever they generate them" (8.550–54). No one else in either the *Odyssey* or the *Iliad* asks about a stranger's name so elaborately. The question, "Who are you?" is usually coupled with a question about parentage (1.170; 14.187; 19.162; 24.298); but Alcinous does not want to know about Odysseus's parents. It is simply the universal practice of particularizing the child that he stresses. For us, his remark reverberates, for we learn that, on the one hand, his grandfather and not his parents gave Odysseus his name, and it was meant to be both significant and unique, and, on the other, Odysseus once gave himself a name that was not a name, and it too was significant and unique. Homer, moreover, had introduced him to us without a name, but simply as "the man who." It seems, then, that what impresses Alcinous about Odysseus is that he is a nobody who both claims to be a somebody and has convinced them that he is; but whoever he is he is not a Rhadamanthys (7.323), someone who was really a somebody.[90] When Odysseus tells lies like the truth to Penelope, he says he is the great-grandson of Zeus (19.178–80). One might suppose that Odysseus unmasked himself when he said he was at Troy and second to Philoctetes in the bow; but Demodocus's songs about him did not or could not make him recognizable in the flesh. Who Odysseus really is slipped by Demodocus. He became who he is only after he had ceased to be the son of Laertes.

5

Odysseus's Own Story

Memory and Mind

The Phaeacians used to see the gods face to face and hear about Odysseus; now they are to hear Odysseus directly and hear what the absence of the gods means. Odysseus tells nine stories. The story about Circe is central; it divides Odysseus's experiences in two: the first four, when he does not know what lies ahead, and the last four, in which there is a double account, what he is told beforehand is going to happen and what in fact happens.[91] The story of Hades is also divided in two parts: what Odysseus tells on his own and what he tells at Alcinous's request. It is in the interval that Arete declares that he is her special guest-friend (11.336–41). Odysseus tells a story that he has had seven years to reflect on and shape. It is not his raw experience, but his understanding of his experience. It can be expected to be at least as different from the experience as his story of how he came to Scheria differed from Homer's story. Here too Odysseus does not quote any speeches he might have made to himself. In this sense, the story belongs to the present and continues the time line of the *Odyssey*. It is therefore in principle possible that Odysseus collapsed his final understanding into his initial experience; but the differences in the character of his actions in the course of his story suggest that whatever he eventually came to understand is not being employed to efface the contemporaneous understanding he displayed in his earlier actions. His actions serve to correct the almost inevitable distortions of hindsight. On the other hand, Odysseus's experiences do not end with his own story, but what he is to experience and how he is to understand it will once more be Homer's story. We do not know as yet whether this represents on Homer's part a deepening beyond Odysseus's understanding or merely the confirmation of it. A token proof that Odysseus's own story is not the end of his story is this. At the beginning of his account, Odysseus praises the singer and goes on to record that he saved a priest; but toward the end of the *Odyssey* he saves a singer and kills a priest. Odysseus saves the priest Maron in the midst of an action that shows he is indeed the sacker of cities, but though prudent not obviously just; he kills the priest Leodes, though Homer tells us that to him alone among the suitors were acts of wickedness hateful, and he was indignant at all the suitors (21.146–47). The problem of the relation between justice and piety, in light of wisdom and prudence, could not be more clearly stated. It is a problem Homer assigns to himself; he does not entrust it to Odysseus.

When Virgil transposes the *Odyssey* into a Roman setting, and thus transforms the mythical into the historical, he has Aeneas tell the story of Troy's destruction and his own wandering to the Carthaginians and not to a people as fabulous as the Phaeacians. Since the Carthaginians were in origin Phoenicians, he seems to have adopted, by a kind of parechesis on "Phaeacians," the Phoenicians from the role they play in the stories Odysseus tells when he is lying. Everything seems real in Odysseus's lies, and nothing seems real when he is telling the truth. It is not enough to say that Alcinous's praise of Odysseus's truthfulness shows the Phaeacians' gullibility, and that Odysseus reels them in on his line of tall tales (11.363–66). It is more helpful to consider the justification Socrates offers in the *Republic* for making up an image to explain the experience philosophers must undergo in relation to their cities.[92] This experience, he says, is unique and there is nothing like it; accordingly, one has to assemble it out of many elements by means of an image, just as painters do when they mix together animals like the goat-stag. The creation of the monstrous, or the putting together of things that do not seem to belong together, is indispensable if one is to understand the unique. Odysseus's singularity, which entails that he not be understood on the basis of any older paradigms, has the further consequence that he can be comprehended only by way of the unreal. The impossible is the sole access into the unprecedented.

Odysseus marks the break with the Phaeacians' former relations with foreigners by saying that he will tell them his name, "in order that I may be your guest-friend even though I shall be faraway" (9.18). The foreigner (*xeinos*) becomes a friend (*xeinos*). A reciprocal relation is to be established that does not require Odysseus to be absorbed into the Phaeacians as a son-in-law. He can now be at home and still be connected with them. Odysseus begins by contrasting as strongly as possible the beautiful with the sweet. Nothing is more beautiful than to listen to a singer like Demodocus in the midst of the good cheer of a banquet, but nothing is sweeter than to see one's own country, and the sweetness of one's country largely consists in one's parents (9.2–36). Odysseus rejected both Circe and Calypso in favor of Laertes: he already knows his mother is dead (11.84–86). Odysseus does not say that he was king of Ithaca, or that his father lost his authority many years before the Trojan War. Odysseus has not been referred to as king since the second book (2.231), and he will not regain the title until the end, when Zeus, in arranging for forgetfulness, ordains his kingly rule (24.483). By that time Laertes has been rejuvenated (24.367–69). Along with silence about his rule, Odysseus does not mention his empire: Ithaca is just one of four islands that lie near one another. He does say that Ithaca is good for raising children; so along with the past the future holds some attraction; but he does not mention Penelope. In Hades, Elpenor appeals to Odysseus in the name of his father, wife, and son (11.66–68). The absence of Penelope in Odysseus's sketch of his background makes one realize that, for Odysseus, home exercises its greater sweetness even for a man who is living elsewhere, apart from his parents, and apparently has no intention of returning (cf. 14.137–44). The fatherland lingers as a taste.

Penelope is not the only omission in Odysseus's tale. It is hard to keep in mind, while we read of the progressive losses he suffers, that Odysseus mentions in the sack of Ismaros that its women were enslaved, and, if one takes him literally, he too received one of the women (9.41–42). Odysseus's twelve ships could have settled anywhere. But Odysseus was fated to return alone. Was he fated to lose 528 women as well? The number would be higher if after their rout the women of the dead were redistributed among Odysseus's men and not let go. It is hard to imagine that they gave up the rest of the booty their comrades had received. As soon as Ismaros is sacked, Odysseus loses control of his men.[93] He cannot persuade them that they are not a match against war-chariots, despite their acquaintance with them at Troy (cf. 18.263–64). He says they were greatly foolish, but he did not reprove them after their defeat (cf. 12.392). He assigns the blame to Zeus, just after he explained their folly (9.52). He does exactly what Zeus complained men always do. He does not say that Zeus punished them for their injustice, not even when Zeus caused a storm immediately afterwards, in which they feared for their lives but sustained only minor damage. He lets the Phaeacians draw that conclusion, in their ignorance of the possible war guilt of the Cicones. He says instead that the evil fate of Zeus stood beside them, in order that they might suffer many sorrows (9.53). Odysseus never again speaks of suffering (*paskhein*) in the remainder of his story; indeed, Homer never says he suffers in the present of the poem.[94] One might say that the "objectivity" of *paskhein* gives way to a more "subjective" mode, in which, unlike in open warfare, there is nothing to show. A sign of this greater inwardness is that though their losses mount, Odysseus's men never again employ the thrice-repeated ritual cry of mourning (9.65), let alone erect a cenotaph, as Menelaus had done for Agamemnon.[95] Elpenor had to remind Odysseus to make a tomb for him (11.53–54).

Odysseus enters upon his adventures proper without the gods. Winds drive him off course as he rounds Cape Malea, and he is then on his own. He begins by making a choice. The Lotus-eaters do not attack the delegation Odysseus sends to them; instead they let them taste of the lotus, "and whoever ate of the honeysweet fruit was unwilling to report back or return, but they wanted to remain there among the Lotus-eaters, nibbling at the lotus, and to forget the return" (9.94–97).[96] The lotus is not just a drug of forgetfulness; it also induces a desire to stay. Odysseus decides in favor of memory, or the limitation of his own tradition, just before he reveals in the next episode the anonymity of mind. Odysseus's greatest triumph, to which he appeals in order to encourage both his men and himself (12.209–12; 20.18–21), involves a declaration of his own non-rootedness in any place or any past, but it occurs after he has used force to bind his men to the nonuniversality of home. The force he uses stands in contrast to the nonviolence of the Lotus-eaters. He renounces both the loss of particularity and peaceableness. Apart from his nipping in the bud the possible spread of rebellion throughout the fleet (9.102), which is all the more likely after the disobedience at Ismaros, Odysseus begins by choosing the fathers. He thus makes tradition the condition for mind. This seems to radicalize the thesis that there is no freedom without restriction, or where everything is possible nothing great can come to be; it even goes deeper than the poet's claim that the wisdom of the Muses has its origin in their mother, Memory. If one casts the Cyclops episode in Platonic terms, it seems to deny the possibility of any escape from the Cave unless there is pure mind; but the preceding episode seems to affirm that it is impossible to confront the issue of escape from the Cave unless one chooses the Cave and does not just find oneself in it. One can go into the light of the sun only if one goes first into the twilight of the Cave. Odysseus's choice of necessity here already anticipates his rejection of immortality.

The juxtaposition of these two first episodes is forced upon us by the absence of any appreciable time interval between them (9.105–7). The Cyclopes seem to be right next door to the Lotus-eaters. We could thus take them as two panels, whose significance does not depend on their sequence but solely on their being constituents in the makeup of Odysseus. There is his past, which he does not try to obliterate, and there is mind, which transcends local time and place, but they are parts of an order that is independent of the temporal order in which they have to be presented. We could then say that Odysseus gives us an exploded diagram of himself, which can in turn be fitted back together in a complete picture wholly free from the arrow of time. As more pieces are given us, the plausibility of this increases. There would still have to be, however, a key piece that would instruct us on how to reassemble the parts, and such a key piece might bring with it an alteration in our bit-by-bit understanding of the parts. It seems, then, at least possible that three factors may be at work in the structure of Odysseus's story: (1) the temporal sequence of parts, (2) the parts in themselves, and (3) the parts in the whole. The last factor, though it is at the moment least visible, must ultimately come to dominate the other two, for it is equivalent to the answer to Alcinous's question, why did Odysseus weep at Demodocus' two songs, and the answer to our question, why did Odysseus choose mortality. These two questions can be posed as one: What was the good he found in the bad?

Odysseus does not arrange his account of the Cyclopes and Polyphemus in the order in which he learned things about them. Prior to his meeting with Polyphemus, Odysseus's account can be cut up into nine distinct sections: (1) the Cyclopes (106–15), (2) the island across from the land of the Cyclopes (116–41), (3) arrival on the island (142–51), (4) goat-hunting (152–69), (5) Odysseus's proposal and its execution (170–80), (6) Polyphemus and his cave (181–92), (7) wine of Maron (193–215), (8) cave of Polyphemus (216–23), and (9) comrades' proposal (224–30).

The Cyclopes have a common way of life without having anything in common. Odysseus first says of them that they are lawless (*athemistoi*), and we believe he means, as indeed he does, that they are transgressors of the law (cf. 17.363). He goes on to say that they have neither assemblies in which they deliberate nor laws (*themistes*), but they lay down the law (*themisteuei*) for their wives and children, and they do not care for one another. Odysseus comes across a prepolitical way of life, which does not suit the political or politicized language of negation.[97] The law of the isolated family is against the law. Odysseus implies that some kind of incest is practiced within each family. They live on the tops of tall mountains in caves, perhaps one to a mountainpeak, so that the bond among them is even less that the link among mountains that the phrase "mountain-range" suggests. They neither sow nor plow: wheat, barley, and grapes grow on their own, which the rain of Zeus increases. The language is the language of Olympian gods, but the gods are the cosmic gods. "Lawless" in its double sense shows up in the difference between and the sameness of "deathless gods" and "rain of Zeus." The ambiguous status of the Cyclopes, inasmuch as they can and cannot be fitted into the standard categories of speech, is symbolized by Polyphemus, whose father is Poseidon but whose mother is a daughter of Phorcys, and either Phorcys still maintains his rule or Poseidon usurped it (1.71–73). A possible translation of "Polyphemus" is "he who is with many voices." Polyphemus was the first intrusion of the Olympian gods into the pre-Olympian world of the Cyclopes (cf. 9.411–12). Odysseus is the second.

The island to which Odysseus first comes is the primary source of his understanding of the Cyclopes. His description of it makes the move of the Phaeacians, led by Alcinous's father, extremely puzzling, since they would have been safe from the Cyclopes there, and the ever-present danger the Cyclopes represent would have kept up their own martial spirit, while their presence in turn might have over time made the Cyclopes more sociable. One cannot rule out the possibility that even at this late date Odysseus is recommending to the Phaeacians the colonization of this island; for the oracle that threatens their future can possibly be thwarted if they accept the conditions of political life.[98] That it occurred to Odysseus to settle there himself might be a passing thought of Alcinous. The all-round suitability of the island—its harbor, fresh water, soil, meadows, woods, and wild game (cf. 13.242–47)—told Odysseus that the Cyclopes had not progressed very far in the arts, of which shipbuilding is for him, as later for Thucydides, the principal sign; and since technical progress requires specialization, the Cyclopes could not be living in cities. The absence of any trails through the brush made it clear to him that hunters had never gone across by raft, and hence that more than the rudiments of carpentry were still unknown to them. Odysseus's interest, then, in seeing the Cyclops for himself is puzzling. Did he not trust the inferences we assume he drew from the state of the island, or did he realize only later what he should have figured out? The second possibility is precluded by his taking along Maron's wine, "for my heart suspected that I would meet a man clothed in great strength, wild, and not knowing well either right or law" (9.213–15). Odysseus, then, just wanted to know whether, in the absence of the city, men can be just, or whether, if the city depends as much on the Olympian gods as on the arts, the cosmic gods suffice to put a limit on human beings. He knows already that men can be completely harmless; but the Lotus-eaters can only absorb the stranger and make him one of themselves; they cannot both accept and dismiss the stranger.

Odysseus's disinterested inquiry into the Cyclopes, as if he were free to experiment, clearly points to the self-identification, at which his heart will soon laugh, of himself with mind (9.413–14). Odysseus is not yet lost. He needs neither directions nor supplies. His morally neutral curiosity about morality has long been familiar to us, but it seems unprecedented. It is one thing to travel as trader or pirate, it is another to travel for fun, as the Phaeacians may be said to do; but it involves a radical reorientation to run risks for knowledge. This aspect of Odysseus, of which Dante knows indirectly, is all the more astonishing in that it anticipates in the element of fiction its reality in a man like Herodotus.[99] The poet imagines a soul of a certain kind before there is, as far as we know, such a soul. If we look, then, at the way in which Herodotus works his way to this Odyssean theme, we get a handle on how Homer conceived of the emergence of an Odysseus.[100] In his prologue, Herodotus first sets out and then sets aside the Persian account of the grounds for the enmity between Greeks and Persians. The Trojan War, the Persians say, put the Greeks in the wrong, since there was such a radical disproportion between the punishment of the Trojans and their guilt. The Greeks assembled a vast armada and sent it overseas to exact justice from a non-Greek city. Odysseus took part in an attempt that necessarily put into question the relation between right and law or ways of life. Zenodotus's reading of law (*nomos*) instead of mind (*noos*) in the third line of the *Odyssey* does not have to be true in order to be true.[101] Accordingly, Odysseus's curiosity seems to be directly traceable to his experiences at Troy. The meaning of the *Iliad* is in this sense to be found in the *Odyssey*. Penelope, who stays at home, seems to be aware of this. She speaks more than once of Odysseus's leaving home in order to take a look at what she calls "Evilium" (19.260, 597; 23.19).

Odysseus's brief description of their landing on the island introduces us to the amazing series of coincidences that permeate the Cyclops episode. He says some god guided them, a heavy fog surrounded the ships, no moon shone through the clouds, and no one saw either the island or the waves as they rolled toward the shore until they beached their ships (9.142–48). The most striking of these coincidences, and perhaps it is all the more so because Odysseus says nothing about it, occurs in the cave. After the very four men Odysseus himself would have chosen are chosen by lot, Polyphemus eats two more, and since by that time he has only eight men with him, sheer dumb luck seems to work in his favor just as effectively as does the unknown god who he acknowledges helps when there is no light from either sun or moon.[102] In that episode in which mind in itself comes to the fore, chance is equally conspicuous, and it runs on a providential bias. One might be inclined therefore to reduce the element of mind and ascribe almost everything to either gods or chance. It is here where we most miss Homer's narrative, which would have told us what Odysseus supplied on his own and what Athena supplied (cf. 9.317). Homer might have told us after all that Athena told Odysseus to give himself the name "No one." Once, however, he turns the story over to Odysseus, there is no going back. Odysseus is fully in control of himself to just that extent he believes he is, regardless of whether there is a higher causality or not.

The fourth episode deepens this puzzle. On the next day, when they wander over the island in admiration, Nymphs, who are the daughters of Zeus, stir up the goats, "in order that my comrades may dine" (9.155). Odysseus has just said that the wild goats on the island are innumerable and have never been hunted; so the hunting of them, one might expect, would be too easy to warrant an explanation. What impresses Odysseus is not that it was like shooting fish in a barrel but that they so quickly shot 109 of them, 9 per ship and an extra one for himself. It is the fact that there was a surplus, so that he could be honored, that seems to indicate that a god presided over the hunt. He seems to be saying that the island, unlike the mainland, is already under the protection of the Olympian gods. The authority he lost at Ismaros, and which his use of force to bring some of his men away from the Lotus-eaters would have damaged further, seems now to be fully restored. The wine they took from Ismaros supplements their meal. No one suspects or objects that Odysseus had twelve amphoras of a special wine. He does not have to distribute them among his twelve ships. On the next day, when he calls his first assembly, he merely has to give orders to be obeyed. His men would not dream of sailing off without him.

Everyone, it seems, was curious about the mainland. They kept on eyeing it while they ate, and noticed the smoke of its inhabitants and the bleating of sheep and goats. Odysseus apparently did not share with his men the inferences he himself must have made; he did not want to test their loyalty that far. As soon as they land on the mainland, they see a cave high up near the shore, whose high wall of stones around the yard informs them that it is inhabited. The size of everything, about which Odysseus says nothing, should indicate what they are dealing with; instead, Odysseus inserts at this point a description of Polyphemus's own size, his isolated life, and his lawlessness. The more Odysseus emphasizes his own shrewdness, by presenting conjecture as fact in the sequence of his narrative, the greater his rashness seems to be. The absence of human sounds amidst those of the goats and sheep no doubt tells Odysseus that Polyphemus is unmarried, and perhaps the distance of the cave from any others he might have seen would have told him of his solitary life. That, however, "he knew lawless things," as Odysseus now phrases it, could only have been inferred from his size. "Might makes for right" is the first principle he must have formulated. The connection between Polyphemus's apartness and his size is expressed in a simile: "He did not resemble bread-eating men but a wooded peak of tall mountains, which appears alone by itself away from the rest" (9.190–92). The class to which Polyphemus really belongs is against appearances. Just as we distinguish between mountain and mountain range, and assign one name for the individual and another for the collection, so Polyphemus seems to be so separated from men that the issue of right is irrelevant. One wonders, therefore, whether Odysseus believes he has a mission to cut Polyphemus down to size and put him in his place. That he tells Polyphemus he and his men were part of Agamemnon's army, which sacked a large city and destroyed many people, suggests that the punitive purpose of that expedition is still something for him (9.263–66).[103] The wild goats on the island could in time have become tame (9.119, cf. 292). Is Polyphemus wild in the same way, and Odysseus just the man to domesticate him? Does Odysseus therefore emerge from this episode with a distinctiveness as marked as Polyphemus's that likewise sets him aside from the issue of right?

The backward order of Odysseus's story seems to be a reflection on and confirmation of the self-sufficiency of pure mind. Pure mind does not need any experience. The seventh part brings out most clearly the backwardness of Odysseus's narration. He ends with an explanation of why he took along Maron's wine: "My heart at once suspected that I would come upon a man clothed in great strength, wild, without knowledge of right and law" (9.213–15). Odysseus's suspicion has already been confirmed for us. He gives himself a decisive edge by arming himself with a skin of wine. He received the wine from Maron, along with other gifts, in gratitude for his not killing him and his family. He spared them out of reverence for him as the priest of Apollo, who had once protected Ismaros. Odysseus is silent about his justice and points up his piety. Was he then under the spell of their virtual identity in the case of Troy? It is, according to the *Iliad*, the Trojans' acceptance of Pandarus's violation of a solemn oath that spreads Paris's guilt to all and dooms them (IV. 155–68). Odysseus, in any case, was very lucky to have spared Maron, for only Maron, his wife, and one housekeeper knew about the wine. In order to be drinkable, the wine had to be diluted by twenty measures of water to one of wine. Odysseus's guess as to the size of Polyphemus proves to be accurate: had he been any bigger, the wine would not have knocked him out. One wonders, however, why Odysseus did not offer him the wine at once so that he would spare them (cf. 9.349–50). Odysseus seems to have been in the position of Maron, and Polyphemus the equivalent of Odysseus's army. Odysseus believes apparently that only gods are to be propitiated before they show their graciousness; but in the case of men gratitude follows the favor and does not precede it. That was a lesson Achilles had to learn (cf. I. 472–74; IX. 300–3).

When finally Odysseus enters the empty cave, he finds something that neither his intuition nor his narrative anticipated. "Baskets were brimming with cheese, and pens were tightly packed with lambs and kids; they had been severally enclosed separately; the older were apart, the middle were apart, and the 'dew drops' were apart; all the fabricated pails, large and small, in which he milked them, were swimming with whey" (9.219–23). Odysseus beholds with pleasure perfect order. Everything is in place by age and kind. Odysseus seems to conclude that wherever there is order, there is justice (cf. 14.13–16, 433–38), but he discovers that law and order can be apart.[104] The very word for law, *themistes*, turns out to be misleading. Though it seems to assume a necessary connection etymologically between order and right, there is none in deed: Herodotus says that *theoi* (gods) was the name given to those who were thought to have put (*thentes*) everything in order (*kosmos*).[105] So Odysseus's decision to stay and not rob Polyphemus, as his comrades propose, is not entirely unreasonable if the random is not a condition for justice. The justice Odysseus has in mind, however, is the justice of exchange, which at any given time is rarely in balance (cf. 21.31–36), for the very notion of the stranger involves a displacement. Only if there were no strangers, as among the gods (5.79–80), or if everyone were to stay in place, and change were wholly compatible with order, would Odysseus's presumption hold. Odysseus thus chose home over immortality: he could not have chosen home unless he had been away from home, any more than he could have chosen memory if he were not in a position to forget. Odysseus had thus chosen both at the start and at the end what either were radically altered through his awareness of what he rejected or could not even exist if he had not been estranged from them. The stranger is the human emblem of the other, and in Odysseus's case, where his being a stranger is grounded in his being a wanderer, error and disorder are built into it. There are forms of the verb "to wander" (*alaomai*) that are indistinguishable from "true" (*alēthēs*), and Homer seems not to have been above suggesting such a connection when he has Eumaeus accuse Odysseus, like all wanderers (*alētai*), of lying when he is for once telling some of the truth.[106]

When Odysseus's men begged him to take some of the cheese and drive the lambs and kids to the ship, he refused and was obeyed. He now admits that it would have been better if he had then left. He does not admit that it would have been better, when he tells him his name, not to taunt Polyphemus a second time. Indeed, Odysseus never admits to another mistake throughout his story, though there are several occasions in which his commissions or omissions are open to question; but his single admission carries with it a price: he implies that it would have been better not to know that there is no necessary link between order and justice. Odysseus gives two reasons for waiting around: he wanted to see Polyphemus and to know whether he was going to give him the presents due to strangers (*xenia*). Odysseus could see that there was nothing in the cave he could not get for himself from the island.[107] Does he want a reward for not stealing from him? Polyphemus knows about piracy. Odysseus wants to see him. On the basis of what he can see, which he has already conveyed to us, he cannot figure him out completely. He knows he is a milk-drinker, and, if there are no traces of blood anywhere, probably a vegetarian.[108] Odysseus should realize that Polyphemus, even if he had any to spare, would not let him have sheep and goats if they are to be killed and eaten. Does Odysseus want to know whether there is a connection between animal sacrifice and the worship of gods? He now mentions that they offered burnt cheese to the gods, though he had not spoken of any sacrifice or libation on the island after the Nymphs had stirred up the goats and a god had quickly granted them a satisfying hunt. Odysseus is going to sacrifice once more, with the burning of thigh bones, after he leaves the cave (9.551–55), but never again to Zeus or the gods above, either in his truthful narrative or when he returns home (cf. 24.215).[109] At the beginning of the *Odyssey*, Athena reminds Zeus of Odysseus's gracious sacrifices to him at Troy, and Zeus acknowledges that Odysseus is outstanding when it comes to mind and sacrifice (1.59–63, 66–67). Toward the end of the *Odyssey*, in the midst of the slaughter of the suitors, Phemius ponders whether he should slip out and take refuge at the altar of Zeus, upon which Odysseus had before the war often sacrificed, or beseech Odysseus directly; he chooses Odysseus and tells him he imagines he is singing by his side as if to a god (22.333–49).

Polyphemus is not one to eat first and ask questions later. He is a casual cannibal. His chores are done in as orderly a way as the order of his cave would suggest (9.245, 309, 342). Only if the order is upset in some way, will Odysseus be able to escape. Polyphemus asks Odysseus, just as Nestor had asked Telemachus, whether he is a merchant or a pirate (3.71–74). In answer, Odysseus boasts: he belongs to the army of Agamemnon, and he has the backing as well of Zeus, who is the avenger of suppliants and strangers. Polyphemus is not impressed; Odysseus's failure to answer his question directly might have led him to infer that the expedition against

Troy was nothing but a glorified act of piracy. He seems to know nothing of Agamemnon, and he says the far more powerful Cyclopes disregard Zeus and the other blessed gods. Whether or not he spares Odysseus and his men depends on his whim. He then asks Odysseus where he moored his ship. Odysseus, who introduced himself to the Phaeacians as famous for his wiles, believes Polyphemus is testing him; but Odysseus, who knows many things, sees right through him and lies. He says that Poseidon smashed his ship. Odysseus's men were prepared to steal, and now Odysseus lies; but he lies in such a way as to tell Polyphemus that he is lying, for his request for a gift makes no sense if he cannot get away (cf. 9.349–50). Odysseus is too sophisticated to understand the simplicity of the Cyclopes. He believes Polyphemus has the nerve to match wits with him of all people, and he could not possibly be asking an innocent question.[110] It is not as if Polyphemus could sneak up on his ship without giving his men plenty of time to cast off (9.315). Polyphemus does not reply to Odysseus's lie; instead, he eats two of his comrades. Odysseus takes certain kinds of wrongdoing so much for granted—the eating of Polyphemus's cheese, for example—that Polyphemus's severe reprisal for lying does not appear to him as a reprisal. Nor does it occur to Odysseus that if Polyphemus believes they cannot get away they have to be disposed of in some way if the order of his cave is not to be disturbed. There is no room here for the permanent stranger. Cannibalism is the strict consequence of Cyclopean tidiness: Polyphemus cuts up the men neatly and leaves not a scrap behind. Nothing in the narrative suggests that cannibalism is anything but a one-time supplement to Polyphemus's diet. The Cyclopes used to harm the Phaeacians when they lived nearby (6.4–6); but we do not know whether they regularly ate them. If they did, it was a generation ago, and it is hard to believe that anyone in the meantime was as daring as Odysseus and risked trying to see them (cf. 9.351–52). When it comes to strangers, the Cyclopes seem to be a harsher version of the Phaeacians. Both get rid of strangers as quickly as they can, but the Phaeacians, with their god-given ships, do not have to resort to Polyphemus's way of maintaining order.

After he and his men had stretched out their arms to Zeus, Odysseus wanted to strike Polyphemus in the chest with his sword. He had already grabbed it when "another spirit" (*thumos*) checked him (9.302): he realized that even if he managed to kill the Cyclops, they could never have moved the stone that blocked the entrance to the cave. The episode recalls another non-completed action: in the first book of the *Iliad*, Agamemnon had so enraged Achilles that he was pondering whether he should kill him or check his spirit (*thumos*), and he was already drawing his sword out of its scabbard when Athena stood beside him and yanked his hair, "appearing to him, and no one else could see her" (I.188–98). Achilles would have proved to be utterly criminal and base had he gone through with the murder. He needed Athena to stop him from doing what would have been entirely in character for him to do; but it takes the rest of the *Iliad* to prove to Achilles that he needs the gods.[111] He cannot be who he is without them. Odysseus, on the other hand, in holding himself back seems to show he does not need the gods; his better second thoughts are his own. It might then take the rest of the *Odyssey* to prove to Odysseus himself that he does not need them, for the evidence and the inference from the evidence are not the same. There is, however, another possibility: Odysseus's self-control is just an illusion of first-person narration. The difference between Homer's account of Odysseus's voyage from Calypso's and his own account now turns out to be of decisive importance, and taken by itself might tend to show that Odysseus is just a more elusive Achilles. This issue—whether all men need the gods, regardless of how different they may be from one another—had already been settled by Nestor's son (3.47–48), whose subsequent acquaintance with Telemachus certainly did not alter his conviction.

Had Odysseus succeeded in killing Polyphemus but died himself, trapped in the cave, it would have been plausible to call it an act of vengeance, heroic and vain. Once Odysseus's "other spirit" alters the issue, and it becomes the practical question of how they are to get out of the cave, necessity overwhelms justice, and nothing Odysseus can do on his own admits of an interpretation in terms of right. When Odysseus does think of vengeance (*tisis*), he couples that thought with the possibility of Athena's help (9.317). That he tells Polyphemus that Zeus and the other gods punished him for his cannibalism may be merely designed to frighten him into submission to the Olympian gods (9.475–79). He does not say a word in that speech about himself; and the next time he speaks to Polyphemus, despite the remonstrance of his comrades, he restricts his own action to the blinding (9.502–5). It is only in his third address to the Cyclops that Odysseus may betray a belief that justice has been done. Polyphemus declares that he is Poseidon's son, and "if he wants, he will cure me himself" (9.520); and Odysseus replies: "It is as certain that not even Poseidon will heal your eye as I wish I were able to deprive you of soul and life and send you to Hades" (9.523–25). Odysseus thus acknowledges that only Polyphemus's death would have *per impossibile* constituted a punishment, and his permanent blindness, with which Odysseus must be satisfied, is not as assured as he claims (cf. 3.228). The speech reveals the great strain the will is under to reinterpret necessity as right.[112]

The question, therefore, of whether Odysseus clearly sees the difference between necessity and right cannot be settled through any interpretation of the Cyclops-episode. It can only be settled once Homer takes over again and we see Odysseus confronted with the same issue at home. The plot of the *Odyssey* and the character of Odysseus are thus seen to merge and diverge in the possible link between punishment and gods, on the one hand, and, on the other, between necessity and the human need of the gods, in which Odysseus may or may not share.

The plan that Odysseus devises cannot of itself free him from the cave, for had not Polyphemus driven in all the flocks, "whether he suspected something or maybe a god urged him," the execution of the plan might have satisfied vengeance but left it up to chance whether anyone could have escaped from Polyphemus's blocking of the cave. So what transforms the intention of the plan into the feasibility of its execution seems to have been an irregularity in Polyphemus's customary behavior. Is it, however, an irregularity? Odysseus has observed him for two evenings and one morning, and his pet ram has evidently been in the cave before. However that may be, there are enough coincidences favorable to Odysseus that a pattern emerges that seems to argue for a disorder, beyond the order Polyphemus knows, that cooperates with mind. Chance and mind are allied in the face of an order without justice (9.352). It thus looks as if Odysseus's pun on *outis* and *mētis*, while being as a pun an exemplification of this principle, puts mind through its radical homelessness together with randomness. The story Odysseus tells would not then be about the miraculous fit of the rational and the irrational, but about the necessary fit of mind and the out-of-place.[113] It is in the stranger, who is as nameless as he is without genesis, that this coincidental necessity would occur. Odysseus is not that stranger but his impersonation. He thus may tell a story the meaning of which is not wholly known to him.

The boldness of Odysseus in reprimanding Polyphemus while he offers him the wine may astonish if one disregards the regularity of Polyphemus's habits (9.350–52). He kills only if he also eats, and once dinner is over he is harmless. He is a monster without cruelty. His orderliness is the background against which Odysseus's name of "Outis" has to be understood. It is another lucky break that Odysseus does not tell him his true name, since Polyphemus knows that an Odysseus is fated to blind him (9.507–12); but it seems to be an extra bonus and not the main intention behind the name Odysseus bestows on himself. He seems to anticipate the use of this name in a sentence the syntax of which will make it vanish as a name. He would then cease to be present, though present, through mind. The uncanniness of this divination makes the supplementary support of chance relatively unimportant. It also makes one overlook the question of how Odysseus figured out that Polyphemus would be misunderstood. Not every sentence with *outis* in it would be ambiguous, particularly if Odysseus altered the accent, as some ancient grammarians prescribe, when he put its two syllables together (οὖτις instead of οὔ τις).[24] The story would then be solely symbolic—the anonymity of mind—and that it shows up in the setting it does would be a purely accidental feature of it—the isolated Cyclopes and the orderliness of Polyphemus; but it seems that just as the apartness of things in the cave echoes the apartness of Polyphemus and everyone else, so the lack of community emerges in the failure of communication.

Now in one sense the Cyclopes' unconcern with one another is decisive for Odysseus's success, for once they conclude that Polyphemus is suffering from a disease from Zeus, they move off and advise him to pray to Poseidon; they do not think of removing the stone from the entrance and trying to help him. Their indifference, however, had to have been triggered by Polyphemus's answer. They did, after all, come from all directions to his cave when they heard his cries of pain, even if they were there only because he had disturbed their sleep. The last ram to leave the cave is Polyphemus's favorite, and clinging underneath it is Odysseus, "λάχνῳ στεινόμενος καὶ ἐμοὶ πυκινὰ φρονέοντι" (9.445). Separately, each phrase has its proper meaning: the ram is burdened by its wool, and the ram is burdened by Odysseus, who has shrewd thoughts. But since πυκινά literally means "dense" and στεινόμενος (burdened) means "tightly packed," the coupling of the phrases assumes another sense: "The ram was oppressed by the density of its wool and the compact texture of my mind" (cf. 1.436, 438). This is no doubt a very strained joke, but it points to Odysseus's undetectability if Polyphemus does not go beyond the literal. Odysseus is at one with the fleece as he fleeces Polyphemus.

Odysseus seems to have made a comprehensive reflection on the double aspect of speech as articulation and communication, and the liability of their interference with one another so as to create ambiguity.[115] What things are apart in their articulation they are not together when they are shared. Polyphemus wants to know Odysseus's name so he can give him a gift due a stranger. His name will single him out and set him apart. If, however, it is not truly a gift Odysseus can delight in, Odysseus must remain a stranger. Odysseus thus makes "stranger" into a proper name by calling himself "No one" or "Not anyone." He assigns to himself the negation that necessarily belongs to the stranger as "not one of us." "No one" names the other. The other is that principle the Cyclopes do not acknowledge. There is for them no one else.[116] Odysseus has incorporated into his name what he has come to understand as the principle behind Polyphemus's cannibalism. He is therefore destined to disappear if the Cyclopes try to communicate with one another. What is apart from them cannot be shared with them.[117]

This transformation from being someone to being no one occurs through a question. The Cyclopes ask Polyphemus after they have gathered (9.405–6):

ἦ μή τίς σευ μῆλα βροτῶν ἀέκοντος ἐλαύνει;
ἦ μή τίς σ' αὐτὸν κτείνει δόλῳ ἠὲ βίηφιν;

ἦ μή introduces a question that expects a negative answer (cf. 6.200): "Surely it is not the case, is it, that any (τις) mortal is driving off your flocks against your will? Surely it is not the case, is it, that anyone (τις) is trying to kill you by trickery or force?" Polyphemus's answer, then, "Oh friends! No one is trying to kill me by trickery or force" (ὦ φίλοι, οὔ τίς με κτείνει δόλῳ οὐδὲ βίηφιν), is completely expected. It is the Cyclopes' confidence in Polyphemus's self-sufficiency and their own that, in making it impossible for them to conceive of the other as a danger, does not allow them to understand him. They already know the answer. Their question, moreover, already anticipates the pun on mind: "Is mind really killing you?" They then confirm the pun in replying to Polyphemus: "Well, if no one (μή τις) is using force against you inasmuch as you are alone . . ." or, "If mind (μῆτις) . . ." It is worth reflecting on that it is only through a question or a hypothesis that the link between *outis* and *mētis* is established. The question is rhetorical; and the hypothesis is framed in such a way that it is the only instance in Homer in which a protasis in the indicative, with the negative *mē*, precedes the apodosis.[118] "No one" comes to light as mind if and only if it is either assumed not to be the case or there is an irregularity in speech.

The pun, which Odysseus accepts with delight, raises this question. Whereas the pun virtually identifies "no one" with "mind," Polyphemus seems to understand *outis* in another way. He calls Odysseus *outidanos outis*, "No one the nobody" (9.460). Perhaps he even took *outis* as a nickname and equivalent to *outidanos*, "The nobody 'No one.' " Odysseus, however, is quite the opposite of a nobody; he is emphatically a somebody, and when he tells Polyphemus his name, Polyphemus admits he was completely fooled, for he thought the Odysseus of the oracle would be a tall and beautiful man, clothed in great strength, and not the nobody (*outidanos*) he is (9.513–15). Odysseus's very name—"Anger" or "Hostility"—points to the anger that he himself admits impelled him to lay claim to the blinding as his handiwork: at the same time that he tells Polyphemus his name he calls himself "sacker of cities" (9.504). The disguise of anger (Odysseus) as mind (Outis) is an extraordinary act of self-sacrifice. "Anger" first wants to punish. "Reason" prevails and devises a scheme of escape in which it declares what it is; but no sooner does the scheme succeed than Anger comes back in the form of a death-defying self-assertion. Odysseus does not explain why he is not satisfied with letting Polyphemus believe the gods punished him. It is as if he felt diminished if the gods took all the credit and he remained unknown. When Odysseus interprets necessity as divine punishment, he says nothing about the future; but when he tells Polyphemus his name, he assumes that a man will ask him about the blinding. He assumes that Polyphemus has been civilized to some extent, and strangers have by then become welcome among the Cyclopes (cf. 9.351–52). The Cyclopes now know that man is a danger, and only if they cease to live apart can they protect themselves against him. Odysseus may well be too optimistic; but it is a curious consequence of Polyphemus's knowledge of his name that he now appeals to his father. He recognizes at least one Olympian god as superior to himself (9.518–21). From this point of view, Odysseus's pride would seem to serve a higher purpose, and at the cost of his own misery extend the sway of the gods.

After Odysseus hears Polyphemus's prayer, he sacrifices to Zeus (9.551–55). Although he says Poseidon heard the prayer (9.536), he does not know that that is the case until Teiresias tells him (11.101–3); and experientially Poseidon does not show himself until Odysseus leaves Calypso, and even then he only knows it through Ino (5.339–40). The loss of his men, which Polyphemus prays for, was already known to him as part of his fate (2.171–76); but Odysseus now attributes it to Zeus: "He refused to regard the sacrifice, but he was pondering, I now realize, how all my ships might perish" (9.553–55). Whatever Odysseus believed before—perhaps the gods, in the self-evident justness of his cause, supported his own ingenuity by way of extraordinary coincidences (cf. 9.381)—is now abandoned. At the time he is telling the story to the Phaeacians, he certainly believes in the malevolence of Zeus. That he came to this conviction before, however, or at least he wishes to insert that conviction or a form of it into his narrative, is indicated by the absence of "Zeus" from the tenth book: only "son of Cronus" occurs once at the beginning (10.21). As the division into books is just a rough guide, it would be more accurate to say that Odysseus, if one disregards what he reports about others, is silent about Zeus for a thousand lines. Agamemnon's story in Hades prompts him to say: "So Zeus really and truly showed his hatred of the offspring of Atreus in a terrifying way by means of the plans of women" (11.436–37).[119]

Nature

After Odysseus leaves the place of perfect order without motion, he comes to a floating island of perfect order (10.1–13). Aeolus, whose name apparently means "Quick," rules a city of only one family. He married off his six daughters to his six sons, and they always dine with him and his wife. The incest, which was implicit in the isolation of each Cyclopean family, now comes to light in another kind of orderly existence. The possibility of maintaining order in the face of constant motion is due to the gods; Aeolus is their friend and Zeus made him steward of the winds (10.21). Because he is not just dependent on the gods, as the Cyclopes are, but an active participant in their order, he is friendly to Odysseus and entertains him for a month. At Odysseus's request for a way home, he ties up, in a leather bag, all the winds, except the Zephyr, and sends him on his way. We do not know whether, when Aeolus asked Odysseus about Troy, the Achaeans, and their return, he included his own adventures (10.14–15). If he did, Aeolus did not take Polyphemus's prayer as either justified or destined to be fulfilled. It was just the idle rage of the frustrated. Odysseus accepts the gift, and then makes an error of commission and an error of omission. He fails to inform his crew about the gift and insists on steering the ship himself, "in order that we may arrive all the more quickly at our fatherland" (10.33). We learn later that he has a competent helmsman (12.217); but something has happened that makes him distrust everyone, and his comprehensive distrust of others is accompanied by an excessive confidence in himself.[120] He believes he can go without sleep for however long it takes to get home, and he believes that either his crew members do not need any explanation for their easy voyage or they would not believe him if he told them the truth.[121] His victory over Polyphemus, it seems, has caused him to exaggerate his own powers—he too does not need to share with other men now that he is the friend of a friend of the gods—and it does not occur to him that his own interest in gifts has rubbed off on his crew. Six of them know he received a special wine from Maron. While he is trying to stay awake in order to get home as quickly as possible, his men believe he is keeping an eye on Aeolus's present.

For the first time Odysseus quotes a speech he has not heard (10.38–45). Even when asleep he knows the evil thoughts of his crew (12.339). If his reconstruction of their speech is accurate, the sacking of Ismaros was designed—unsuccessfully as it turns out—to lessen the disproportion between his share of the booty from Troy and theirs; if it is not accurate, it represents Odysseus's understanding of their resentment, which he expresses as their coming home emptyhanded even though they accomplished the same journey as he did. His men are willing to honor him—after the escape from Polyphemus's cave they gave a choice piece of lamb to him alone (9.550–51)—but they are not willing to let honor slide over into an undistributed reward. Odysseus now reveals that had his men managed to get home, he would have found it difficult to treat them still as children. For good or ill, their experiences have made them wiser. Odysseus has just left a "city" in which Aeolus rules, not as a father, but he is the father. At Ithaca, the time for paternal rule, even in a nonliteral sense, is past. An independent demos is in the process of formation. Odysseus calls them evil (10.68).[122]

Ten years after this episode Athena tells Zeus that Odysseus, then trapped on Calypso's island, in his eagerness to see merely the smoke rising from his country, desires to die (1.57–59). The truth of that extravagant flourish is now confirmed in Odysseus's account of his journey from Aeolus's island. Athena seems to have read his thoughts at the time. Odysseus does get close enough to Ithaca to see the inhabitants tending their fires (10.30); and when his men unleash the winds, he wakes and ponders committing suicide (10.51). Odysseus does not say why he chose the alternative of survival, any more than he says why this setback put him in such despair. Did he believe the perfect cooperation of chance and mind in the Cyclops episode was then crowned with the reward of the perfect control of chance? Odysseus does not just call his men bad, he also curses sleep (10.68–69; cf. 12.372). He does not blame himself, but a condition of being human. The pun on "no one" and "mind" was more than a pun for Odysseus. He seems to have taken it as a sign of his own unconditionality. Mind fused with will dispenses with the body and its limitations. Whatever checked Odysseus and made him endure, he endured in silence: he gives up control of his ships and men. He asks no questions and utters no reproaches, but after having wrapped himself up he lies in the hull of the ship. He lets things take their course. He becomes indifferent. He did not, then, choose life so much as resignation. He was not going to interfere regardless of whether it concerned himself or others. This choice of nonintervention has consequences far more terrible than the inquisitiveness of his men.

Despite Odysseus's labeling of the blast of winds as evil, the ships are carried back to Aeolus's without sustaining any damage. They are just back where they started. They are now in a position to profit from their experience. When, however, Odysseus makes his case for another chance, he is rebuffed. Aeolus tells him: "Leave the island at once! (Ἐλέγχιστε ζωόντων!) You are of all living beings the one who least deserves to live.

It is not lawfully sanctioned for me to care for or send away men who incur the enmity of the blessed gods. Be off! You have come here an object of enmity to the immortals" (10.72–75). Aeolus infers this from the failure of perfect means to reach their end. A Sisyphean action, one might say, entails suicide.[123] It seems that Odysseus at first and on his own drew Aeolus's conclusions. He does not deserve to exist unless either he himself is perfect or he commands total trust on the part of his crew; and he cannot command such trust unless the derangements of generational time are eliminated through incest. Aeolus's children have no weight in their father's house. Aeolus's inference follows if and only if there is no room for trial and error. Aeolus does not conclude that he was at fault in giving perfect means to fallible beings. To be fallible is the greatest disgrace to life.

In the summary Homer gives of Odysseus's rehearsal of his adventures, there is no mention of his second landing on Aeolus's island (23.314–17). Its suppression is in accordance with his silence about the successful counterattack of the Cicones and the presentation of his escape from the Cyclops solely as a punishment. The rehearsal thus neglects the decisive change that Aeolus's peremptory dismissal signaled. Odysseus is told that he now is on his own, and no divine support is to be expected. This turn to complete self-reliance emerges as the necessity for his men to row for six days straight (10.78–80). It recalls the proverb "second sailing," which applies to those who cannot employ the best means possible but must be content with whatever means are available. What is now available are their own efforts. The feasible replaces the ideal.

This replacement alters the very character of Odysseus's narration. The city of the Laestrygonians is a city of cannibals, and again, unlike Polyphemus, they attack without first asking questions. Odysseus's delegation learns about them from the daughter of the king, and her normal size deceives them as to the normality of this city-dwelling people. Odysseus was not warned by the absence of agriculture (10.98). The daughter is either a lure or indifferent. She directs them to her father's house, where the queen, as tall as a mountaintop, summons her husband from the assembly. Everything that in its absence made the Cyclopes uncivilized is in place among the Laestrygonians, but they are more brutal than Polyphemus. There is none of that elephantine playfulness and moderate gluttony Polyphemus displayed. The Laestrygonians simply destroy all the ships in the harbor; and just as if they are piercing fish they eat up all the men and women on the spot. They evidently are not vegetarians (10.82–85). They resemble the Giants, but they do not suffer the fate of the Giants. Odysseus does not say a word about their injustice or wickedness.

He does not even pray for their destruction. His account is as neutral as Homer's description of the carnage of war (cf. XVI. 404–10).

This neutrality points two ways. Eleven foreign ships with almost a full complement of men in the harbor of a city look like an invasion force and not at all like a friendly flotilla. The city is necessarily geared for war, and everyone is an enemy who is not a friend. The innocence of intentions does not count in the face of a presumption of hostility. It is unclear therefore whether the Laestrygonians are not somewhat justified in their response because Odysseus has been so Homeric in the narrative. This possibility leads to the second. Odysseus shows his usual caution in mooring his ship outside the harbor; but just as obviously he abandoned the rule of his men. He did not even advise them to follow his example. One wonders, therefore, whether the neutral tone he employs throughout does not arise from a resentment against his own men and a corresponding satisfaction in their "punishment." That he has to take out his anger on others and not on his own crew, who undid the knot of the bag of winds, would be merely a consequence of his need of them if he himself is to get away. He would thus be accepting the principle of Aeolus, who condemned everyone for the fault of a few.

That his own negligence or dereliction of duty could be defended at home if any managed to survive is inconceivable. The indictment would run: "The wise Odysseus, after walking into the cave of the Cyclops, with his eyes wide open, suddenly suspects nothing, and he the sacker of cities!" One only has to think of what use Eupeithes would have made of it had he known (24.426–28). None of this indictment has to have a word of truth in it in order for one to concede that Odysseus has had a potentially grave problem solved for him, to which he himself called attention when he reconstructed the speech of his own crew. That Homer began the *Odyssey* with their wicked folly, from which Odysseus could not save them, now seems trivial in comparison with the losses Odysseus had already sustained; and it is all the more shocking when one considers that Homer's beginning backed Zeus's general observation about human responsibility. It seems that the Laestrygonians, who dwell in a region where the days follow one another with but a sliver of night between them, dwell beyond the rule of the Olympian gods. That Odysseus had a herald accompany two of his men would have been meaningless to them (10.102). Odysseus, then, would not have experienced the active hatred of the gods, but the absence of the gods, whose influence does not extend as far as Odysseus might have thought. He now believes, it seems, that Zeus, "who rules over all," devised the destruction of his ships (9.551–55); but his own narrative, stripped as it is of any mention of the gods, whether by name or anonymously, does not support this belief. Zeus had been invoked to account for Odysseus's defeat by the Cicones, even though it was wholly superfluous; and in the Cyclops's cave a god (*daimōn*) had breathed great confidence into his men only after he had himself given them confidence (9.376, 381). So it is not as if Odysseus were reluctant to indulge in overdetermined causal accounts. It seems, then, that he blames Zeus in order to cover up his own responsibility, and in a terrible way, Zeus is once more proved right.[124]

The Laestrygonian disaster alters Odysseus. For the first time he addresses his men as friends (10.174).[125] Down to his last ship, he knows he must share. He shoots a mighty stag and offers it to them; they do not give him a choice cut. He then divides his forty-four men into two equal groups, and assigns Eurylochus to be the captain of one group and himself of the other. He follows up this split in the rule with a lottery. Eurylochus's group is thus elected to make inquiries. Odysseus does not say that the lot came out as he wanted, even though the story, as it develops, would have allowed him to make the remark. These democratic concessions are more or less forced upon him; but they are connected with two others that are not. One is a matter of speech, the other of deed. Now for the first time Odysseus tells us the name of one of his crew, and he ends his stay at Circe's with naming the nobody Elpenor and honoring him (10.552–53; 12.8–15). He had not told us the name of the far superior Antiphus (2.17–20).[126] Eurylochus is the first whose name is given; the second is Polites, "Citizen" or "Fellow-citizen" (10.224). When, moreover, Eurylochus comes back alone and reports on the disappearance of his fellows, Odysseus decides to rescue them, despite Eurylochus's refusal to guide him and despite his plea that they flee, "for," as he says, "a mighty necessity is upon me" (10.273). This is the first time Odysseus does anything that does not involve his own advantage. He risks his life for his "evil" comrades and trusts that those he leaves behind, with the unreliable Eurylochus, will not desert him.

This completely just and daring action, with its implicit recognition of what he shares with his fellow human beings, is instantly rewarded. Hermes reveals to him that things have natures. From every point of view, both intrinsically and extrinsically, this revelation is the peak of the *Odyssey*. It comes after a series of encounters with men who illustrated the character of the bestial in the composition of man and thereby exposed the conditions of political life. The swine Odysseus's men become complete the series. After Circe, Odysseus encounters only various forms of the divine—Hades, Sirens, Scylla and Charybdis, and the cattle of the Sun. Odysseus's narrative thus shares in his own experiences at sea after he left Calypso. He had then chosen first the divine and last the bestial. That split within his choice of home and mortality turns out to have been anticipated in the shape he gives to his story.[127] And at the same time, his story contains versions of both "Nestor" and "Menelaus," insofar as Nestor had tried to fit everything that had occurred after the fall of Troy into a pattern of divine justice, and Menelaus and Helen had supplied respectively the notions of becoming and of will. Menelaus had come closest to suggesting a comprehensive understanding of becoming, which Helen had deepened with her suggestion of the inscrutable heart behind all appearances. Hermes' showing of the nature of the *moly*, however, seems to be of a different order. It lets Odysseus share in the knowledge the gods have without his having to share in their being.

In the *Politics*, Aristotle speaks of man as a political animal by nature inasmuch as he is "rational animal," an animal with reason and speech; but he almost immediately weakens the connection between rationality and the political (or the just as the common good) by speaking of the additional need for law, if man's bestiality, whether it show up in a sexual or other form of lawlessness, is to be held in check (1253a1–37).[128] Odysseus's adventures so far seem to have unfolded as if they were meant to illustrate Aristotle. Not only does he encounter cannibalism and incest in a political and a nonpolitical setting, but the problematic relation between law and reason was at the heart of the tension between Odysseus's choice of memory and the selflessness of mind. It does not have to be stressed again how mind showed up in the ambiguities of speech. All of these Aristotelian elements in Odysseus's experiences, however, are not grounded in an Aristotelian understanding of nature. They came to a head with the Laestrygonians, who shattered any vestige of hope Odysseus might still have had in the necessary justice of political life.[129] The Cyclops had disillusioned him about the connection between justice and order, and the Laestrygonians had disillusioned him about the connection between justice and community. The rule of a king with an assembly can be infinitely worse than the isolated and whimsical Polyphemus. It now seems that the way to the discovery of nature has been decisively prepared for, on the one hand, by the unsupported human effort to reach the Laestrygonians, and, on the other, by Odysseus's uncompelled choice to be just.

There are two accounts of Circe and her ways. The first, from 10.210 to 10.243, includes both what Eurylochus saw and what he did not, for it tells what happened to Odysseus's men after Eurylochus held back and the rest accepted Circe's invitation. The second account, from 10.274 to 10.347, includes Hermes' report of Circe's drug and his own antidote.

Circe's actions are more or less the same in the two accounts, but Odysseus, unlike Eurylochus, does not see, around Circe's dwelling, any enchanted wolves and lions, which like dogs fawned on the men (10.212–19; cf. 433). Although his men were afraid when they saw the terrible beasts, Odysseus does not react at all; he is neither afraid nor indifferent, but without seeing anything his heart heaves (10.309). It is unclear whether the beasts disappear in fact or in narrative; but if they disappear in fact, Hermes' intervention would seem to have something to do with their disappearance: Hermes too does not mention them. Although he tells Odysseus to take the *moly* and go with it, Circe does not apparently see it, for else she would have known at once that he was proof against the drug as well as that he was Odysseus, about whose coming Hermes had already informed her. If, then, Odysseus was not carrying the *moly*, he would have had either to swallow it or rub it on himself like a salve (cf. 10.392).[130] Neither action is at all likely; Hermes dug the *moly* out of the ground then and there. What Hermes does with the *moly* is to show Odysseus its nature (*phusis*): "It was black in its root, and its flower like milk; the gods call it *moly*, but it is hard for mortal men to dig up, but the gods can do everything." If the decisive action is the showing forth of its nature and not the revelation of its divine name, as if it were a magical charm, then the *moly* in itself is irrelevant. What is important is that it has a nature, and the gods' power arises from the knowledge of its nature and of all other things.[131] To dig up the *moly* is to expose to the light its flower and its root; they belong together regardless of the contrariety in their colors. It is this exposure and understanding of the nature of things that is difficult but not impossible for men. Odysseus, then, would be armed with knowledge. This knowledge saves him from Circe's enchantment. Her enchantment consists of transforming a man into a pig, with its head, voice, bristles, and build, but the mind (*noos*) remains as it was before. His knowledge, then, is the knowledge that the mind of man belongs together with his build. They are together as much as the root and flower of the *moly*. There cannot be a change in one without a corresponding change in the other. Menelaus's encounter with constant becoming, in which there are no natures, must have been an illusion. "There is in your breast," Circe tells Odysseus, "a mind that does not admit of enchantment" (10.329).[132]

It has often been remarked that, while the prephilosophic term for the whole is "heaven and earth," the philosophers call it *kosmos*, an ordered composite whose structure is intelligible only to the mind but is not apparent to the eye, which cannot go beyond its two most conspicuous parts.[133] There is "day and night," and there is "day," which comprehends both day and night and can no longer be seen. Heraclitus uses it as an example of what Hesiod did not know, for day and night are one (fr. 57). The unity that logos discovers can be sounded but never without ambiguity, for day and night are still two.[134] "The way up and the way down are one and the same," Heraclitus says (fr. 60), but there are still two contrary ways, and one has to go one way or the other, even while one knows they are one.[135] It now seems that Homer was the first, as far as we know, to have come to an understanding of this philosophic principle, to which he gave the name "nature."[136] The experiences that had to precede its discovery are a measure of the difficulty of its discovery. It is unclear whether Odysseus extends the principle beyond this one insight, but he does have it confirmed. In Hades, he learns, there are recognizable images of men and women, but, with the exception of Teiresias, they have no mind (10.492–95). Odysseus himself had claimed that he was nothing but mind; the ghosts in Hades are everything he then denied. Between the two episodes "Cyclops" and "Hades," he was shown the nature of the *moly*, and saw his men in an unrecognizable form but with their minds intact. He therefore must realize later that Calypso's offer to make him deathless and ageless cannot be genuine.[137] His shape and his mind make him the mortal he is, and only at the price of losing that unity could he survive such an alteration.[138] Calypso probably does not know this (cf. 5.170), but Circe does: although she too wants to have Odysseus as her husband, she does not offer to make him immortal.

After being a witness to the inhumanity of which man is capable, Odysseus might believe that only a drug as powerful as Circe's could fully domesticate man.[139] The price would be the loss of speech (cf. 10.408–20). The possibility of such a "city of pigs" is shown to Odysseus after he has democratized his rule and thereby allowed not only for occasional rebelliousness, which he can for the moment suppress, but also for his defeat when the going gets too hard for his men and numbers count more than sense (10.428–48; 12.278–97). Homer has thus juxtaposed two political considerations that seem to be of different orders. The theme of bestiality culminates twice, first among the Laestrygonians and then with Circe's swine. The latter points, by way of contrast, to a humanity that, though it belongs to man as man, is not open to every man, since what he is necessarily he is not necessarily unless he knows that that is what he is necessarily.[140] Without that knowledge he can be enchanted and made subject to perfect rule; but it is unclear whether the apparent connection between justice and knowledge, which Odysseus's daring action and the insight he is then granted seem to suggest, is as tight as that between ignorance and bestiality. The insight might be implicit in the action, but

the action is not guided by the insight. Is the necessity Odysseus acknowledges he is under to rescue his men ultimately the same as the
knowledge of the necessity of the togetherness of looks and mind?

If man cannot live except politically, he must live with men who, if they
do not know what constitutes man, must have a version of the knowledge
of what constitutes man that does not preserve, however much it may
reflect, the nature of man. Homer indicates that a most powerful version
of that knowledge is summed up in the word "Hades." "Hades" splits
body and soul apart in a peculiar way: the soul retains the looks of the
body, and the mind vanishes entirely. Hades distinguishes man from everything else. Men go to Hades, all other animals just die (10.174–75).
This distinctiveness of man, whether exaggerated or not, imposes on man
certain constraints. The prohibition against cannibalism takes the form of
a general prohibition, whether it be through inhumation or cremation,
against man being consumed by any wild beast.[141] Hades is a negative
determination of man, and, as such, a lawful equivalent of Odysseus's
knowledge of his nature. Its invisibility, which seems contained in its
name (*Aïdēs* or "Unseen," V. 846), seems to displace the invisible bond in
the nature of man. Hades, therefore, is not a deduction from the knowledge of that bond. Elpenor has to remind Odysseus to bury him and
threaten him with punishment if he does not (11.71–73).[142]

Odysseus's knowledge of nature does not go beyond the knowledge of
man in general. It does not protect him against the possibility that if he
sleeps with Circe she may unman him (*anēnōr*). A difference seems to be
implied between the intelligible *eidos* of human being (*anthrōpos*) and the
visible species (*eidos*) of man (*anēr*) and woman (*gunē*).[143] If Odysseus is
naked, he is helpless against Circe unless she first swears an oath not to
harm him in some other way (10.296–301). To be naked probably has a
double meaning—to be without clothes and to be unarmed. Circe understands sexual love as a way of their shedding their mutual distrust
(10.334–35); but Odysseus is told that she would still have an advantage
over him. There is in man some capacity to resist, a strength of soul or
whatever we choose to call it, that can be lost or diminished regardless of
knowledge. It seems to comprehend more than the shame and the weakness that, in the case of men, might be thought to accompany sex: as a
goddess and a daughter of the sun, Circe has nothing to lose and nothing
to hide.[144] After Circe swears an oath, Odysseus does go to bed with her;
but though a bath has later refreshed him, he refuses to eat: "I sat dis-
traught, and my heart imagined evils" (10.374). Circe does not know and
cannot figure out what is distressing Odysseus. She in fact guesses wrong
and believes he suspects another trick. Odysseus has to explain: "What

man, whoever should be just (*enaisimos*), would bring himself to taste of food or drink before he had arranged the release of his comrades and saw them with his own eyes?" (10.383–85). Odysseus informs Circe of something she does not know: he shares something with his fellow human beings that she does not. For her, his men are no different from domesticated animals (cf. 10.283). He pities them, she does not. Only after she sees each one clasp Odysseus's hand and hears the house ring with the lamentations of longing does she too take pity (10.399). This is an extraordinary thing; a god learns from a man. Hermes did not tell Odysseus how or when he was to gain the release of his men. Even Odysseus perhaps, once granted a share in the knowledge the gods have, if it were then coupled with access to the bed of a goddess, might have been dehumanized if the oath, peculiar to gods, which Circe swore, had not reminded him of his own justice. In the absence of that oath, he might have suffered another form of enchantment as debilitating as his men had suffered. Perhaps he no longer would have had the heart or manliness to resist a version of Calypso's temptation. We know that Menelaus, a "soft warrior" (XVII.588), did not resist.

Odysseus, at Circe's urging, goes back to his ship to bring the twenty-two men he left behind. He describes their welcome of him in a way that might lead one to believe he has a certain contempt for them: "Just as calves jump and skip about a herd of cows, who have come into the barnyard when they are sated with grazing, and the pens no longer hold them but they run around their mothers lowing intensely, so they, when they saw me, poured around me in tears, and their heart imagined that it was just as if they had come home to the city of rocky Ithaca, where they had been born and raised" (10.410–17). A uniquely human response is transformed by Odysseus into a picture of domestic cattle, in which he is no longer their father but their mother. Odysseus distinguishes between his own picture of them and their imagination; that it is indeed their imagination and not his own that likens Odysseus's return to them to their own return home, is made explicit (10.419–20). It would not have escaped him that only in their imagination were they ever to get home (cf. 23.233–40). Odysseus's sense of superiority is plain; it recalls the simile, whether Eurylochus's or Odysseus's, used to describe the enchanted wolves and lions around Circe's house: "Just as dogs fawn around the master when he leaves the table, for he always brings them heart-appeasing scraps" (10.216–17). The perfect rule, however, which Odysseus's image suggests, is immediately shattered. Eurylochus urges the crew, whom Odysseus left with the ship, not to go to Circe's; and Odysseus is prepared to kill him, even though he is a relation by marriage. Eurylochus accuses Odysseus of rashly leading them into a trap, where they would end up as swine or tame wolves and lions and be set to guard Circe's home. Eurylochus must have inferred that the wolves and lions he saw were once men, for he assumes that only men are tame.[145] Odysseus's anger is aroused not only to divert attention away from Eurylochus's shrewd guess that their comrades were turned into swine—the others would certainly not have gone had they known—but also because Eurylochus adds that it was by Odysseus's wickedness that their comrades perished in the Cyclops's cave. This charge, which casually attributes criminality to the desire to know, is too close to the truth to be answered effectively. It reminds one of Eupeithes' charges to which the only answer was his death. Odysseus must at all costs prevent Eurylochus from commandeering the ship and leaving him and the rest of his men stranded. He knows that his simile is inadequate against the combined force of terror and indictment, not despite but because of their falseness.

The discovery of nature is clearly linked with the problem of rule. There is not only Odysseus's condescension—his men are friends and Eurylochus gets for a time to rule half his men—but along with the herdlike character of his subjects there also are sharply edged portraits of individual natures. Eurylochus was put in charge, but Polites was the dearest and most thoughtful of Odysseus's comrades (10.225); and Elpenor—the man of hope—was the youngest and least equipped with either brains or brawn (10.552–53).[146] Odysseus ultimately loses out to Eurylochus. The second time Eurylochus rebels, Odysseus knows better than to threaten him with force (12.297). The assent of his men had in the meantime drained away. Odysseus loses control at Circe's. Although she urges him to stay as long as it takes to recover their spirit completely, so that they will be as they were when they left Ithaca (10.460–65), his men demand to return home after a year.[147] He admits to Circe that they have been wearing his heart out with their persistence (10.484–86). Odysseus, to be sure, is not reluctant to go home, but the decision is not his. Perhaps he lost control at the moment his men had to restrain him from killing Eurylochus. If he had not been restrained, he might have been able to save most of the rest. The obstacle Eurylochus represents points directly to the suitors.

Hades

Circe is the daughter of the Sun. She belongs in herself among the cosmic gods, but she acts as Odysseus's guide to the Olympian gods, of whom

Hades can be said to be the most potent symbol. To see the light of the sun is to be alive, for the sun does not shine in Hades (10.498; 12.383). Circe, it turns out, knows the way home for Odysseus, but she does not know his future. The difference recalls the error Croesus made when he wanted to test the oracle at Delphi.[148] He arranged for his envoys to ask the oracle what Croesus was doing on the very day they were consulting it; but they only had to ask what he was going to do on the morrow to make sure that Apollo knew not only the present but the future. Odysseus is about to enter upon his fate (cf. 11.139). Once he goes to Hades he has no choice. The two main elements of his fate then become known to him. One involves his justice, the other his piety. He must return home if his wife and son are to be saved, and he must leave home if he is to make his peace with Poseidon. The riddle of the *Odyssey* largely turns on the disunion and union of this double task. Odysseus's life begins to make sense once Teiresias reveals the future to him; but it is unclear whether the sense it imparts to his life is unequivocal and comprehends everything he has experienced and is going to experience in the course of his completing his life. It has often been remarked that when Achilles gazes at the shield Hephaestus made for him, he knows everything he sees depicted on it; but when Aeneas gazes at the shield Vulcan made for him, on which is shown the battle of Actium, he cannot understand it, and, although he rejoices in the image despite his ignorance, puts on his shoulders the fame and the fate of his descendants.[149] Odysseus is in this respect more like Aeneas than Achilles. A shape is given to his life that fits and does not fit his life. Only if he had seen and suffered what he has would he be prepared to put on his fate; but one cannot help suspecting that his fate, like the ghost that instructs him in it, is no more than an image of his life.

The difficulty we have in understanding Hades is reflected by Odysseus himself. When Odysseus learns that he must go to the house of Hades and terrible Persephone, he weeps, "and my heart was no longer willing to live and see the light of the sun" (10.497–98). He speaks as if to go to Hades and not to see the light of the sun were not the same (cf. 12.21–22). Both are just expressions; they would carry no weight separately, but once they are juxtaposed they recharge each other with their literal meaning and render ambiguous what would otherwise be plain. Shortly afterward, Odysseus tells of the mischance of Elpenor. In order to sleep off his drunkenness he went up on the roof of Circe's house, "desiring coolness (*psukhos*)," and when he heard the bustle of the men preparing to leave, he forgot to go down the ladder backward, broke his neck, "and his soul (*psukhē*) went down to Hades" (10.560). In the *Odyssey*, no soul goes to Hades before Elpenor's does, and Odysseus himself never speaks in this

way again. It is Homer who bears witness to Hades. It is the only one of
Odysseus's tales that Homer retells: the souls of the suitors go to Hades.
Odysseus himself, however, seems to believe the soul to be no more than
the fact of breathing (*anapsukhein*), and the soul as something separable
and in itself merely the hope of the foolish "man of hope" Elpenor.[150]
Odysseus's despair would then arise from his being told, after he had
realized the necessary togetherness of human shape and human mind, that
the gods can separate them, and in the case of Teiresias put them together
again apart from life and away from the light of the sun. Odysseus is
properly introduced into the power of the gods through two events.
Circe, without being seen, brings to the ship the sacrificial animals Odysseus needs for Hades, "For who would see a god go either here or there
against his will?" (10.573–74). And at the end of the journey to Hades, he
comes across a people at the edge of Ocean upon whom the sun never
shines either when it is rising or when it is setting (11.13–19). To be alive
is not the same as to see the light of the sun (cf. 24.263–64). Night belongs
to the gods.[151]

Odysseus's account of Hades falls into four sections: Elpenor, Teiresias,
and Anticleia form the first, the heroines of old the second, Odysseus's
former comrades at Troy the third, and the heroes of old the last. It is no
doubt due to the second section that some ancients say that underworld
stories are particularly suitable for women.[152] Odysseus, at any rate, wins
Arete's support and more gifts after he speaks of the heroines, and before
he tells, at Alcinous's request, of the treachery of Clytaemestra.[153] He had
prudently broken off his recital of the women with an allusion to hateful
Eriphyle (11.326–27). From the point of view of strict economy, the account of Hades should not have included any of the last three groups.
Once he talks with Elpenor, Teiresias, and his mother, he should return
to Circe. From Elpenor he learns about the divine duty he owes to the
least important of men; from Teiresias he learns his future; and from his
mother he learns there is no embrace in Hades. This is something Agamemnon does not know (11.392–93). Once they are dead, Odysseus and
Penelope will be eternally apart.[154] Odysseus's first and last experience of
Hades is of fear (11.43, 633); but he overcomes his initial terror and cannot overcome the last. He seems to have put himself to a test he finally
failed, even though he knew everything he might have seen thereafter
would have been as much a phantom as all he had seen already. No god
ever sends Odysseus a dream; Hades is his nightmare. Odysseus's persis-
tent curiosity in Hades needs to be explained. It recalls his refusal to leave
the Cyclops's cave. If one says that he has a purely mercenary interest in
speaking of the second group, and the third cannot be avoided once Alci-

nous asks about them, then only the fourth is strictly something he wishes to tell. What he has learned up to that point does not satisfy him, and what he learns later suggests to him some further inquiry that he cannot stand to continue. One might suppose that what he learns from Achilles would have been enough to make him quit the place at once, and if it did not reverse his acceptance of his fate, it would at least have made Calypso's offer more tempting than he seems to have ever treated it. Odysseus's choice now appears to have been of neither home nor mortality but of Hades.

Just as Circe had come to the ship sooner than Odysseus had, Elpenor arrives in Hades before he does. Elpenor adds nothing to Odysseus's account of his death except that a god had doomed him (11.61). Odysseus attributed it to a lack of brains. Elpenor requests that his armor be buried with him, a tomb (*sēma*) be built near the seashore, and an oar be fixed on top with which he used to row when he was alive (11.74–78). It is easy to understand what he wants. He wants to be known to people in the future as a somebody, even if he is not a name to them. They will know who he was from what he did. It is not much, but it is something.[155] The sign of the tomb cannot be misunderstood. Odysseus's second journey, on the other hand, will take him to a people who do not know the sea and do not salt their food; they do not know of ships or oars. The clear sign (*sēma*) to Odysseus that he has reached his goal will be when a traveler meets him and, on seeing the oar Teiresias has told him to carry on his shoulder, says he is carrying a winnowingfan (11.121–31).[156] On the spot of this encounter, Odysseus is to fix the oar in the ground and make a sacrifice to Poseidon. The sacrifice, which is to consist of sheep, bull, and boar, is too elaborate for Odysseus to have brought the victims with him. He will have to explain to the inhabitants what he wants to do. "There is a god," he will say, "who presides over something you cannot see." Odysseus, who was chosen to bring home to the Phaeacians that the gods have ceased to be manifest to them and are essentially invisible, is destined to extend the Olympian gods into a region where the sign of their being will cease to point to their being.[157] He will break the connection with the cosmic gods that still lingers, in the element of metonymy, among the Olympian gods. The oar will be a sign with a displaced significance. That significance is of a radically new kind. Teiresias says of this landlocked people that they do not know of oars, "which are wings for ships." The analogical function of wings and oars allows Teiresias to speak poetically; but the poetry implicit in the word for winnowingfan (*athērēloigos*)—it is literally a "chaff-destroyer"—does not offer a way to explain the oar. The oar does not separate the good from the bad. When stuck in the ground, it points to something it is not meant to point to; and what it is meant to point to is unknown. The oar partly functions in the way in which the proper name Outis did. Once it was communicated to the other Cyclopes, it designated no one; but in designating no one it signified mind. So the oar, which in the proper setting designates either the tomb of a sailor or Poseidon, will alter its significance and either designate no one or get a new label.

It seems to be altogether fitting that in the region of the invisible Odysseus learns of the need to bury the dead and to be a messenger of the Olympian gods. Between these two forms of piety, one of which lies in the immediate and the other in the distant future, he learns of the content of Polyphemus's prayer, that the suffering at home will consist in arrogant men who will eat up his livelihood and woo his wife. This is a new kind of suffering. It has nothing to do with any visible injury he will sustain; it is not as plain as either the tears he will shed on Calypso's island, where the emptiness of his life is obvious, or the wear and tear of war and sea, of which the Phaeacians know nothing. The equivalent to the pain that Polyphemus experienced goes deeper and depends entirely on how Odysseus treats it. The violent acts of which Teiresias speaks and that Odysseus will avenge turn out to be one: Antinous hits Odysseus with a stool. Between, then, Odysseus's appeasement of Elpenor with a sign and his appeasement of Poseidon with a sign, Odysseus will experience another sign that requires the killing of 108 suitors in order that there be a requital for it. Teiresias speaks concretely of a symbolic act, which, it seems, Odysseus cannot possibly interpret correctly. The sign of the oar, with its double meaning, is simple in comparison with what we learn Teiresias intended.

The apparent disproportion between the crime of the suitors and their punishment is underlined by the language Teiresias uses to describe what we would call their freeloading: "They eat up your livelihood (*biotos*)." We have heard this before (1.160; 2.123); but for Odysseus, who has seen the Cyclops and the Laestrygonians eat his men, it must be either an exhausted metaphor or meaningless. His vengeance, however, seems to demand that he react to it as if it were literal, as if *biotos*, in other words, meant life (as it sometimes does), so that he should take out on the suitors what he could not exact from Polyphemus.[158] If *biotos* just meant his property, it is hard to see why Amphinomus' last-minute proposal should not be accepted, that they pay back what they ate and drank plus damages (22.55–60).[159] It seems, then, that they must be punished for the thought that lay behind their gobbling up of his goods. They treated him as if he were no longer alive (14.89–92; 22.38–40). Not to be alive would mean to them to be helpless. The suitors do not believe in Hades. Whenever they threaten anyone, they speak of the bogeyman King Echetus, who is baneful to all mortals (*brotoi*); he cuts off the nose and ears, and draws out the genitals and feeds them to dogs (18.65, 116; 23.308). Echetus is a kind of pre-Olympian Hades who sets no limits on mortals. Nowhere else do the suitors ever speak of *brotoi*, which in these passages seems to have restored to it some of the sense of the noun from which it is derived: *brotos* means "gore" (cf. 11.41).[160] More significantly, the suitors never speak at all of men as mortals (*thnētoi*), though Odysseus himself uses the word some thirty-one times. The suitors do not believe that men are constituted by the contrariety of the pair immortal (*athanatos*) and mortal (*thnētos*). They therefore do not acknowledge "mortal" as the marked term of that pair, with "Hades" and all it entails standing behind it. The vengeance with which Elpenor, a nobody, threatens Odysseus if he does not bury him, presupposes that though dead he is not helpless. He is something.

Despite what Circe and Teiresias tell him, Odysseus does not yet understand Hades. He knows from Circe that souls are shadows (10.495), while he himself calls Elpenor's soul his image (*eidōlon*, 11.83). Teiresias explains that once a soul drinks blood it will be able to see and speak to him; but neither prepares him for his failure to embrace his mother. He thinks it possible that Persephone sent him a phantom (*eidōlon*). Anticleia tells him that she is not an illusion, but the soul hovers like a dream. There is nothing to it. She urges him to seek the light at once and tell everything she told him to his wife. What she tells him, apart from reporting the faithfulness of Penelope, a proleptic truth about Telemachus, and the miserable life of his father in the country, is that she died out of longing for him, for his understanding and kindliness (11.181–203). Odysseus realizes at once the difference between his mother and his father: his absence more deeply affected her than Laertes. The frustration of her wish killed her. His refusal to follow his mother's advice and leave at once seems to have been prompted by a guess he wishes to confirm: Hades is a place of eternal frustration.

The souls he first saw were for the most part those who had been cut off early in life: warriors, brides, bachelors, and young girls (11.36–39). The heroines of old are as a class stamped with one characteristic: none of them are known to him by sight. He has to ask them who they are (11.233–34); he does not have to ask the heroes of old who they are. No woman is called famous (1.308, 310). Odysseus goes out of his way to give the women some measure of glory. They are dependent on him for their afterlife. Odysseus becomes the Muse for women. It really is true that Poseidon was the father of Neleus, that Antiope slept with Zeus, that

Zeus fathered Heracles, and that Epicaste married her son out of ignorance. Odysseus, however, never allows the women to speak for themselves.[161] Most of these stories are not really about themselves, but their
husbands, lovers, and children (cf. 11.227); and the only ones who are
not passive are Epicaste (Jocasta), who hanged herself, and Eriphyle, who
betrayed her husband, and with whom Odysseus ends. He does not mention that her son killed her. Hades is a place of the strict segregation of
the sexes. Only there can women be seen for what they are, but precisely
for that reason they cannot come fully into their own. Odysseus should
know already that Penelope is finished once Telemachus grows up and he
comes home. To judge by Homer's summary, Odysseus did not tell Penelope about his encounter with the heroines (23.322–25).

The heroines' stories, which fall into nine groups, are all, except for
the last, connected with gods, whereas neither Agamemnon nor Achilles
assigns any role to the gods.[162] Agamemnon perished simply by the will of
an evil woman (11.384). This difference between men and women perhaps
explains why in the fourth group no women are being punished. They are
not judged. One wonders whether this indulgence is going to end, and
Hades is destined to become gender neutral. In which group will Clytaemestra be? Will another Odysseus ever learn her side of the story?
Odysseus, in any case, seems to take Agamemnon's advice to heart: "Do
not ever be gentle to your wife, and do not tell her everything you know
well but speak part of it and keep part of it hidden" (11.441–43). By
following this advice, Odysseus makes his task at home infinitely more
difficult. Amphimedon, one of the suitors and a guest-friend of Agamemnon, tells Agamemnon in Hades a version of the *Odyssey*, in which everything runs smoothly in the plot to kill the suitors simply because he assumes that Penelope was in on it from the start (24.127, 167–69).
Odysseus's distrust of everything and everyone seems to have become a
settled conviction once he hears Agamemnon's story. His own indifference to certain issues of right shows up in the neutral tone of the question
he puts to Agamemnon: "Did Poseidon destroy you at sea, did enemies
injure you on land, when you were rustling cattle and sheep or fighting
over a city and women?" (11.399–403). What Odysseus himself did and
suffered at Ismaros could have gone worse for Agamemnon elsewhere.
Agamemnon's story subordinates Aegisthus to Clytaemestra. She is his
damned wife; she killed Cassandra; she was the bitch who refused to close
his mouth and eyes as he went to Hades: "there is nothing more terrible
and low than woman" (11.427). Clytaemestra dooms to disgrace all
women in the future, even if any is good (11.432–34). Agamemnon's universal indictment of women, though he makes an exception of Penelope,

seems to have fixed Odysseus's decision to proceed in secret.[163] The days of alliances are over; the city is too divided, and Penelope has become inscrutable. The resentment his own men have already expressed is as nothing to the discontent Penelope might harbor.

The Circe episode is framed on both sides by the same line: "There is no possibility of accomplishment (*prēxis*) for those who weep and mourn" (10.202, 568). In Hades, Agamemnon weeps (11.466), Achilles mourns (11.472), and everyone else grieves (11.542). Nonaccomplishment characterizes Hades (cf. 11.464). Agamemnon regrets most of all that Clytaemestra killed him before he could see and embrace his son (11.452–53). Hades is dominated by the demand for the satisfaction of right (*themis*). Achilles, whose claim to be the rightful leader of the Achaeans was the armature on which the *Iliad* was built, now finds in Hades that claim realized—all the Argive heroes are with him—and he is still not satisfied: he wants to live again just for a short time so that he may punish anyone who is dishonoring his father (11.494–503).[164] Whatever vestige of anger remains undischarged in life lingers in Hades. Minos is still adjudicating suits (*dikē*) that must have arisen after the plaintiffs came to Hades (11.569–71). Everyone in Hades still has concerns (11.542). There are still scores to settle. One wonders, then, whether Odysseus believes he will not go to Hades, if his fate is to punish all those who dishonor him and his family. His choice of home gives him the chance to accomplish what Achilles' choice kept him from accomplishing. He might thus believe there is a completeness granted him that does not leave anything undone. Odysseus seems so certain that he alone never does anything in vain that when he is confronted with the silence of Ajax, who still cannot forget his anger over the "damned armor" of Achilles, he expresses confidence that he would have answered him sooner or later (11.553–65). He seems to take the privilege of having seen Hades once as a sign that he will not see it again. It is uncertain whether Homer agrees with him. Elpenor seems to stand for the truth of Hades. What never dies is ungrounded or senseless expectation, whether it be of good or evil: "We are always full of hopes."[165] If, however, Odysseus were convinced that his life would be fulfilled, it would serve to explain his tears of frustration on Calypso's island, as if the gods were determined to break that conviction, and it would go far to explain as well his rejection of Calypso's offer.

It is the sight of Heracles that seals Odysseus's decision to turn Calypso down (11.601–26). Heracles is the last in the series of heroes whom Odysseus was so impatient to see that he could not wait for Ajax's reply. Three of them illustrate the fruitlessness characteristic of Hades—Tityus, Tantalus, and Sisyphus.[166] Heracles illustrates the unreality of Hades: it is im-

possible to tell apart Heracles the *eidōlon* from what is depicted so artfully on his golden shoulder strap. Just as the other souls are still fleeing
in terror before him—he looks like dark night and as if he were ever about
to shoot—so Odysseus is frightened by the picture of wild beasts and
"struggles, battles, and human slaughter."[167] Heracles in Hades unites the
absence of the good with the absence of the real. He is still complaining
about his former subjection to an inferior. Odysseus does not speak to
him; he says that Heracles himself (*autos*) is among the gods.[168] Odysseus's silence seems to be due to his recalling his friend Iphitus, who gave
him the bow with which he kills the suitors, and whom Heracles slew in
his own home when Iphitus was a guest-friend (21.11–14). The gods reward injustice with immortality. The very principle for which Odysseus
fought for ten years proves to be as vain as everything else in Hades,
Agamemnon dead and Heracles deathless. This is the low point of Odysseus's narrative. His desire to see others is not unreasonable if he wants
to know whether any just men are being punished, but Persephone frightens him off before he can find out. Perhaps he fears he would have seen
Iphitus.

Destiny

What Teiresias tells Odysseus extends from the island of the Sun to Odysseus's double future, and what Circe tells him extends from the Sirens to
the island of the Sun, but neither tells him about Calypso. Calypso is
hidden from view. She is the most mysterious part of Odysseus's life. She
represents all that we do not know about Odysseus. She slips out of sight
between the story Odysseus tells and the story Homer tells. She is the
personification, as it were, of the difference between story and life, of
everything that eludes both Homer's presentation of causality and Odysseus's understanding of his experiences. Not only is she the lie of poetry,
which must hide whatever it cannot make shine, but possibly also the lie
in the soul, whatever it has that is truly false and is not just the impure lie
of speech.[169] That Calypso cannot budge Odysseus from the necessity of
either his fate or his human nature does not mean that these two constituents of his knowledge are so perfectly joined that there is not a shadow
between them. Odysseus's refusal to retell the story of Calypso, on the
grounds that he told it to Alcinous and Arete the day before, calls attention to the possibility of this shadow. In saying that he hates to repeat
what was clearly stated, he only underlines the obscurity of Calypso
(12.450–54).

Teiresias picks up Odysseus's fate at the point where the piety or the impiety of Odysseus and his men will decide whether or not he arrives home aboard his own ship. Teiresias treats as unimportant whatever will occur between Odysseus's departure from Circe's island and his approach to the island of the Sun, as though his survival up to then were assured and he had no choices to make. Circe certainly seems to chart his course at first as if that were true; but no sooner does she tell him how to escape from the Sirens than she gives him a choice and refuses to advise him (12.55–126). One way is through the Planctae, the other between Scylla and Charybdis. The way of Scylla and Charybdis carries with it the necessary loss of six men; the way through the Planctae has been successfully crossed only once, by Jason's ship the *Argo*, for he was dear to Hera. Odysseus chooses Scylla and Charybdis; he rejects out of hand divine support. This rejection does not check him from speaking to his crew about Zeus, on whom, he says, their escape from destruction depends (12.215–16). After Hades, Odysseus is quite candid about the half-truths he tells them. He does not speak either to them or to Penelope of the choice Circe gave him (23.327–28). It is as if Odysseus generalized Agamemnon's advice and extended it to everyone. His policy leads him to soften the dire consequences for his men if they eat the cattle of the Sun, so that it is left to Eurylochus to formulate as a possibility what Odysseus was told was inevitable (11.112–13; 12.275–321, 348–49). A certain resignation creeps over Odysseus. He picks up a line of Nestor: "Then I knew that a god (*daimōn*) was devising evils" (12.295; 3.166).

The first alteration Odysseus makes in Circe's advice is to present as a command what she gave as a choice to listen to the Sirens (12.49, 160). There is certainly no necessity to be tempted by the Sirens. Odysseus could easily have plugged his own ears and calculated how far they must row beyond the Sirens. Odysseus, in any case, does not tell his men of either the Sirens' charm or the danger. The Sirens address Odysseus; they know his men cannot hear. They design a speech meant for him alone: "We know everything the Argives and Trojans suffered at Troy by the will of the gods, and we know everything that happens or comes to be on earth" (12.189–90). Odysseus knows that if he succumbs, his wife and son will never greet him (12.41–43). He discovers, after he knows his fate, that his strongest and deepest desire is not for home but for knowledge. Odysseus can resist the enchanting speeches of Calypso, which offer him immortality, but he cannot resist the enchantment of omniscience, and he is willing to give up his life for the chance. Justice is not at the heart of his nature. It is perhaps for this reason that, when he tells Penelope about his second journey, he adds to Teiresias's prophecy words that echo Homer's proem: "He commands me to go to very many cities of mortals" (23.267–68). That his men must double the bonds is not designed to prevent him from breaking them, but to drive home to him that the Sirens have hit upon a truth about him that Hades, as the locus of frustration, might have hidden from him.[170] His thirst for justice may very well be sated, but not his desire to know. He is going to die not knowing.

The Sirens represent the first of three limitations Odysseus experiences. The second concerns his wish to thwart Scylla as he steers clear of Charybdis. He wants to wage war even against the gods. Circe warns him not to arm himself against a deathless evil but to call upon Scylla's mother; but Odysseus forgets to hearken to Circe's painful injunction. He does arm himself uselessly and fails to invoke Scylla's mother; but he does not get off any the worse than if he had followed Circe's instructions, and he can come away with the belief that at least he was doing something and not giving up without a fight. Scylla eats the six strongest men in a single pass. Odysseus did not try to arrange for her to take the six weakest. His reluctance to acknowledge necessary evils bears directly on the problem the suitors pose. It begins to look, in any case, as if Odysseus is being made to experience the living equivalents of underworld frustration. First, he learns he cannot know; next, he learns he cannot defeat evil; and finally he will learn the limits of persuasion: the force of the majority is stronger than any eloquence or sacred oath. First himself, then the gods, and third other men stand in his way. He is being forced to submit to his fate.

Odysseus does not say for how many days, after the supplies Circe had provided were exhausted, his men fished and caught birds (cf. 4.360–69); he must realize that however long they would have held out, the gods would have prolonged their stay on the island until they succumbed. What looked in the perspective of Homer as criminal wickedness, and which Odysseus at first accepts as such (12.300), though Eurylochus, in pleading for a respite and warning of the risks of their sailing at night, is only being sensible (12.279–90), proves to be a necessity that makes his men helpless and innocent (12.330). They would have had to let themselves be bound voluntarily, as Odysseus had, in order for Odysseus to rescue them. That their craving was for meat and his own for knowledge merely shows a difference in natures: Odysseus can be saved against his will, they cannot be saved against theirs. Indeed, a scruple of a religious kind might be involved. Perhaps they feel uneasy about taking the life of fish, for which no appropriate sacrifice to an Olympian god can be made.[171] Eurylochus, in any case, proposes to sacrifice to the gods the cows they slaughter; and the men go to some trouble to find substitutes for what a lawful sacrifice requires. What seals their fate, however, is Eurylochus's promise, once they come home, to establish a temple to the Sun and put in it many noble things to delight the Sun. Since it turns out that Circe is right and not Teiresias (11.109; 12.131–36, 374–75)—the Sun does not see and hear everything—the Sun does not know about this promised reversion to the cosmic gods, just after Odysseus has been given the task to extend the realm of the invisible Olympians. When, therefore, the Sun asks for a fair recompense for the death of his cattle, we do not know whether he would have regarded his worship to be equitable.[172] Zeus decides on his own to destroy the ship. Zeus was under terrible pressure: the Sun had threatened to descend into Hades and shine among the dead.

6

Odysseus's Lies

From the thirteenth book on, the *Odyssey* is lengthened beyond what seems to be required for the story once Odysseus returns home: four books at Eumaeus's, four at home in disguise, and four for the killing and recognition.[173] A less roundabout way of accomplishing the same ends could easily be imagined. One wonders, then, whether there are not obstacles of a hidden kind that did not allow for a straightforward narrative. The first obstacle seems to be Odysseus himself. For all his impatience to get home, it is not obvious that he will be at home once he is at home; and this alienation is not due solely to the necessity he is under to ship out again but also to the issue of whether his experiences and his understanding of his experiences are wholly adapted to his homecoming and the reestablishment of his rule over his house and his city. The anonymous Odysseus of mind had yielded in a moment of defiance to Odysseus the sacker of cities; but the Odysseus of pure mind had been corrected, by Hermes' instruction, into Odysseus the human being. Odysseus, now, however, seems to revert to the at-home equivalent of "sacker of cities" and to give up his "hermetic" knowledge. Homer suggests, at any rate, that Odysseus undergoes, on his passage home, a death and a rebirth. His pleasant sleep on board the Phaeacian ship is most like death, and while the ship carries a man with thoughts like unto the gods', he sleeps undisturbed, having forgotten everything he had suffered (13.79–92). From the island of the Concealer Calypso, the navel of the sea (1.50), to the land of the Phaeacians, or the Grays, and from there to Ithaca, Odysseus is on a course of emergence into the light, but whether that light is the light of the sun or some other kind of illumination is unclear. Although he does not recognize anything when he wakes up on the beach, he accepts at first Athena's assurance that it is Ithaca as long as he does not know that the young shepherd he meets is Athena (13.250–51). Odysseus started out by choosing memory; when he gets home, he sees nothing of what he knew as home, and takes as gospel the word of a stranger that he is home. If hearsay thus replaces memory, and Odysseus becomes as unknowing as he is unknown, then the rebirth of Odysseus, at which Homer hints, amounts almost to a reinvention. This reinvention seems to take place without Odysseus being aware of it and certainly without his being in control of it. He could make himself pass for no one, but he does not remember his scar.

Odysseus would become a completely tragic figure, if it turned out that the connection between his name and his scar, which Homer, in juxtaposing the stories about them, seems to be urging us to make, were as tight as that between Oedipus's name and lameness, and he were as oblivious as Oedipus of what was right before him. The double meaning of "Oedipus"—"Know Where" and "Swollen Foot"—has its counterpart in Odysseus's chosen name "No one," with its shadow "Mind," and his given name "Anger." If one adds the anger of Oedipus, the resemblance becomes uncanny. In the case of Oedipus, the solution to the riddle "Why must he who solved the riddle of the Sphinx kill his father and marry his mother?" lay in the difference between species and genesis, for while Oedipus could figure out man in time he could not comprehend the end points of birth and death, at which the sacred, in the form of a divine prohibition at one end and a divine injunction at the other, intrudes on human life. Oedipus could not bring himself to will retroactively the conditions for what he claims to be, the outsider wholly devoted to the city; for those conditions were patricide and incest, or the annihilation of the family on behalf of the city. The theoretical disposition of Oedipus, which showed up in his disregarding himself in discovering "man," was put in the service of a political end with which it had to be forced to fit. The force required for the fit was made manifest in Oedipus's anger. In the case of Odysseus, on the other hand, for whom the gods reserved the discovery of nature, he is fated to vindicate the family at the expense of much bloodshed in order that he may safely leave the kingdom in the hands of his son. That the fit between Odysseus the knower, however, and Odysseus the king is no less forced than in the case of Oedipus, the anger of Odysseus equally shows. Odysseus, who is "No one" by mind, experiences what it means to be a nobody and demands the recognition due to a king. Odysseus in his own country duplicates what he is destined to do for Poseidon. Poseidon is to become known while he remains unknowable, and Odysseus, who had already among the Phaeacians rehearsed his task, wants to be acknowledged to be, while concealed, what he would automatically be conceded to be were he to be revealed; but we do not know whether Odysseus can be revealed. Did not Helen indicate that he was transparent only to her?

While Odysseus is sleeping on the beach, Poseidon and Zeus first discuss the punishment of the Phaeacians, and then Poseidon, in accepting Zeus's suggestion, turns the ship that transported Odysseus into stone. Zeus does not forbid the expression of Poseidon's anger; he refines it. The stone ship becomes a permanent sign of Poseidon's displeasure: the Phaeacians can never forget that they are not to be friendly to strangers. Zeus's alteration of the prophecy Alcinous knew from his father presupposes that its second part, that a mountain will surround them and cut them permanently off from the sea, will not be fulfilled. The threat is a far more effective restraint than its reality. One wonders whether this interlude, in which we leave the Phaeacians standing around Poseidon's altar, does not symbolize the new relation Zeus is preparing between gods and men. The essence of this new relation will be one of terror. There will be warnings, either to be seen or to be heard, of the consequences of disobedience to the gods (cf. 24.537–44). That the Phaeacians were just and friendly in escorting Odysseus home and heaping gifts upon him would be irrelevant: they defied in their hearts the clear intention of the prophecy. They chose to appease Odysseus in his wrath rather than Poseidon.

The new principle that the punishment of the Phaeacians establishes seems to be wholly at odds with the sacred obligation of guest-friendship to which Odysseus appeals as soon as he wakes and fails to recognize the distinctive landscape of Ithaca (13.200–216). Since Athena altered the appearance of things, Odysseus believes that the Phaeacians did not bring him home and possibly robbed him as well, and he wishes that Zeus might punish them. Zeus, it seems, anticipated Odysseus's wish and thereby accepted the false premises of his wish. If the Phaeacians had done what Odysseus believed they did, then their punishment would have been just according to Odysseus; but since the appearance of things is not the truth of things, Odysseus is unjust in his will and still the Phaeacians are punished. They are punished not for what they did but for the hidden ground of what they did: they put man ahead of god. This cancellation of the obvious, or the denial of the possibility that human beings can read correctly the significance of things, recalls both Telemachus's error in believing that Athena, disguised as Mentes, was waiting long at the threshold and Athena's insight that the suitors, who were listening in silence to Phemius's song, were really extraordinary in their insolence (1.119–20, 227–29). It seems, then, that the punishment of the Phaeacians points directly to the punishment of the suitors: whatever they are being punished for cannot be interpreted by way of the manifest. The signs of the gods have become as hidden as the gods themselves. Odysseus in disguise reflects and is meant to reflect the permanent disguise of the divine.

The inevitable consequence of the occlusion of the gods is the necessary misreading, on the part of men, of the gods and their intentions. The oar Odysseus will carry on his shoulder, and that will be mistaken for a winnowing fan, does not just hold among a people who do not know the sea; the effect of that misreading will spread everywhere and put everyone in fear and trembling. This new "theology" is encapsulated by a remarkable sentence in Herodotus.[174] Herodotus reports what he learned from the Egyptian priests about the Trojan War. The Egyptians say that Helen never went to Troy but was detained in Egypt by Proteus, who took her away from Paris when he was blown off course on his way back to Troy. When the Greek army showed up at Troy along with Menelaus and demanded the return of Helen, the Trojans denied under oath that they had her; and the Greeks, in the belief they were being mocked when the Trojans asserted that Helen was in Egypt, besieged Troy. On capturing it they discovered that the Trojans were telling the truth and sent Menelaus to Egypt to recover her and his goods. Now Herodotus backs up this Egyptian tale with his own reflections: the Trojans would not have fought for Paris's sake at such great suffering to themselves even if Priam were sleeping with Helen, for the kingdom was not going to devolve on Paris but on Hector, and Hector would not have helped his unjust brother. So, Herodotus concludes, "the Trojans could not give Helen back, and though they were speaking the truth the Greeks could not trust them, since the divine was arranging by the Trojans' total destruction that it become manifest to men that for acts of great injustice the punishment of the gods is equally great." The Trojans are completely innocent and still they are punished. The crime is not theirs, but they must perish in order that the magnitude of Paris's crime be properly appreciated. To kill Paris alone would not do. It would have seemed to be a lucky blow and not significant (cf. III.439–40). A whole people must be wiped out if men are going to be impressed.

On the same principle, it seems, the killing of Antinous, the ringleader of the suitors, does not suffice. Antinous, after all, does not even know why he is killed or who killed him. If anyone had asked him when he got to Hades, he would have said a beggar got drunk and killed him by accident, carried away by his successful stringing of Odysseus's bow and straight shot through the axes.[175] Odysseus's killing of the suitors, then, seems designed to establish the principle, "Fear the gods and the future indignation of men" (22.39–40). Such a principle needs to be illustrated on a grand scale. It needs in particular a poet to make it known every-where and always. If Zeus's initial complaint against the unjust blame of the gods on the part of men really involved, as we surmised, a complaint against the singers, whose way of telling a story induced men to lay the blame for their own wickedness on the gods, then the *Odyssey* seems to be meant to coax Zeus into looking more kindly on them. The *Odyssey* displays Homer's self-censorship.

Homer let Odysseus take over his own story for four books. Odys-seus's story was part of Homer's story. Now that he is home, Homer lets him take up another of his own traits: Odysseus impersonates other men and tells lies like the truth (19.203). This is a privilege Homer accords to no other human being: Menelaus lied in deed and not in speech, and Helen imitated the voices of others but not face to face. The gods, how-ever, often impersonate.[176] The different men, whom Odysseus claims to be, seem to be not so much different men as the same Odysseus we al-ready know in different circumstances. Odysseus presents himself in a series of possible worlds. He is transportable but does not alter. It thus seems possible to detect amidst the lies he tells distinctive characteristics of Odysseus, that, stripped of the circumstances in which Homer placed him, reveal the man himself. His signature is readable away from Homer's plot. Homer thus gives us the opportunity to pull apart what he wove together. Odysseus through his lies emerges as a free man, someone whom we could imagine choosing another life.[177] This possibility shows up most clearly in the complete life he sketches for Eumaeus; but even in the very first of his lies, which he tells to a disguised Athena, one can discern Odysseus's reflection on the life he has led and his rejection of it (13.257–86). The difference between the lie Odysseus tells and the truth about Odysseus finds its counterpart in the difference between the expla-nation Homer himself gives for Odysseus's failure to recognize his own countryside and Athena's transformation of the landscape so that it would appear totally different to its king (13.189–94).[178] Odysseus did not recognize his own country, Homer says, because he had been away from it for so long; and during the time in which Odysseus does not know that Athena is speaking to him, he accepts her assertion that he is in Ithaca. He interprets his failure to know it to the lapse of twenty years since he last saw it. Purely human considerations determine Odysseus's failure of recognition and cautious response to the joyful confirmation of his return home. With the apparent removal of the oppressiveness of both fate and gods, Odysseus can stand back and look at what he might have been. Homer's request to the Muses, to pick up Odysseus's story at some point or other, now takes on a different meaning. Odysseus is not at one with his own life. Odysseus is the sort of man before whom there is at every stage another branch open to him.

In Odysseus's first lie there is no mention of either gods or fate. It is not everyone who in lying would say he was guilty of murder in the first degree. Odysseus seems to be telling the shepherd, to whom Athena has likened herself, that he would kill him without a moment's hesitation were he to make a move against the goods the Phaeacians left on the beach and Odysseus has not had time to conceal.[179] He killed the son of Idomeneus on a dark night with the help of a companion, and though there were no witnesses he obviously did not trust his accomplice but went on board a Phoenician ship that was forced by adverse winds to abandon him here while they went on to Sidonia. The economy of the lie has to impress: Odysseus needed an accomplice because Idomeneus's son was the best runner in Crete. Odysseus, moreover, does not want to appear completely unjust; he left as much property to his children as he took with him. He must have made a deal with the Phoenicians and secretly stored his goods on board their ship before he committed the murder. Idomeneus's son wished to deprive him of the booty for the sake of which he had suffered at Troy. As far as this pseudo-Cretan is concerned, the Trojan War was a drawn-out pirate raid and no sacred principle was at stake. Odysseus's casual demythologization of the Trojan War goes even further. He says that Idomeneus's son, in wishing to make him give up the booty, alleged that he had not served his father but ruled over his own men. Odysseus did not show the proper respect to Idomeneus; he refused to gratify him (χαριζόμενος). Now Thucydides, in trying to cut away the poetry from the history contained in the *Iliad*, argues that it was Agamemnon's overwhelming power that allowed him to gather so large an expedition against Troy, and he did it "not more by favor (χάρις) than by fear."[180] Here Odysseus rebels against the principle of authority that even Achilles acknowledges (I.158–60; cf.14.70). He refuses to be a subordinate to anyone and, unlike in Achilles' case, there is no Athena to pull his hair and check him from murder. Odysseus reimagines the beginning of the *Iliad* and on a smaller scale lets Achilles win. Since Odysseus stresses now merely the suffering he underwent and not his merits as the ground for his deserts, he betrays, voluntarily perhaps, a certain sympathy with his own men, who had remarked that though they had accomplished the same journey as Odysseus they were returning home with empty hands (10.41–42).

Before Athena, Eumaeus, and Telemachus tell him about the circumstances at home, Odysseus declares in his first lie that his dignity and his property are so tied together that any attempt either to disgrace or rob him will involve a fight to the death, and he is prepared to kill and get away with it. It turns out, however, for all the talk about the suitors' consumption of his property, that Odysseus admits, when he is disguised as a beggar, that that is a spurious issue, and the spring of his actions is solely the suitors' failure to see through him and recognize him for what he really is. After Antinous hits him with a stool, Odysseus tells the suitors what his heart bids him: "There are no grounds for grief or any mourning whenever a man, in fighting for his property, whether it be cattle or white sheep, gets hit, but Antinous struck me on account of my wretched belly—an accursed thing!—that gives many evils to men" (17.470–74). This is an extraordinary admission. In one sense, the admission does not go further than the implication in the lie Odysseus told Eumaeus, which he abbreviated just before this in begging for food from Antinous (17.415–45): the suitors are nothing but imprudent and cowardly pirates. They do not set up the proper guards for their theft, and they do not knowingly risk their lives in raiding the property of others (cf. 2.237–38); they feast before they kill. Now, however, Odysseus admits much more. All property is theft, and one cannot complain if another tries to take it away; but Alcinous attacked him because he was hungry and asked for food. Odysseus dismisses the one charge against the suitors that is manifest to all and replaces it with another that in the form in which it is expressed is completely spurious. However little every other suitor gave him, Odysseus would certainly not go hungry. His son is there to supply whatever his appetite demands. Odysseus, rather, uses his belly as a cover for his dignity. He is in the same situation as Plato's Glaucon, who rejects Socrates' "true city," which he calls a city of pigs, because ostensibly there is no meat in it and he is hungry, but really because he cannot imagine himself to be eating off the ground, without tables and couches, and have no opportunity to be something.[181] Odysseus claims to be a nobody and appeals to the gods of beggars, if they exist, to kill Antinous before he marries; but he is not a beggar and hardly speaks like one. The young suitor, who rebukes Antinous, seems to sense what it is that Odysseus is really seeming to be: "He may be a god who dwells in heaven. The gods also resemble strangers from elsewhere, and being of every kind they frequent cities, surveying the hubris and the lawabidingness of human beings" (17.484–87). Odysseus, the suitor seems to be saying, is exactly what one would expect of a god who was on a mission to spy on human beings. Odysseus so impresses him that he uses the word ἄνθρωπος (human being) to characterize man in general. It is the first of only two occasions on which any suitor uses the word (21.364). The highest of the high has taken on the guise of the lowest of the low in order to vindicate human dignity as such.

"It is hard," Odysseus tells Athena, "for a mortal who is even very knowledgeable to recognize you, for you make yourself look like anyone" (13.312–13). Indeed, this encounter on the shore of Ithaca seems to be the only occasion on which Athena deceives Odysseus completely; and once she has changed from a shepherd into a tall and beautiful woman, Odysseus no longer believes he has come home. It is unclear why Athena did alter the landscape; but it seems she wanted to be sure that Odysseus would trust no one, neither herself nor his wife (cf. 13.335–38), and in not taking anything for what it appeared to be, would trust her to have the capacity to make him unrecognizable to everyone else.[182] Odysseus believes he would have met with the evil fate of Agamemnon in his own house had Athena not explained the situation to him (13.383–85). The heightening of his inborn distrust, by making Ithaca appear to be someplace else, increases the difficulty of anyone passing the test of loyalty Odysseus devises. Although Eumaeus tells him that slavery takes away half of a man's virtue (17.322–23), the twelve servant girls who are now sleeping with the suitors are not given any credit for resisting their advances for some three years. If the suitors learned about Penelope's nightly unraveling of Laertes' shroud from one of them (cf. 19.154–55), they could not have given in at first. If one also adds the plausible assumption that the suitors went after the younger servants, none of the twelve who succumbed would have ever known Odysseus, and they would be punished for disloyalty to a master who has always been absent (22.497–501). That Odysseus accuses the suitors of rape can be set aside; he obviously intends to arouse Telemachus's sexual jealousy (16.105–9; 20.315–19; 22.37): he must have known about Laertes' attraction to Eurycleia (1.433). If, moreover, slaves are held to so high a standard of chastity, does not Odysseus necessarily degrade Penelope's (19.45)? Agamemnon of course finds her exceptional; but if slaves are expected to match her (cf. 18.324), it is a good thing if the gods do not take on too often the appearance of strangers. The only time Athena can be strictly said to be a stranger, she sees right through the suitors and against the evidence (1.227–29). Justice, if it is not confined to broad daylight but seeks instead to comprehend the secrets of the dark, is of necessity unforgiving.[183] Penelope knows nothing of the punishment meted out to her servants; she would, it seems, have let off even the worst of them with a stinging rebuke (19.89–95). They were the children, after all, of her slave and not of Odysseus (4.735–37).[184] Her resistance to an immediate acceptance of Odysseus as Odysseus, which her son finds so unfeeling, might be grounded in resentment: she who had wept for her husband for twenty years had still to be tested.

Before Odysseus tells Eumaeus the story of his life, he swears an oath that Odysseus will return within a short time, and after he tells the story he makes a wager and proposes that Eumaeus throw him down a high cliff if Odysseus does not return, "in order that another beggar may avoid deceitful speech" (14.151–64, 393–400). Odysseus tells Eumaeus in effect that he does not have to wait for punishment from Zeus if he lies, but he can carry out the punishment himself and turn Odysseus into a deterrent. Eumaeus declines to take justice into his own hands. He is not yet prepared to be as vicious as his dogs, which like wild beasts he cannot control except by throwing stones at them (14.21, 35–36). He seems not to be a suitable instrument of Odysseus's revenge. One of the reasons for the postponement of the punishment of the suitors is Odysseus's relatively late recruitment of Eumaeus; he does not reveal himself to him until the last moment (21.207), and only after he has learned of the cowherd Philoitius's support as well (20.235–39). Odysseus feels his way very cautiously. He knows what his fate is, but he does not yet know what it means. He is to kill the suitors, extend the worship of Poseidon, and die at home. His second journey seems to be as convenient as his first. It too will be a form of exile and will allow the hatred, which the killing of his fellow citizens will arouse, to die away. Odysseus's first attempt to make sense of himself consisted in the first five episodes of the story he told the Phaeacians; but his destiny, which Teiresias revealed to him, was not obviously connected with his self-understanding. His self-understanding involved a parallel understanding of the elements of political life, but those elements were universal in their scope and could not lead directly into his destiny or its meaning. Odysseus's first attempt to come to terms with his destiny shows up in his invention of another life for himself. In that life he never stays home.

The story Odysseus tells Eumaeus falls into two parts (14.192–359). The first part concerns the life he led before the Trojan War; the second deals with everything that happened to him in the aftermath of that war. The first part explains who he is; the second imposes on his adventures a theodicy. The pattern he presents seems meant to remind us of the difference between "Menelaus" and "Nestor," on the one hand, and the difference, on the other, between the first and second parts of his own story.[185] This Aristotelian differentiation of character and plot shows the difficulty any poet faces in putting them together. Odysseus seems to take the Trojan War as the turning point, which transformed a freebooter's life into an illustration of divine justice. Without giving himself a name, Odysseus tells Eumaeus that he was the bastard son of a wealthy Cretan, but his father honored him no less than his legitimate brothers. (Are we meant to suspect, as Megapenthes, the son of Menelaus and a slave, would already suggest [4.10–12], that a prudent motive lies behind the pitiless slaughter of the slave girls?) Once, however, his father went to Hades, the estate was divided among the legitimate heirs and little was given to him; still, his virtue won him a rich wife. At this point, Odysseus challenges Eumaeus to recognize what he once was in the dry stalk he sees before him. He seems to be testing the effectiveness of Athena's disguise; but Eumaeus is no Helen. One wonders whether any disguise at all was necessary. Would it not have been enough to say he was a beggar? Odysseus, in any case, refuses to cast himself simply as a nobody. He must always be either a prince in disguise, like Eumaeus, or somebody to be reckoned with. He cannot be someone whom anyone can push around, even though he thereby runs the risk of being exposed. His vindication of Everyman is not a role that comes easily to him.

"Odysseus" of the story owed his virtue to Ares and Athena.[186] They gave him confidence and ῥηξηνορίη, the ability to smash through armed ranks of men: ῥηξήνωρ is an epithet Homer assigns exclusively to Achilles (4.5; VII.228; IV.324; VI.146, 575). "Odysseus's" heart never imagined death in front of him, whenever in an ambush he devised evils for enemies. "Enemies" (δυσμενεῖς) is a word that in the *Odyssey* Homer never uses himself but always assigns to the speeches of others (it occurs fifteen times); and in the *Iliad* it is only once in his own mouth: "Zeus handed Hector's corpse over to his enemies to be maltreated in his own country" (XXII. 403). Clearly, Odysseus is sketching a character like Achilles, a man whose birth does not exhaust his superiority. "Odysseus's" claim to have been fearless in ambush recalls Achilles' branding of Agamemnon for cowardice (I.226–28). He was not fond of agricultural work, "Odysseus" goes on to say, nor of anything that increases a household's wealth (he means, of whatever is commonly understood to be a just way of increasing one's wealth); ships, wars, and the instruments of war, things that make other men shudder, were his sole interest; "but what was dear to me was no doubt what a god suggested to me: different men take delight in different deeds." "Odysseus" does not defend his makeup; he was a pirate and good at it. Prior to the Trojan War he mounted nine successful raids against foreign peoples, and as a result was feared and revered among the Cretans. The gods made him what he was; but after that his life was his own. Neither his failure to get a fair share of his father's estate nor his string of successes, from marriage to piracy, is presented as anything but his own or others' doing; but as soon as Zeus devised that wretched expedition to Troy everything changes. At first, Troy seems to put the cap on his career: the Cretans appoint "Odysseus" and Idomeneus the joint leaders of the Cretan contingent. It was impossible to back out: "The hard voice of the people held fast" (14.239). This is the only hint Odysseus ever gives that his going to Troy was not entirely voluntary.[187] It shows besides that the character he has assumed is not modeled entirely on Achilles. Achilles jumped at the chance to distinguish himself in war; "Odysseus" was more interested in gain. It was a trait he could not even hide from Euryalus (8.159–64). "Odysseus," in any case, then found himself to be part of a divine plan. That plan, as we know it, was designed to vindicate right. "Odysseus," however, does not preface the post-Trojan part of his life as if he acknowledged that. When a god scattered the Achaeans, Zeus was devising evils for him. He tried to resume his old life. He stayed home for a month, taking pleasure in his children, his wife, and his possessions. Odysseus, it seems, is looking forward to a short stay in Ithaca before he ventures forth once more; but Athena would not have had to hold back the dawn, after the killing of the suitors, if he really had so much time. Penelope will have him home, we suspect, for one day.

In setting out for Egypt, "Odysseus" entertained for six days the crews of the nine ships he had equipped and offered sacrifices to the gods. Up to a certain point, the account of this Egyptian foray has as its model Odysseus's account of the sack of Ismaros (9.39–61). There is a comparable lack of foresight on the part of his men, and Zeus in both cases is said to cause a defeat that is sufficiently explained without him. "Zeus" seems to be inserted in order to exclude the slim chance of success that could always be the outcome in the face of the greatest certainties. This time, however, "Odysseus" does not get away. Many of his men are killed, and some enslaved; and unlike the first time, when he wished for his death in the past, so that he would not then undergo death at sea (5.299–12), "Odysseus" now says he should have died then in order not to experience his future. There is nothing ignominious about surrender. So far, Odysseus's story has been amoral; but from this point forward two themes emerge: the superior piety of kings to their people and the divine bafflement of the wicked. The king in Egypt pitied Odysseus when he knelt before him—"he was in awe of the wrath of Zeus the god of strangers, who is particularly indignant at wicked deeds" (14.283–84)—and protected him from the people who in their great anger wanted to kill him. Are we to suppose that Odysseus would spare the suitors if they grab his knees? Leodes does and is killed (22.310–11). Odysseus imagines a case in which his men devastate the fields of a country, enslave women and children, and kill the men, and he still charges the people who want to kill him with wickedness. The criminal Odysseus claims the protection of Zeus who watches over strangers. This is perverse. It does not even have the truth to justify it. If, moreover, the injustice of the Egyptians is granted, what can possibly be the justice of Odysseus, who certainly cannot believe that the crimes of the suitors are of the same order as those he imaginatively ascribes to his own men? It seems, strange though it may be, that Odysseus's own criminal negligence in the Laestrygonian disaster is the true counterpart to his men's assault on the Egyptians, and that the suitors are not to be compared with his crew but with the Egyptians who wanted to kill him. Each of them has done something—or better is someone—impossible to understand in terms of any conceivable criminal code. We are dealing with a new kind of delict.

After staying in Egypt as long as Menelaus had, and gathering much wealth, "Odysseus" is lured by a Phoenician into going to Phoenicia. After a year's stay there, he goes on a voyage with the Phoenician, who intended to sell him into slavery for a great profit; but Zeus devised his destruction when he caused a storm off Crete. Zeus sent thunder and lightning, and the ship was struck by the thunderbolt of Zeus, and while the gods took away their return, Zeus himself placed a mast in Odysseus's hands so that he could be saved. For a simple storm at sea the gods are surprisingly active. It would be impossible to find a comparable density of "Zeus" and "gods" anywhere else in the *Odyssey*: "Zeus" and "gods" occur eighteen times each in the course of Odysseus's narration. Odysseus makes himself out to be a favorite of Zeus and assigns the death of everyone else to divine punishment. This would be an extreme case of theodicy of Nestor's type were it not for Odysseus's assumption that he knows the unfulfilled intentions of the Phoenician. The narrative sequence makes Odysseus privy to the Phoenician's plan prior to a retrospective interpretation of it: he does not reason from his death back to the justice of it but uses the death as confirmation of his guesswork. Odysseus's story thus combines "Nestor" with "Helen": his knowledge of the heart and will is as keen as Helen's, but it serves a narrative that discovers in events a moral purpose. Odysseus seems to be rehearsing out of town a version of the story he is to play for real in his own house. Does Homer accept Odysseus's insight into the suitors and the necessity of their execution as following from that insight? Or is it just the kind of story Odysseus needs in order to bring himself to do what necessity requires?

It could be argued that Odysseus's story is just a lie and, far from its being a rehearsal, it contains everything he rejects in truth. If, however, one denies to Odysseus any elements of the fictional Odysseus, the story would be designed solely for Eumaeus's consumption. He takes it straight and obviously approves of its moral. It certainly echoes his own low view of the Phoenicians (15.416); and the satisfaction he expresses when his Phoenician nurse breaks her neck—Artemis caused it—and is cast overboard to be eaten by seals and fish (15.478–81), agrees with the tenor of Odysseus's tale.[188] If, then, Odysseus is just trying to hook Eumaeus and convince him of the divine support he enjoys—the gods themselves allowed him to slip out of his bonds (14.348–49)—the issue would turn on how important Eumaeus is in the future scheme of things. If he is just a tool of the moment, to be discarded after he has done what he must, it would make no difference what line Odysseus feeds him. If, however, this prince in disguise will become Telemachus's brother and live next door to Odysseus with his wife and goods (21.213–16)—if he lives in town he will cease to be a swineherd—then the story he now hears will become an authoritative version of Odysseus's past and as widespread at least as whatever Penelope chooses to disclose. In this version, Odysseus consulted the oracle of Zeus at Dodona to find out whether he was to return openly or in secret (14.327–30).

Odysseus does not convince Eumaeus that he is telling the truth about Odysseus; but the rest of the story moves him, and he later tells Penelope that the stranger is as good at enchantment as any singer (17.513–21). The gist of this enchantment is the moral dimension Odysseus adds to his story once he has passed through the ordeal of the Trojan War. The curious spin the story puts on morality, however, so that, on the one hand, Zeus as the guardian of suppliants takes precedence over any ordinary understanding of justice, and, on the other, the wickedness of the heart is as punishable as any action, forces us to leave in doubt the extent of Odysseus's own investment in his story. This doubt is increased by his next story (14.459–506). It differs from the earlier one insofar as Homer tells us its purpose; it is designed to discover whether Eumaeus would give the shirt off his back to a complete stranger. From this point of view it is not a success, and Eumaeus says there are limits to what he will do for a guest-friend. The answer shows Odysseus that Eumaeus, despite his reverence for sacred obligations, is not simply a pushover for just anyone (cf. 14.379–81), and he can be tough if need be.

The story serves other ends as well. Eumaeus accepts that the stranger was an intimate friend of Odysseus; and the story itself seems to inspire him to sleep among the pigs and protect them from thieves who would take advantage of the winds and rain. Odysseus is delighted by the swineherd's concern for his property even though he is absent (14.526–27). The Cretan "Odysseus" reports how Odysseus arranged for "Odysseus" to get clothed when he had inadvertently left his cloak behind when he went out on ambush on a cold and snowy night. We note once more that the folly of "Odysseus" is translated into a divine deception when he has to explain to Odysseus his fear of freezing to death. "God" is just a way of hiding from others one's own lack of caution: no one had to invoke god to explain their correct forecast. Odysseus saves "Odysseus" by telling the patrol that he had a divine dream; they advanced further into enemy territory than they should have, and someone ought to run back to ask Agamemnon for reinforcements. Odysseus seems to drop his guard and tell Eumaeus that divine causality is always fraudulent, whether it be exculpatory or motivational. He seems to let Eumaeus into his workshop and show him how he constructs an effective story. We wonder, then, whether Homer has given us side by side two different Odysseuses, one of whom seems to be in conformity with the agent of revenge he becomes, while the other seems to stand at a distance from any such role and regard it as nothing more than popular rhetoric. Odysseus presents "Odysseus" in a guise that perfectly fits the Odysseus of the later books, but it is not the Odysseus who finds it so easy to make up stories about gods.

7

Nonfated Things

Theoclymenus and Eumaeus

Aristotle uses the *Odyssey* to illustrate the difference between plot and incident.[189] Its Homeric equivalent is the difference between Odysseus's fate and everything the *Odyssey* contains that his fate does not either include or entail. A further division within the second class ought to be made, but it resists any attempt to make the cut as clean as one can in separating fate from nonfate. This second division should put everything the gods arrange on one side in order that one may look at the rest as the simply human, in which either chance or mind and will exercise their power.[190] The best illustration of the obscurity with which Homer seems deliberately to surround the simply human occurs in the fifteenth book. Telemachus is still at Menelaus's and, while Nestor's son is sleeping next to him, anxious thoughts about his father are keeping him awake; Athena comes and stands near him; her speech, apart from the advice to avoid town and go to Eumaeus's, seems to be nothing but his own thoughts (15.10–42).[191] This is not new; something similar had occurred in his first encounter with Athena; but what is new and unprecedented is that Athena comes without any disguise and in pitch darkness speaks to him without Telemachus either seeing her or reacting to her presence in any way (cf. II. 172 [=15.9]-82). We know that he does not have the gift to detect Athena even when she is carrying a golden lamp (19.33–43), let alone when Odysseus and Eumaeus's dogs see her plainly as a tall and beautiful woman (16.157–64). Telemachus's imperceptible experience of Athena, in which she is nothing but a voice, seems to herald the next stage in the gods' withdrawal.

Athena tells him the suitors are plotting to kill him on his way back, and she advises him to sail at night and steer clear of the islands where the suitors have laid their ambush. The last we know about Telemachus's voyage, Telemachus has aimed for the islands, pondering whether or not he is going to be caught (15.297–300); and the next we hear about him, his crew is anchoring the ship at Ithaca (15.495–98). The interval of the voyage is taken up by Eumaeus's story of his life, in which the providential order of things is at a minimum, and nothing shows the justice of the gods except the death of Eumaeus's nurse (15.403–84). It does not occur to Eumaeus, who prefers to wait for Odysseus than return home a free man to a land where no one dies in sickness, that the Phoenician nurse might not consider it unjust to use him as a means to regain her own freedom. However that might be, the only other report we get of Telemachus's voyage is from Antinous. He explains that despite his crew's constant watchfulness, a god brought Telemachus home (16.364–70). We do not usually have to rely on hostile witnesses to fill in a narrative gap. Homer, it seems, leaves it up to us to round out his story in whatever way we want (cf. 16.355–57). We can take Athena's assurance that a god protects Telemachus, and Antinous's surmise that Telemachus could not have otherwise evaded him, as evidence that the gods do not leave any chink in their plans; or else we can chalk it up to chance and as one of those details, which, like Athena's failure to conceal Odysseus's scar, or Telemachus's failure to lock the door of the room where the arms are stored, does not affect the outcome but adds suspense to a foregone conclusion.[192]

Telemachus belongs more to the divine scheme of things than to Odysseus's fate, in the various reports of which he has no part. Two favorable omens, one at Sparta and one at Pylos, show the difference between them. While Telemachus is preparing to leave Sparta, an eagle swoops down and carries off a tame goose from the courtyard (15.160–62). Helen interprets it by way of a proportion: "Just as the eagle, raised in the mountains, seized a goose, grown plump at home, so Odysseus, after much suffering, will return home and take revenge, or maybe he is home already and devises evil for all the suitors" (15.174–78). This is a straightforward interpretation of Odysseus's fated return, though slightly sinister: Odysseus does not belong to Ithaca and is as different from the suitors as savage is from tame. The second omen occurs when Telemachus is about to cast off; a hawk sweeps by with a pigeon in its claws; it is plucking at the feathers, which are falling to the ground between Telemachus and the ship (15.525–28). Theoclymenus calls Telemachus aside, grasps his hand, and says he realized by looking straight at the sight that it was an omen: "No other race is more royal than yours in Ithaca, but you [plural] are always mighty" (15.533–34). Theoclymenus does not explain how he figured this out—he later gives another interpretation of apparently the same

omen[193]—but it convinces Telemachus to alter his plans and have Theoclymenus lodge with one of his companions rather than with one of the
suitors.

Theoclymenus is the most mysterious character in the entire *Odyssey*.
His name recalls by way of contrast Proteus's daughter Eidothea, who
helped out Menelaus. Her name is readily decompounded into "looks"
(*eidos*) and "goddess" (*thea*); Theoclymenus's name means "He who
hears or hearkens to gods" (cf. 15.271).[194] He seems to symbolize the shift
from visible gods to gods of hearsay. He is the only character who remains a complete stranger to everyone: Homer himself refers to Theoclymenus as the "stranger" even after we know his name (17.72, 73, 84); he
never so refers to Odysseus (cf. 13.47–48). Only we know Theoclymenus's name and genealogy (15.223–56), and not even we know whether
Apollo made him, as he did his father, the best of diviners (15.252–53):
Theoclymenus suspects but does not know that the kinsmen of the men
he killed are in pursuit. Not even when Theoclymenus prophesies later to
Penelope and the suitors does he ground his prophetic authority (cf.
17.154 with 1.200–2). All that Telemachus knows is that he killed a man;
neither Homer nor Theoclymenus says whether he acted justly or not. If
we cut him out of the narrative, nothing alters. He stands outside the
action of the *Odyssey* and still belongs to its theme. He represents another
kind of anonymity than the anonymity of mind. It is mind so possessed
by the gods that it can "see" what no one else can. In his one prophecy
to the suitors, he uses the verbal cognate of mind (*noeō*) in a unique way.
The prophecy itself is unique. Athena has just caused the suitors to laugh
and distracted their minds. They were eating meat contaminated with
blood; their eyes were filled with tears, and their hearts forebode lamentation. "Oh miserable ones!" Theoclymenus says, "What is this evil you
are experiencing? Your heads, faces, and knees below have been wrapped
in night. Lamentation has flared forth. Your cheeks are drenched with
tears. The walls and beams are sprinkled with blood. The porch is full,
the courtyard is full of phantoms rushing to darkness; the sun has been
lost from the sky, and evil mist has spread" (20.351–57). This quasi-Bibli-
cal prophecy pulls the future into the present: the descent of the suitors
into Hades is being prepared.[195] It is a vision without the visible. It turns
hearing into sight—"lamentation has flared forth"—and sun and night
into metaphors. When the suitors laugh good-humoredly at Theoclymenus, and Eurymachus suggests he needs an escort, "since he likens
everything here to night," Theoclymenus says he has his eyes and wits
about him. His mind (*noos*) is sound: "I sense (*noeō*) an evil is approach-
ing you, which no one of the suitors would escape or avoid" (20.367–68).

This is the only occasion where *noeō* is ever used in either the *Iliad* or the *Odyssey* about the future; it is most commonly used for discernment through the eyes.[196]

In the larger scheme of things, one might say that Theoclymenus is the *Odyssey*'s equivalent to the Hermes whom Zeus sent to warn Aegisthus; but no one sends Theoclymenus, and his warning to the suitors is timed to come too late. Theoclymenus, in being outside of plot or fate, divine or human action, seems to be nothing but his meaning: he embodies the future rule of the prophet, who will be the sole intermediary between gods and men once the gods have completed their withdrawal. Indeed, Theoclymenus is so much of the future that though Odysseus is present throughout the scene in which Theoclymenus proclaims his vision, he does not say a word. He prepares the way for Theoclymenus, but Theoclymenus belongs to another story. Theoclymenus's arrival on the shore of Pylos coincides with Telemachus's prayer and sacrifice to Athena. The coincidence suggests that he is the answer to the prayer, though we do not know whether Telemachus prayed for such a sign. Theoclymenus seems to be the replacement on the voyage home for Athena's presence in the guise of Mentor on the voyage out. Theoclymenus would make up for the divine providence one has to infer in the face of the puzzling failure of Homer to fill in Telemachus's miraculous escape from the ambush of the suitors. His presence on board would be the meaning of Athena's assurance to Telemachus that some god protects him. Theoclymenus would be the "idea" rather than an agent of divine causality. He is a trace of providence. Insofar as Athena and Zeus are able to infuse Odysseus's fate with a purpose that serves them, Theoclymenus is a necessary consequence of that purpose. He is a deduction of an argument.

For all his significance, Theoclymenus is situated on the margin of the *Odyssey*; Eumaeus is central to the *Odyssey*, but his significance is obscure. That there is something special about him Homer indicates by addressing him directly some fifteen times, as if he were still alive and as much his favorite as Patroclus is in the *Iliad*. In being Homer's sole addressee within the poem, he is comparable to Theoclymenus, whose name only we know. The role Athena assigns Eumaeus is modest. His place is convenient for the secret meeting of Odysseus and Telemachus; but the further purpose Athena designs for him, to report to Penelope the safe return of her son, simply duplicates the arrangement Telemachus's companions make on their own to inform his mother (16.328–41): it did not occur to either Telemachus or Athena to plug this leak (16.130–34). Plato hints at Eumaeus's importance when in the *Statesman* he has the Eleatic

Stranger exercise the method of division, which is designed to isolate the statesman, in such a way that up to the final cut the swineherd proves to have been a concurrent of the king.[197] The Stranger seems to be alluding to Eumaeus's regular epithet, "leader of men," which his rule over four subordinates barely justifies (14.24–28).

Without Eumaeus's participation in the killing of the suitors, it is hard to imagine that the goatherd Melanthius would have played any role in the story. Melanthius is as much outside the apparent fatefulness of things as Theoclymenus. Odysseus and Eumaeus meet up with him on their way to town, and it is clear that the enmity between swineherd and goatherd has been longstanding (17.204–22; 22.195–99). Melanthius insults Eumaeus and Odysseus, kicks Odysseus, and wishes for the death of Telemachus; but though he is a thoroughly bad sort, he proves to be quite intelligent (22.135–41) and not one to mix up the rhetoric of insult with knowledge: his report to the suitors about the beggar Odysseus is a model of conciseness (17.369–73). His sister has been sleeping with Eurymachus and has an equally nasty tongue (18.325–36; 19.65–69). Why should Odysseus suggest the torture of Melanthius to Eumaeus (22.172–77)? It is of a piece with that suggestion that the dogs of the household devour him (22.474–77). Odysseus makes a concession to Eumaeus that violates the principle behind the divine law of burial: hatred is to stop with death.[198] What Achilles had to learn so painfully is wiped out in an instant (cf. XXIV. 406–9).[199] The threat Antinous utters—he will ship Irus to the bogeyman King Echetus, in order that he may cut off his nose and ears and feed his genitals raw to the dogs (18.84–87; cf. 21.363–65)—is executed against Melanthius. It would seem that Homer's own presentation of Hades in the last book is meant primarily to revindicate that for which it stands over against Eumaeus's assault on it: Eumaeus, unlike Philoitius, never speaks of Hades (20.208).[200] None of this is easy to understand. It seems to violate Odysseus's prohibition to Eurycleia, that she must not express her joy at the death of the suitors openly (22.411–12), unless one should suppose that silent gloating has worse consequences (cf. 23.45–47), or that Odysseus, practical as ever, does not want any sound to alert the people or wake up Penelope.[201] These considerations make one curious about Eumaeus. Since Eumaeus falls below the horizon of the gods' concern, he is entirely in Odysseus's power to use or discard. Odysseus does not disapprove of Telemachus's decision to arm him (22.103–4; cf. 23.368–69): Eumaeus takes part in the final battle against the Ithacans (24.497).

The narrowly political problem Odysseus faces is how to secure the throne for Telemachus. If all the traits in which Telemachus resembles his father were substantially of the same order, there would have been no need for Odysseus to return, and Telemachus could have disposed of the suitors years before. Telemachus admits as much (2.58–62; cf. 4.818). Odysseus, when he was no more than a boy, had been sent by his father and the elders to recover three hundred sheep and their shepherds from the Messenians (21.16–21). Odysseus has the further problem of killing the suitors without having to go himself into exile. He admits to Athena that this is of greater concern to him than the apparent impossibility of killing the suitors all by himself (20.41–43). Telemachus had already agreed with Odysseus that if Athena and Zeus were on their side they could not fail, and Odysseus had asserted they would be present whenever the need arose (16.259–69; cf. 13.389–94); even now he confirms that his success in killing the suitors depends on the will of Zeus and Athena (20.42). Athena gives him an oblique answer: "Scoundrel! One is wont to trust an inferior companion, who is merely a mortal and does not know as many wise counsels [as I do], but I am a goddess and in all toils I guard you continuously. Now I shall tell you straight out. If fifty companies of men should surround the two of us and be eager to kill us in war, then even so you would drive off their cows and fat sheep" (20.45–51). Athena seems to be talking about the actual killing of the suitors, which she casually assimilates to a cattle raid, in which by implication the suitors are not at least in the wrong. Her guarantee seems to have nothing to do with Odysseus's anxiety. Even if Athena is alluding to the armed struggle against his fellow citizens, which Odysseus might have to wage after the killing, the extinction of his own people seems to be a rather drastic way of avoiding exile.

The key words of Athena are not, I think, her offer of help but the apparently pointless preface to them: "One is wont to trust an inferior companion, who is merely a mortal and does not know as many wise counsels." On the surface, they are irrelevant. No trust in a mere mortal is going to make up for Odysseus being outnumbered. Shortly afterward, the cowherd Philoitius comes. His friendly address to Odysseus seems to convince Odysseus to bring him and Eumaeus into the conspiracy. They are the inferior to whom Odysseus believes Athena was alluding. He offers them the equivalent of their freedom—marriage, wealth, and a house next to his. They are to be the brothers and companions of Telemachus (21.213–16; cf. 16.115–21). Odysseus democratizes the regime. They, and perhaps whoever else in the country prove loyal, are going to be rewarded by having a share in the power. Even if he wanted to disarm them after their usefulness was over, Odysseus is outnumbered, and someone has to replace the princes he killed.

When Odysseus landed on Circe's island, he was also forced to relax his rule. The consequences, though they were as fated as they were convenient, were disastrous. His men, however, had been free. Eumaeus's fear at an empty threat of the suitors, shortly after Odysseus reveals himself to him, seems to confirm his own view that slaves lose half of their virtue (21.359–67). We know from the second book of the *Iliad* that Agamemnon did not know how to speak to the assembled army at Troy after Achilles had shattered confidence in his leadership; and we know that on the same occasion Odysseus spoke in one way to men of the people and in another way to the kings; and he proved to have the requisite address to put Thersites in his place when he voiced the secret sentiments of the army; and we also know that neither Hera nor Athena had this knowledge (II. 110–78).[202] Odysseus's political skill, however, which he displayed on that occasion, did not involve any real compromise with the commoners. Now the situation is quite different. He is not dealing with a temporary disaffection but a festering resentment that has taken a particularly difficult form. At its head are all the princes of his empire, but behind them, waiting cautiously for the outcome, are all those who do not remember the goodness of his rule and have the loss of their relatives and of the booty they would have brought back with them to feed their anger. That Odysseus waits until the last minute to recruit Eumaeus and Philoitius shows how reluctant he is to establish Telemachus's rule with such allies. They have to be paid for their loyalty, and Melanthius is the price.[203]

The new order Odysseus allows to form behind his back, as if it were not of his own doing, does not just involve a raising up of Eumaeus and Philoitius but also a lowering of Telemachus.[204] Odysseus realizes that the loyal female slaves are also due something. This means in particular Eurycleia. When she recognizes Odysseus and offers to distinguish between those who dishonor him and those who are sinless, Odysseus refuses her help and says he will make the judgment on his own (19.496–501); but when the suitors have been killed, Odysseus allows Eurycleia to make the selection, and the twelve she chooses refused to honor either her or Penelope (22.417–25). Eurycleia has her own score to settle, just as Telemachus has (22.462–64). He claims that the slaves had insulted him as well, though we have not heard anything about it (cf. 22.426–27), and decides to disobey his father and give them an unclean death, not by sword, as Odysseus had ordered, but by hanging. Odysseus's contemptuous reference to Aphrodite makes Telemachus's disobedience all but inevitable (22.444–45). That Odysseus anticipated his disobedience would not surprise anyone. Telemachus gets his hands dirty and joins in the punishment of Melanthius. The triumph of the swineherd is now complete. His title, "leader of men," is not so much an allusion to what he would have been, had he inherited his father's kingdom (15.412–14), as it is to the future. Homer's address to him indicates that the *Odyssey* is primarily for him.

Two different kinds of killing are involved in the reordering of Odysseus's house. The suitors are killed, and the slaves are punished. Only in Homer's simile, in which Odysseus looks at all the suitors fallen in blood and dust as if they were fish caught in a net and gasping for breath on the sand as the burning sun takes away their lives (22.383–89; cf. 12.251–59), is any indignity visited on them. Only the slaves are paid back in accordance with the insults in which they imitated their betters. Their suffering matches in some sense the hubris of the suitors, but the suitors themselves are not meant to experience a literal equivalent of their outrageous behavior. It is reserved for Philoitius to declare to the already dead Ctesippus that his present of a cow's hoof, with which he tried to hit Odysseus, is now balanced by the gift of a spearcast in the chest (22.285–91); and Ctesippus was not noble but trusted to his great wealth in wooing Penelope (20.287–90). That the herder of cows is allowed to pay back the insult of a cow's hoof is not only a piece of grim humor, but a symbol as well of the rearrangements of power that are to come. It is only on the level of a story that the suitors are punished.[205] Their deaths belong to the pattern, at which one can look and invest with one's own indignation; but insofar as punishment is a matter of deed and the victim can believe that the justly condemned experiences in kind what he himself had inflicted, then the slaves alone are punished. They bear the brunt of the story.[206]

The Slave Girls

When Eurycleia proposes to wake up Penelope, presumably so that she too may choose the sinners among the slave girls, Odysseus forbids it (22.428–32). Penelope is not going to be a member of the new regime. Athena and Odysseus between them make sure that she never sees the ugliness of the event she believes is ordained (17.537–47). As far as we know, she never gets to see the corpses of the suitors, though she comes down to do so (23.83–85). By the time she comes down, the corpses have been piled up in the courtyard, and the slave girls, shortly before Telemachus hangs them, have washed away any trace of blood (22.448–53). In shielding Penelope from any unpleasantness, Odysseus also excludes her from any say in his plans. Penelope's fate is also not a part of his fate. When Teiresias speaks of the time when Odysseus finally comes home, and the people are happy around him, he does not say a word about her

(11.136–37). If Penelope can be said to have a fate of her own, it is to be unhappy. Odysseus's decency in keeping her in the dark goes along with the indecency of the treatment of the slave girls. Their execution is settled long before Odysseus orders it. What seems to be decisive in sealing their fate is Odysseus's accidental encounter with them in the dark, when he is lying awake thinking evil thoughts against the suitors, and the girls slip out to go to their lovers, laughing and cheering one another (20.1–8). Odysseus is torn between killing each one of them or letting them sleep with the suitors one last time: "His heart was howling within; and just as a bitch stands guard over her tender puppies when she fails to recognize a man, howls, and is eager for a fight, so his heart was howling within in his indignation at evil deeds" (20.13–16). While the dog may or may not be right about the evil intentions of the intruder, Odysseus seems to have no doubt; but what exactly is he defending? If it is the integrity of the house, where does the failure of recognition enter? What could it be that he, like the dog, does not know? Odysseus himself also understands his experience by way of a comparison: "He struck his chest and rebuked his heart. 'Endure, heart! You once put up with something else more disgraceful, on that day when the Cyclops ate my mighty comrades. You endured, until mind (*mētis*) brought you out of the cave though you thought you were going to die' " (20.17–21).[207] Odysseus admits that his heart is exaggerating. The crime of the slave girls falls short of Polyphemus's. Odysseus alludes to his immediate impulse to kill the Cyclops when he saw him eat the first two of his men; but he checked himself with the thought that even if he were successful he would remain trapped in the cave (9.299–305). Odysseus calms himself now when he realizes that if he kills the slave girls he cannot kill the suitors. His restraint in the cave redirected his goal from vengeance to survival; and the setting aside of his impulse to kill the slaves would likewise serve the necessity to rid his house of the suitors without any thought on his part that he was punishing them. The execution of the slaves also belongs to necessity; that Odysseus hands it over to Telemachus and his slaves shows that he is well aware of this. It satisfies their sense of justice.

The issue thus becomes once more how Odysseus understands his escape from the Cyclops's cave. If he now thinks of the blinding of Polyphemus as merely the indispensable means of escape, then his self-address on this occasion would involve the admission that whatever insults he received from the suitors are strictly irrelevant. Their deaths are not designed to pay him back. Homer seems to favor this more rational interpretation of Odysseus. He follows up Odysseus's address to his heart with an identification of Odysseus himself (αὐτός) with the Odysseus who meditates on how he might kill the suitors, outnumbered though he is; and he couples this pure calculation with the problem of how Odysseus can avoid going into exile (20.22–43). Athena comes to Odysseus when he is rational and not when he is angry. It would thus be settled that Odysseus kills in cold blood. He comes back, does what he has to do, and moves on. Indeed, if the killing of the girls corresponds to his initial desire to kill Polyphemus, then Odysseus accepts exile as the equivalent of his escape from the cave. Whether he can avoid exile is not up to him. Athena is needed for this last miracle. The *Odyssey*, however, ends before we find out whether Odysseus's fate to go on another journey is not just a pretext for exile.[208]

If Odysseus's citation of Polyphemus bears this way of reading his relation to his fate, then all the indignation Homer had ascribed to him, and that Athena still aims to provoke (20.284–86), would now fall away. He would now acknowledge that it was spurious. Apart from an ambiguous answer to Eumaeus, when he questions him whether the suitors continue to dishonor him as they did before (20.166–71), Odysseus does nothing but glower and smile once sardonically throughout the day of the killing (20.183–84, 301–2; 22.34, 60, 320). The more Odysseus seems calculating, however, the more terrible he becomes. It is one thing for us to accept the political necessity that dictates all that Odysseus does; but we are not being overly squeamish if we find Odysseus repulsive because he can bring himself to realize an argument. So much evidence, however, has mounted up against a cold-blooded Odysseus that perhaps one should not put together the Odysseus who speaks to his heart and the Odysseus whose main concern is whether he can avoid exile. It is at least possible that Homer's juxtaposition of Odysseus's heart with Odysseus's mind is meant to point to the conclusion we rashly assigned to Odysseus himself; but the significance of Homer's splitting Odysseus in two is to deny that Odysseus sees that the solution to his present quandary must be strictly in conformity with the way he devised out of Polyphemus's cave. Odysseus would then be postponing the slave girls' punishment in order to punish the suitors first, and he would be acting in this case under the same delusion he experienced when he eluded Polyphemus. Such a reinterpretation would underline how closely anger can pose as reason, and at the same time restore to Odysseus the righteousness that then animates his execution of right. This reinterpretation is not meant to make us feel any better about Odysseus, but rather to bring into relief the unblinking gaze of Homer, who would in this way be distinguishing the bow from the lyre.[209]

There are two episodes after Odysseus's return to Ithaca that seem to be essential for understanding Odysseus. They are both outside his fate, and one does not involve any divine intervention. The first concerns Melanthius. Odysseus and Eumaeus meet him on the way to town at the common spring. Melanthius kicks Odysseus on the hip as he passes by him. Odysseus stays his ground and ponders whether he should kill him in one of two ways; but he checks himself, and Eumaeus prays to the Nymphs of the spring that they allow Odysseus to return and punish Melanthius (17.233–46). One is not puzzled by the restraint Odysseus exercises, but why it ever occurred to him to consider killing him at all, and not simply as an alternative to keeping his cool. Although Melanthius's intention was to injure him, the result is no more than a slap in the face, and it is hard to see why Odysseus should react to someone like Melanthius. As a king he ought to have brushed it off, as a beggar he ought to have cowered in fear, or at the least taken a fall. Homer does not say that Odysseus got angry; he presents the twofold possibility of killing Melanthius as if it were solely a matter of reflection. Odysseus's plans would be rendered null and void before he started. Odysseus seems to forget himself, or rather he fuses the man he is with the man he is pretending to be, whether that is the beggar Athena made him into or the once-successful pirate he told Eumaeus he was. Whoever he is, Odysseus's reaction to Melanthius's kick seems to anticipate the killing of the suitors.[210] They too get one hit against him. It is as if he saw through Melanthius to the suitors he has not yet seen, and he checks himself from killing him in just the way he puts off the killing of the slave girls, so that he can dispose of the suitors first. Melanthius would thus sink in importance and be no more than a preliminary irritant of Odysseus's appetite for revenge.

Irus seems to be another story. He is a real beggar and, as his nickname indicates, a figure of fun (18.1–7). He is big but weak, and Odysseus knows he is a coward for all his bluster. He should be under the protection of the gods of beggars, about whom there is so much talk and whose existence Odysseus seems called upon to prove. It is against Irus that the suitors first show their deep impiety when Antinous threatens him with King Echetus (18.83–87, 115–16). Odysseus must knock Irus out and get rid of him before the killing begins. Odysseus saves his life. Odysseus, however, thinks about killing him, but he treats him gently, "lest the Achaeans take note of him" (18.90–94). Odysseus's prudence is no surprise, but his murderous thought is. He is not angry, though he warns Irus against getting him angry (18.20). It is not as if even on this trivial occasion his strength was his own (18.69–70). After he beats Irus up and drops him outside, he tells him in effect that he was punished for affecting to be the prince of beggars and strangers (18.106–7). Odysseus boasts to

Eumaeus that no one is a better servant than he (15.318–24; but cf. 17.20–21); he challenges Eurymachus to compete with him in successive contests of mowing, plowing, and war (18.366–80); and he offers to take over the duty of the slave women in keeping the torches alight no matter how long the suitors stay up (18.317–19). "I am the best inferior there ever was," Odysseus seems to assert. "No one, high or low, can beat me."[211] The dignity of the human, to which everyone seems entitled, shows up to-gether with the pride of Odysseus, to which no one else can lay claim; and everyone is punished who does not acknowledge the coincidence of the class-characteristic of man with the highest representative of man. No body (οὐτιδανός) is No one (οὔ τις).

The Name and the Scar

Eustathius raises the question of how Odysseus managed to conceal his scar when he exposed his legs and thighs prior to his match with Irus (18.3755–56). The answer, no doubt, is that he did expose it, but no one was present who knew anything about it. A more pertinent question is how Odysseus himself failed to notice it and so prevent Eurycleia from washing his feet. Odysseus's and Athena's joint oversight of this sign, without which, it seems, Odysseus could not have convinced Eumaeus and Philoitius that he was Odysseus (21.221–22), is as puzzling as the context in which Homer tells the story. Eurycleia assumes that Odys-seus's refusal to allow any of the younger women to bathe him has to do with their insolence (19.370–74); but it is more plausible to suppose that Odysseus would find it difficult to order the killing of anyone who had performed one of the customary offices due a stranger. Whichever is the case, Homer interrupts the story of the bath to go back to Odysseus's birth, so that he can explain the meaning of his name, before he goes on to account for his scar (19.392–466).

The story seems designed to connect the Odysseus we know with the true Odysseus, who really was born in Ithaca, received his name from his grandfather, and was once wounded by a wild boar. It is as if with the death of Argus, there would otherwise have been no way for Odysseus to cast off his disguise and prove he really is not either a clever adventurer or a god. It seems that we too need some assurance of his identity. Lies like the truth have become so widespread that there has to be an anchor-ing in something that remains the same in spite of any disguise. In the case of Odysseus, such a mark seems to be known only to Helen and Argus. Argus's knowledge in particular seems to be the standard against which the failure of the suitors to acknowledge their master is to be judged. Nothing less than a doglike loyalty seems to be the demand behind the testing of the suitors; but it seems to follow from the convenient death of Argus that loyalty based on knowledge is incompatible with secrecy, and Odysseus seems to want the unrecognizability that goes with complete concealment along with the recognition that would unintentionally betray him. He threatens to kill Eurycleia after he succeeds in killing the suitors if anyone overhears her (19.487–90). Odysseus does not admit that he simply made a mistake and had forgotten about the scar; he tells Eurycleia that a god arranged for her discovery of it (19.485). Odysseus, then, does not remember the one piece of evidence he needs to convince the skeptical. He is so sure of himself that he finds it irritating that Telemachus cannot believe he is who says he is, even though Athena has just transformed him into a beautiful youth (16.172–89). What seems to convince Telemachus is that he is looking at himself, for he had been told several times that he looks exactly like Odysseus (1.208–9; 3.120–25; 4.141–50). In any case, regardless of what prompts Telemachus to take Odysseus's word for it, the dismissal or the discounting of appearances, which emerged with Athena's presence at a sacrifice to her, only goes to emphasize the importance of the scar, which keeps Odysseus attached irrevocably to his past, before his own experiences away from Ithaca and Athena's interference have combined to wipe out that past almost completely.

If, then, Odysseus's scar is indispensable if enchantment is to leave some loophole for truth, Homer's intention in linking it with how Odysseus got his name becomes all the more difficult to make out. The nominal and the real belong apparently together. Odysseus obviously does not resemble his father at all; he takes after Autolycus—"A wolf in itself"— who excelled in theft and swearing. Hermes, who showed Odysseus the nature of the *moly*, bestowed this twofold ability on Autolycus. Autolycus was able to steal with impunity, it seems, because he formulated his oaths in such a way that their literal interpretation, contrary to the unexpressed intention of the witnesses to them, granted him the right to take what was not his.[212] Accordingly, Autolycus had incurred the enmity of many men and women; and when Eurycleia asked him to name his grandson in light of the fact that he was much prayed for (*poluarētos*), he took her at her word, interpreted it as "much accursed," and named him "Odysseus." "Odysseus" seems ominous. The name predicts not the away-from-home Odysseus, though on his homeward voyage there are already enough signs of its suitability, but the Odysseus Odysseus is once he has returned home and carries out his fate, as if that meant that he must be the embodiment of anger in itself—"Autothumos," as it were—whose sole purpose is to punish. What to the understanding appears as the twin forms of shame and pride—and it was as well the Phaeacians' introduction to the human by itself through Odysseus—has its genealogical equivalent in the descent of the pseudobeggar (Odysseus) from the lying thief (Autolycus). Homer tells a story in which what Odysseus made of himself falls away and what he was from the start reemerges and confirms his name as his fate. It is perhaps this more than anything else that makes Eumaeus, who knew Odysseus from the time he was a boy, the most appropriate audience of the *Odyssey*.

8

The Suitors and the City

The Suitors

The sole justification Homer gives for the killing of the suitors seems not to amount to much. It occurs in one of several passages in which killing is assimilated to eating, as if Homer, in constantly reminding us of the acts of cannibalism to which Odysseus was a pitying witness, wanted to suggest how the unlawful gets absorbed into and lodges in right.[213] The ideality of right is experientially the bestial.[214] As Odysseus's failure to tell Polyphemus the truth brings on a silent requital, so the suitors' failure to see the truth of the hidden sets them up as a feast for Odysseus's singing bow (21.406–11). Such a proportion, however, between the appropriate punishment for falsehood and insult respectively lies below the surface argument. "There would not be another dinner less without grace [more disagreeable] than the one the goddess and the mighty man were about to prepare, for they [i.e., the suitors] were the first to contrive unseemly deeds" (20.390–94; cf. 21.428–30; 22.400–6).[215] The unseemliness cannot consist in their wooing of a presumed widow, for even Odysseus thinks it possible that Penelope married again soon after the Trojan War (11.177–79; cf. 13.42–43; but 22.35–38). It would seem, then, that what Homer refers to must be the suitors' plan to kill Telemachus; but the suitors formulate that plan only after they realize Telemachus intends to kill them (2.325–30; cf. 17.79–83),[216] and we know that Athena planted that idea in Telemachus and drove out his own wish that Odysseus return and merely disperse the suitors (1.116, 295–96). The drastic measures taken are in retaliation for a series of apparently petty offenses that do not add up to anything criminal enough to make the justice of their punishment self-evident.[217] The disproportion between the base fate of the suitors, which Teiresias predicted years before they began to woo Penelope, and its coloring by justice seems to be almost as great as that between the fate of Odysseus's companions, which Odysseus knew of before the start of the Trojan War, and the death of most of them at the hands of the Laestrygonians, which Odysseus does nothing to prevent and in some sense must regard as a fitting punishment for their wickedness. If, however, the suitors are not comparable to the majority of Odysseus's companions, but to the survivors, who violate their oath and eat the cattle of the Sun, they, unlike the suitors, will their own fate. It is, however, not obvious whether the necessity Odysseus's men feel does not absolve them, to say nothing of Odysseus's failure to impress upon them strongly enough the certainty of their doom (12.273–76). Their destruction, in any case, became Zeus's punishment and not just either an accident at sea (12.288–90) or Poseidon's fulfillment of Polyphemus's curse because Odysseus learned years later from Calypso what had determined the outcome. The suitors are marked for death regardless, and it seems not to make much difference what charges are discovered or invented to cover over this necessity.

The suitors are aware in some sense that they are in an absurd position (cf. 2.205–7; 16.387–93; 21.249–55). If Penelope does decide finally to marry one of them, she would leave Odysseus's house (18.269–70), and the truly important issue, who gets to rule Ithaca, would be once more up for grabs. If the future husband plans to stay (15.522), he must kill Telemachus and Laertes and usurp power in just the way Aegisthus had; but why anyone should help him in this enterprise is not at all obvious (cf. 2.335–36).[218] The division of the estate would not be in the interest of Penelope's husband. If the suitors had a ringleader who was evidently as superior as Odysseus was to Laertes, he would have taken over the kingdom long ago, and Odysseus's family could have been allowed to sink away into insignificance (cf. 21.91–95, 323–29). Perhaps one should set aside the absurdity that whoever finally gained the kingdom would have looked on with equanimity as his own future property was being consumed over a period of three years. The wooing of Penelope is a Sisyphean labor (cf. 16.111, 373). Nothing can be permanently achieved if anyone either succeeds with her or continues to try to wear her down. The suitors are suspended in a vain action. If they saw their own interests clearly, they would have formed an oligarchy and ignored Penelope entirely. Indeed, the fact that Leocritus, a minor member of the gang, can dismiss the assembly Telemachus summoned shows that they already are a successful oligarchy, and nothing more can be or needs to be done (2.257–58). They can only lose their authority if they persist in harassing Penelope and Telemachus (16.375). Penelope's distraction of the suitors, so that they do not know what they are about, is the highest achievement of enchantment that can possibly be imagined. Without the assumption of such a power on Penelope's part, the premise of the *Odyssey* would be fundamentally ridiculous because it would be impossible. The continuous weaving and unraveling of Laertes' shroud should have told the suitors they were in the grip of a delusion.

If, then, we should look in vain were we to peer inside the suitors in the hope of finding there a coherent motive or plan of action, we have to look at their constant feasting at Odysseus's expense as containing in itself a significance that is independent of intention. They would be in that case the unwitting protesters against the loss of every able-bodied man in Ithaca, which can be laid at Odysseus's door, especially since everyone now knows that Odysseus knew he was going to return alone (2.171–76). This political background turns the suitors—everyone in town, with few exceptions—into the spiteful embodiment of the resentment Odysseus's own men experience; but it must be hidden and replaced by an account that will restore to the punishment of the suitors a justice that, it seems, it cannot possibly have. The task Homer has set for himself can be formulated more precisely as follows. He must convince us or at least Odysseus that the perspective of Eumaeus obtains in truth for the suitors. Odysseus's acceptance of that perspective becomes clear when he asks Zeus for a twofold sign, one a human speech and another from Zeus himself, and after Zeus has thundered in response, a slavewoman, who was the weakest of twelve millers and alone had not yet ceased grinding her portion of grain, asked that the coming day bring the last dinner for the suitors (20.98–21). Odysseus hears the prayer but does not know the reasons for it: he responds to a general right stripped of its particular grounds. The prayer expresses essentially the point of view of Eumaeus, who is at least as angry about the extra labor the suitors have imposed on him as he is about the losses Odysseus's estate has incurred (14.415–17). The extraordinary wealth in flocks that Eumaeus attributes to Odysseus does not help his case against the suitors (14.91–106; cf. 20.211–16). That case becomes spiritualized as soon as Odysseus enters his home in disguise; but at least on one occasion Odysseus fails to detect the criminality of the suitors, even though Athena was urging him to discern the difference between the just and the lawless (17.360–64).

Homer seems to offer two solutions to the problem the suitors pose. One is to subordinate Odysseus to the divine plan—the withdrawal of the gods and the consequent demand for a new kind of piety; the other is to make Odysseus central, and thus have him discover a new kind of justice, which is no longer dependent on or essentially connected with piety. The feeding of Melanthius to the dogs points to this second way; but insofar as Odysseus does not participate directly, one cannot take the Melanthius episode as more than a sign of the radical disjunction between justice and piety to which Odysseus himself might subscribe. He kills a priest.[219] He does it on the basis of a moral certainty (22.321–25), but possibly against Athena's intention that the priest alone survive, for it is only to his justice that Homer bears witness (17.363–64; 21.146–47). Odysseus himself has not forgotten the gods' own disregard of the sacredness of guest-friendship in the case of Heracles, and if he vindicates some version of it, he must be trying to establish it on a new basis. The most obvious difference is that the suitors are not strangers. The internationality of the principle in the case of the Trojan War, which involved a common effort on behalf of a common cause, is not at stake in Ithaca.

The *Iliad* seems to show the simultaneous triumph of the just and the beautiful: Achilles' withdrawal opens the way for the attainment of glory by everyone else. In the *Odyssey*, the just is no longer beautiful, and the beautiful itself changes. Insofar as anyone corresponds to Helen in the *Odyssey*, it is Eumaeus's Phoenician nurse who, once she has intercourse with a Phoenician trader, is seduced into betraying her master (15.419–22). The Phoenician nurse is obviously the model of the Phoenicians' Io, with whose story Herodotus begins his *Histories* (1.1.2–4, 5.2). The *Odyssey* demythologizes the *Iliad*. Penelope is no Helen, who instantiates the beautiful to such an extent that the rights and wrongs of the case do not matter. Demodocus's song reflected that understanding; but it was sung among the Phaeacians and has no echo in Ithaca. When Penelope first faces Odysseus after the killing of the suitors, he is covered with blood (22.401–6); but after she refuses to recognize him, Eurynome bathes him, Athena pours overwhelming beauty down over his head, and he comes out of the bath like unto the immortals (23.153–56, 163). Odysseus has split apart Ares and Aphrodite; they are not going to be put together again in Ithaca. When Athena had bestowed on Penelope all the charms of Aphrodite, and the suitors to a man were bewitched by desire and prayed to sleep with her, Homer does not say what Odysseus experienced (18.190–96, 212–13).[220] The last to mention Aphrodite is Odysseus (22.444), but she is no longer golden.[221]

The suitors seem to follow a path of degeneration: they begin by planning a murder and end up by failing to be properly respectful. Amphinomus for one refuses to kill Telemachus, "for it is a terrible thing to kill one of royal blood," and all the other suitors accept his proposal that they first consult the plans of the gods, and only if the ordinances of great Zeus consent to it, will they go ahead with the killing (16.400–6; cf.

20.273).[222] Amphinomus's phrasing is obscure enough to guarantee that they will do nothing. Before Odysseus ever crosses his own threshold, then, the suitors have ceased to be a real threat; an unfavorable omen will later deter their last attempt to kill Telemachus and send them off to dinner (20.241–47). Their ready acquiescence in any obstacle that comes up, so as to have an excuse to put off any decisive action, is due to their vague realization that Telemachus's death could only put one of them on the throne, or else start up a deadly contest with no clear winner among themselves. Murder, then, recedes as a real possibility only to be replaced by insult. Telemachus, when he meets his father at Eumaeus's, is reluctant for them to go home together, lest they insult Odysseus (16.85–89). The insult would not be aimed so much at the beggar Odysseus as at Telemachus, who would be shown up thereby to lack the capacity to defend his guests. To insult a beggar is a safe way for the suitors to insult Telemachus (16.71–72; 18.223–25); it is not directed against Odysseus. Odysseus, in reply, puts himself in the place of Telemachus or of Odysseus himself, and denies that he would put up with seeing unseemly deeds, even if he were to be killed (16.99–107). Telemachus does not answer Odysseus directly, but he seems to excuse himself by shifting the blame onto Penelope: her refusal to decide one way or the other ties his hands (16.126–27). Either Telemachus is lying, and he believes Odysseus mistaken to be willing to risk his life on behalf of whatever principle is involved, or the suitors have, as they claim, some vague right on their side (2.123–25; 20.328–32).

If Telemachus has any reservations, whether they arise from the suitors' rights or from the weakness of his own right, he admits that the situation in his house is not one of war, in which men are perfectly willing to risk their lives for the sake of right (cf. 18.265–66). Now Odysseus does not believe in his own brave utterance either; he is willing to kill the suitors only if he survives and not if Penelope alone survives. Odysseus's prudence seems to weaken necessarily the passion that he invests in right. The more, it seems, right is on one's side, the less one is willing to pay for it. Or, inversely, the less one has to pay for the vindication of one's right, the more one proves that right is on one's side.[223] It is remarkable, then, that not everyone in Ithaca acknowledges that the success of Odysseus's plan makes his right self-evident (24.463–66). Antinous turns out to have overestimated the goodwill the people have for Telemachus (16.380–82). He has no understanding of the strength of his own right. It is left to his father to appeal to it (24.426–29).

Polyphemus prayed for Odysseus to find sufferings at home (9.535); but there is a strange unreality to them, as if Odysseus stood apart from the abuse directed at him and condemned the suitors for an intention that was incapable of being realized. "The swineherd," he tells Telemachus, "will bring me later to town; I shall look like a wretched beggar and old man. If they dishonor me at home, let your heart put up with it while I am being ill-treated, regardless of whether they drag me by the feet out of doors or hit me with spears. Put up with seeing it. Urge them, however, to stop their folly with soothing words. They will not obey you, for the fatal day has come for them" (16.272–80). If, Odysseus implies, Telemachus got angry and spoke harshly to the suitors, the suitors might stop, and then the evidence of their wickedness would be lacking (cf. 20.322–25). They are doomed in any case. Nothing they do or do not do will make the slightest difference; but they still must show who they really are. To whom, however, are they to show it? Is the charade designed for Telemachus, so that he can kill men with whom he has been in daily contact for three years (cf. 18.231–32)? Telemachus has never yet killed anyone; he believes it calls for an explanation if an inferior kills a superior (3.250). It is even unclear whether he ever has gone hunting (cf. 17.312–19). If that is Odysseus's intention, Telemachus's knowledge of who the beggar really is must fuse with the appearance of ill-treatment of a beggar, so that he can condemn the suitors for a crime they cannot possibly know they are committing (cf. 21.99; 22.38; 24.159–63).

What is still more curious is that the suitors themselves, and only the suitors, accept the possibility that this kind of entrapment is a practice of the gods. Whereas Telemachus knows that the beggar is his father, the suitors believe the beggar might be a god (17.483–87). Odysseus was suspected of being a god by Alcinous, and he had denied he looked like a god (7.208–10); Telemachus says he is a god, after he sees him transformed into a young man, and Odysseus denies it without offering any proof (16.183–89). Odysseus seems to imply that appearances do not count, and he is just what he is regardless of what he looks like (16.205); but he admits in the case of his dog Argus, who knows who he is despite appearances, that he cannot tell from his beautiful if decayed appearance whether he was a hunting-dog or was merely kept for show (17.306–10). Indeed, Odysseus's claim to be himself, in response to Telemachus's suspicion that he is a god, turns on the absence of aspiration:

οὔ τίς τοι θεός εἰμι . . . : I am not any god, you know . . .
ἀλλὰ πατὴρ τεός εἰμι . . . : But I am your father (16.187–88).

The placement of θεός (god) and τεός (your) in the same metrical position seems to underline the evident closeness of god and Odysseus, while the two speeches assert the absolute separation between them.²²⁴ Odysseus's first sentence, however, could be heard as saying, "I am, you know, the god No one." His enmity, which originally testified to the character of mind, would now take on its other valence, the nothingness of the no-body, as the proper form for the maintenance of divine justice. So at least a nameless suitor believes, and in this case Odysseus cannot deny it. He has to let the error pass. The suitors do not behave as if their supposition were true, nor is it true in this case or in any other that we know of. There is, in speech but not in deed, an interpretation of Odysseus that has him fulfill a purpose that would perfectly conform with his second journey but that makes the justice of the punishment of the suitors an irrelevant issue. The suitors would be sacrificed to the truth of a principle the evidence for which would be lacking.²²⁵

The City

Once Odysseus kills the suitors, he becomes remarkably indifferent to the future. When he goes off to the country, he makes no provision for either the safety of Penelope, against whom the citizens might vent their anger, or the defense of his actions. He arranges that the city first see him as ready to kill them. The corpses of the suitors who were not from Ithaca are shipped back to their several homelands (24.418–20), but no envoys are sent with them in order to placate their families. Odysseus knows there will be an armed struggle, but he does not have any interest in what his opponents will say. He gives the impression that he agrees with his father, who, immediately after he accepts the death of the suitors as a proof that the gods still exist, expresses the fear that all the Ithacans will come against them, and they will summon help from every other Cephallenian city (24.351–55). Laertes takes it for granted that no one else will count the slaughter of the suitors as evidence for the gods' existence. When Odysseus had asked Telemachus what he thought they should do, now that they had killed not just one man but the very support of the city, Telemachus had deferred to Odysseus, whose craftiness (*mētis*) was reputed to be the best (23.117–22). Odysseus was able to suggest how to postpone for a time the discovery of the murders—he seems to have spared the singer and the herald for this purpose—but he has nothing to propose after they get to the countryside: "Afterwards, we will devise there whatever gain Olympian Zeus puts into our palms" (23.139–40). It is possible that Odysseus has something in mind that he does not wish to disclose as yet to Telemachus; but at the end he is on a murderous rampage and has to be stopped by the joint action of Zeus and Athena (24.537–45). Odysseus did not understand Athena's shout to the Ithacans, to abstain from war and be reconciled, as applicable to himself (24.528– 36).[226] Odysseus, then, seems to have given no thought to the solution of the political problem his son and father are going to face once he leaves home again. A resignation in light of his fate seems to have come over him.

The task of reconciliation in the city, which happens without his knowledge nor at his behest, is left to Odysseus's partisans (24.439–64; cf. 22.372–80). They are not entirely successful, but they do manage to win over more than half the people, so that Odysseus's ragtag army is not so greatly outnumbered that it could not have killed them all (24.528). It seems, then, that the political solution falls into two parts, an internal and an external one, and Odysseus is involved only with the external, even though one might have thought that his eloquence was especially needed inside the city, and a rejuvenated Laertes, with Telemachus's help, could easily have taken over the field operations. The case against Odysseus is stated by Eupeithes; in its simplicity it is very powerful, and it would take the entire *Odyssey* to blunt if not refute it (24.426–37). They will be humiliated forever, Eupeithes says, if they do not avenge their sons and brothers. He seems to divine what will characterize Telemachus's rule. Eupeithes is particularly concerned about the possibility that Odysseus will get the jump on them and either go into exile voluntarily or send for allies from abroad; but Odysseus seems to have forgotten the former possibility, and he has certainly made no provisions for the latter.

Eupeithes' speech is met with universal pity (24.438). There is no one who believes that Odysseus has right on his side. They are as convinced of this as they once had been persuaded by Telemachus that the suitors were entirely in the wrong (2.81). In neither case does their pity lead anywhere. It is a vague sense of right that would need something else to stir it to action. Before that can happen, Phemius and Medon come in the nick of time. Medon speaks: "Listen to me now, Ithacans. Odysseus did not devise these deeds without the will of the deathless gods. I myself saw an immortal god: he stood near to Odysseus and resembled Mentor in all respects. Sometimes a deathless god was manifest in front of Odysseus and was encouraging him, sometimes he was stirring the suitors and was storming through the hall, and they were falling one after the other" (24.443–49). Now we know that Medon had crept under a chair at some point in the fight and had covered himself with a freshly flayed hide (22.362–64); and whatever he saw from that position he could not have seen a god if he saw Mentor (cf. 4.653–54). Medon's assertion is in a way the climax of the *Odyssey*, for it transforms inference into sight and passes itself off as having the certainty of the evident. Nothing in Homer's narrative corresponds to the second half of Medon's account: Athena sat high up in the rafters, shook her aegis, and terrified the suitors into flight (22.297–99). Medon's fusion of opinion and sight is what Plato calls at one point *phantasia* or imagination.[227] It is the highest achievement of the Cave.

Medon's speech turns everyone around. It is met with universal fear (24.450). Pity for human beings is driven out by fear before the gods. Right as men understand it is opposed to right as gods are seen to understand it. Each experience seems to cancel the other, though the sequence in the *Odyssey* is necessary for their resolution. That resolution is supplied by Halitherses, who had foretold part of Odysseus's fate before the Trojan War and predicted the imminent downfall of the suitors as well as disaster for many others in Ithaca (2.161–76). Halitherses now comes forward to separate pity from fear and introduce a third experience: "Listen to me now, Ithacans, to what I say. These things occurred, friends, by your own baseness. You refused to be won over by either me or Mentor to stop your sons from their folly; they did a great deed by their wickedness, ravaging property and dishonoring the wife of the best man. They thought he would not return. Now let it be as I say. Let us not go, lest one no doubt find an evil one has drawn upon oneself" (24.454–62).

The effect of Halitherses' speech was for more than half to leave the assembly with a great shout. He had assumed that the citizens' fear would not suffice to deter them from marching against Odysseus; it required the supplement of guilt. Guilt tilts the balance between pity and fear in favor of fear. The majority acknowledge their own baseness (*kakotēs*). *Kakotēs* had occurred seventeen times before this, and never with any other meaning than distress and misery. It was always "objective" and never received any personal pronoun; it was always something in whose grip one was held or from whose grip one had escaped. Now, however, it has been internalized, and one is fully responsible for one's own misery. The importance of this cannot be stressed too much. It brings an end to Zeus's complaint, with which the *Odyssey* began, about men always assigning blame to the gods for a misery they themselves have brought about. It consequently explains how the gods can withdraw and still be effective in the support of right. The pity that belongs to purely human right, and that by itself would necessarily lead men to holding the gods responsible for the failure of its vindication, is not commingled with fear in its reevaluation by guilt; rather, pity is then separated out entirely and overwhelmed by terror and remorse. The people are made to experience in a single burst the drawn-out course of Odysseus, who, with right entirely on his side against Polyphemus, was and is being led to undergo a formal conversion: he must appease Poseidon. Whether that conversion involves remorse is left in the obscurity of his stay with Calypso.

While Eupeithes has the prior mourning of the crowd to support his appeal (24.416), to say nothing of the sight of the corpses, Medon and Halitherses induce the experience of fear and guilt entirely through speech, though a certain amazement at Medon's survival may have forestalled any precipitous action and allowed him time to counteract the impression Eupeithes left (24.441). The crowd sees neither the god whom Medon says he saw nor Odysseus. Odysseus in fact is as unseen by the people as the god was to Medon. Perhaps, then, Odysseus is just as effective, or even more so, because he is not seen. It is difficult, in any case, to imagine his giving a version of Halitherses' speech without raising all sorts of awkward questions. Odysseus seems to be needed where he is, for the induction of terror and remorse does not work on everyone. It works, one might say, on the soft part of the population. The smaller but tougher part follow Eupeithes into battle. Against them the gods must act directly. Athena frightens them into dropping their weapons and threatens Odysseus with Zeus's anger. If the text is sound, Athena had always intended to establish peace; otherwise, it is a last-minute arrangement of Zeus (24.473–87). That Zeus should interfere in this way agrees with his modification of Poseidon's original intention in regard to the Phaeacians (13.146–58). "Now that Odysseus punished the suitors," Zeus says, "let them swear (ταμόντες) trustworthy oaths: let him be king for always (ὁ μὲν βασιλευέτω), and let us in turn (ἡμεῖς δ' αὖ) make them forget the murder of their sons and brothers. Let them love one another as before, and let there be wealth and peace in abundance" (24.482–86). The syntax of Zeus is confused. He starts out in the main clause with the Ithacans as subject (ταμόντες), proceeds to split the oath-takers in two, with Odysseus as subject of the first subordinate clause (οἱ δέ), himself and Athena (ἡμεῖς δ' αὖ) of the second, and when he resumes the main thread, Odysseus and the Ithacans are jointly the subject (τοὶ δέ). The suppressed clause should have been on the order of "and let them obey" or the like; but, by the replacement of the "intended" subject, Zeus makes himself and Athena those who are to swear the trustworthy oaths, and the Ithacans are not part of the agreement. The confusion in which Zeus gets himself unnecessarily entangled seems to be due to the imbalance between Odysseus's resumption of his rule and the Ithacans' induced forgetfulness. Is not Odysseus to forget his vengeance? Zeus seems to imply that he has in his arsenal a drug more powerful than Helen's, which could make one forget terrible things but only for a day (4.220–26). We do not know whether the Ithacans ever did forget, or whether Athena believes that the oath was sufficient. She administers the oath between both sides, but she does so in the likeness of Mentor (24.546–48). She thus makes the gods participate in the oath. The gods uphold the reconciliation between Odysseus and his enemies without either establishing their friendliness in more than a formal sense or guaranteeing that the oath will not be broken at some later time. We have Odysseus's grandfather and his own men to remind us of the fragility of oaths. Zeus's wish that the people be as loving as they were before cannot be fulfilled: since he must be referring to the time before the Trojan War, when Odysseus was as gentle as a father, there cannot be any recovery of that time. There were then no oaths between the father and his children.

The formal solution to the political problem is now complete. It consists of two kinds of divine terror, one by hearsay, the other manifest. The first kind of terror becomes, under the proper circumstances, guilt; the second assumes the form of the law.[228] The first is effective against unarmed men, the second against those who have to be disarmed. The punitive rhetoric of the first does not require divine intervention, the lawful consequences of the second need the gods to be ever-present though concealed: we are meant to be reminded of Athena's presence and nonpresence at the sacrifice Nestor made to her. Odysseus gladly accepts the conditions that the second kind of terror brings about, he knows nothing about the first. He has already made arrangements with Eumaeus and Philoitius that are destined to introduce another kind of terror and disturb the distribution of power. Odysseus believes he can make up in part for the losses he sustained from the suitors by exactions from the people (23.355–58; cf. 13.14–15). To experience guilt is one thing, to have to pay for it another. There are, besides, the disloyal male servants to take care of. Many of them will probably get off easy. Odysseus had wanted to find out, while he was still in disguise, whether they feared and honored him; but Telemachus dissuaded him (16.305–7; 318–20). Despite what Zeus says, Ithaca will never be as it was.[229]

9

Recognitions

Penelope

If the suitors were not shameless, the contest of the bow would have gotten rid of them without bloodshed (21.153–62). Antinous's proposal to put off the trial gives them only one more day (21.256–68). Antinous, however, never does get the chance to string the bow, and for all we know he might have succeeded, with Apollo's help (21.267–68), had not Odysseus and Athena diverted the purpose of Penelope's plan (21.1–4).²³⁰ Penelope is perfectly willing for the suitors to be killed, but not apparently by a human being. Although she rejoices when Eurycleia, in order to confirm the truth of her first report, invokes Telemachus's prior knowledge of the identity of the stranger, Penelope doubts again as soon as she learns that Eurycleia did not see with her own eyes how one man killed so many (23.11–57). Penelope in fact never does learn about it; Odysseus does not discuss the killing with her, and she does not ask. In answer to her assertion that a god must have done it, Eurycleia appeals to Odysseus's scar; but Penelope implies that a god could have faked that as well, for the plans of the gods are nearly inscrutable (23.81–82). Penelope recognizes and fails to recognize Odysseus; she is put off by his appearance: she had never seen him before in rags and covered with blood (23.94–95). It is as if the unseemly (*aeikelios*) were not to seem and to be unlike (*aeikelos*; cf. 4.244–49). Penelope is not Helen. She cannot see through appearances to an unchangeable nature. There must be a showing of it if she is to be convinced. She says there are signs that are known, apart from all others, to herself and her husband alone: her use of the dual "we" would seem to indicate that she has already been won over (23.107–10). After his bath, Athena enhances the beauty of Odysseus and gives him back the looks he had twenty years before (23.175–76). Penelope ac-

143

knowledges the resemblance, but she still does not give in. Athena's intervention seems to make the recognition of the real Odysseus impossible. Her intervention implies that had Odysseus been allowed to appear as what he had become through his experiences, he would have been unrecognizable. Penelope has to fall back on an external sign, the marriage bed, which Odysseus constructed in so preposterous a way that no one but a god could have possibly known of it. Odysseus, by limiting a god's power to the moving of the bed, seems to deny that a god could have known about his irrational procedure, whereby he roofed the bedroom, with the branches of the olive tree still intact, before he cut it down to size (23.183–204). It is Odysseus, then, who puts the question of his own identity in doubt; but Penelope accepts him anyway, for, as has been often remarked, it is not his artfulness that stamps him as the real thing but his anger (23.182). His indignation at the humanly impossible melts Penelope's iron heart (23.172).

Whether Penelope intended the bed to be the only sign she wanted is unclear; she had spoken of what only she and Odysseus knew, but the character of the bed was also known to Actoris, and she may still be alive (23.225–30). Neither the bed nor Odysseus's anger quite measures up to the intimacy one might expect between husband and wife. She is won over, she says, despite her cruel or unfeeling heart (*apēnea thumon*); and she herself had contrasted the cruel (*apēnēs*) with the blameless (*amumōn*), and asserted that all men curse whoever is cruel while alive and mock him when dead (19.329–31). In a sense, "unfeeling heart" is in quotes, since Telemachus had said it of her and reviled her for her aloofness (23.97–103). His remarks echo Athena's, who had said, in praise of Odysseus's distrust, that any other man would have rushed to his wife and children and not first tested his faithful wife (13.330–38); and Telemachus now says that any other woman would not have had so stony a heart if her husband had returned after twenty years.

Odysseus and Penelope are of a piece, but their suspiciousness does not have the same source. His seems to be due to the demand that he be known while he is unknowable; Penelope explains hers in a surprising way (23.209–24). She begins by asking for his understanding. The gods, she says, begrudged them to enjoy their youth and to advance to old age together. She now acknowledges the reality of time and resents it (cf. 19.358–60); she seems to suspect, even before she learns of Teiresias's prophecy, that not even their future will be shared. His homecoming cannot make up for lost time. As Homer says in the simile that follows her speech, only a few survive the shipwreck Poseidon caused (23.233–40). Penelope then asks that Odysseus not be angry with righteous indignation because she did not embrace him at once. Penelope distinguishes between Odysseus's mind and heart. Odysseus's mind is needed to acknowledge what they both have lost; Odysseus's heart has to be held in check while he hears what holds only in her case: "My heart was always in a shudder of fear lest some mortal come and deceive me with words—many plan acts of evil gain. Not even Argive Helen, born from Zeus, would have had intercourse with a man from elsewhere in sexual love had she known that the warlike sons of the Achaeans were going to lead her home again to her own country, but a god, you see, had stirred her to do an unseemly deed, and she did not set in her heart the mournful doom before it happened, which grief came to us too at first" (23.215–24). Penelope, it seems, should have expressed herself differently: "Otherwise, Helen would not have slept with Paris"; but by adding a condition—"had she known the consequences"—she not only absolves Helen—How could she have known what the Achaeans would do?—but she implies that the only defense against seductive speeches is radical distrust. She denies, at least in her own case, that it would be impossible to be seduced. She vindicates the power of Aphrodite.

Eustathius remarks that the puzzle Penelope and Odysseus have jointly raised does not admit of a solution; but he proposes, as the only way out, that Penelope would not in the strict sense be violating her wish not to please the mind of Odysseus's inferior (20.82) were she to welcome a god instead (1940,19–34). Penelope herself seems to separate the killing of the suitors from the recognition of Odysseus: a god could have done the killing, a man could have deceived her. She thus refuses to associate the Odysseus she accepts as her husband with the Odysseus everyone else assumes did the killing. She does not pay any attention to the arrangements Odysseus makes with Telemachus about its aftermath (23.130–40), and she does not respond when Odysseus tells her as he leaves that he killed the suitors (23.363). Had Eurycleia told her why Odysseus sent for her, after the killing of the suitors, she would certainly have accepted the hanging of the slave girls as all the evidence she needed that no god could have given the order. As it is, if a god did not kill the suitors, then a stranger, taking advantage of the terms of the contest he himself had urged her to hold, comes forward to claim his prize, something she denied he had even hoped for (21.312–19). The most seductive speeches she ever heard were his.

In the absence of any explanation from Odysseus of why he refused to reveal himself to her and trusted their son and slaves instead, some shadow of distrust must linger even after she recognizes him. Her refusal to sleep with him until she hears in detail what immeasurable suffering awaits him seems to confirm it (23.248–62; cf. 10.334–35). She says it is better to know at once what she will learn about eventually. She does not want to be left in the dark a second time. That Odysseus will leave again seems decisive for her acceptance of him. This is the Odysseus who went to take a look at "Evilium" (23.19). He cannot be an impostor if he has no interest in staying. She now knows where she stands; she is to suffer shipwreck again and never reach shore (23.233–40). Her reply to Teiresias' prophecy is brief: "Well, if the gods are going to effect a better old age, then you can expect that you will have thereafter an escape from evils" (23.286–87). Now that she knows that she will get nothing, she lets the imitation of her former marriage go forward (23.142–51, 295–99). Odysseus's last order to her is strict: "Do not look at anyone, and do not ask any questions" (23.365). We have heard this line before; Athena said it to Odysseus when she warned him against the unfriendly Phaeacians (7.31).

Hades

Were Penelope to have had among the Ithacans the authority Arete exercised among the Phaeacians (7.67–74), or even perhaps were Odysseus merely to have honored her in the way Alcinous honored Arete and to have conferred upon her the regency when he left for Troy, she would have been immune from unwanted attentions and kept the household safe from spoliation. Given the circumstances and the weakness of her own position, she had for three years, by surrounding herself with a large number of suitors, protected Telemachus from the assault of any one of them alone, and she had prevented any concerted effort by making secret promises to each (2.91–92; 13.380–81). Odysseus never praises her for what she did, and Telemachus does not even realize it. Odysseus does seem to praise her once, but then he is in disguise and tries to catch her offguard: in praising her happiness in contrast to his own misery, he intends to expose her pride and have her confess that she is well content with her situation (19.107–22, cf. 19.45, 541–43; 2.125–26). It could be said, in Odysseus's defense, that any acknowledgment of Penelope's action would be tantamount to an admission that the status of the suitors thereby falls under the sacred principle of guest-friendship, whose violation by Odysseus would make Aegisthus's and Heracles' crimes pale into insignificance. However that may be, Penelope's real praise is reserved for Hades. This is the penultimate surprise of the *Odyssey.* Just as Penelope forced Odysseus to repeat the story of his descent to Hades, first in order to know his future and then in Odysseus's recounting of his adventures, so something forces Homer to pick up that episode alone and give his own account of Hades.

Homer's resumption recalls the two discussions of poetry in Plato's *Republic*, first in the context of morality and then in light of philosophy. In the first of those discussions, Achilles' rejection of Hades and his own life is taken by Socrates to be the model of what he finds most objectionable in Homer; but the very same lines he originally censored from Achilles' speech he later puts in the mouth of the one who has ascended from the Cave.[231] Although it seemed that Odysseus had accepted Hades when he rejected Calypso's offer of immortality, Odysseus in fact accepted death while rejecting the law and its meaning, for which Hades can be said to stand. Homer, then, sets out to restore Hades. The theme he assigns to it is burial and song. What emerged from Odysseus's descent was that Hades is the region of dreams and frustration. Nothing there is real and nothing there is good. Odysseus, we thought, was not going back. Those who do descend are the souls of the suitors. Hermes, the god who showed Odysseus the nature of nature, conducts them: he who pointed to the inseparability of mind and shape as that which constitutes man, the knowledge of which was proof against enchantment, now brings the separated souls of the suitors to Hades. He holds a rod in his hands by means of which he enchants the eyes of anyone he wishes; and on this occasion he uses it to stir the souls as if they were bats in a cave, which squeak and take to flight whenever one of them falls away from the cluster (24.1–10).

The souls of the suitors meet up with the heroes of the Trojan War, who gather about Achilles. The suitors, it seems, are not going to be tortured (perhaps Aegisthus was); they are allowed to join the best of the Achaeans (24.107–8). They are acknowledged to be the last vestiges of the heroic world Odysseus was either destined or designed to destroy. Should Odysseus ever descend again to Hades, he would find the hostility of Ajax multiplied a hundredfold. In Hades, Achilles is king, and Agamemnon comes to him. Agamemnon's soul is still distressed. No matter how much time passes, Agamemnon will still be found rehearsing his misery. The same privilege is apparently going to be extended to the suitors. In their generosity, the gods grant those who were the victims of right the right to put forward their own claim to right. The spokesman for the suitors was once the host of Agamemnon and Menelaus when they came to Ithaca to persuade Odysseus to join the expedition to Troy (24.114–19). We learn that not all the suitors were as young as Antinous, who knew Odysseus when he was a child; Amphimedon was not much younger than Odysseus and knew firsthand Odysseus's beneficent rule (24.159–60). Could it be that the suitors, far from forgetting Odysseus's

gentleness, were counting on it and expected no more than a reprimand
and a beating if by any chance Odysseus were to return? Amphimedon,
in any case, is allowed to tell the story his way, but not before we hear
what Achilles and Agamemnon still have to say to one another. Their
discussion prepares us for Agamemnon's praise of Penelope.

Achilles seems now to be at peace with Hades. Whatever resentment
Odysseus's visit stirred up is not present in his speech to Agamemnon.
His solicitude is all for Agamemnon's fate. He expresses regret that Agamemnon could not have died at Troy, so that all the Achaeans could have
built him a tomb and his son basked in reflected glory. Such an end would
have been in conformity with the favor the Achaeans thought Zeus had
bestowed on him, because he was the ruler of so many. Achilles' words
remind us of Odysseus's rejection of his own life and momentary prefer-
ence for a death at Troy while fighting over Achilles' corpse (5.306–12).
Odysseus then expressed a wish that would have reabsorbed him into a
world from which he had always been apart; but the wish is consistent
with Achilles' understanding of Agamemnon, and Agamemnon seems to
acknowledge as much when he reverts to the same occasion and the subsequent burial of Achilles (24.36–97). The worst day in Odysseus's life is
the prelude to the highpoint for Achilles. There never would have been an
end to the struggle over his corpse, Agamemnon tells Achilles, had not
Zeus sent a whirlwind. To learn at last that Achaeans and Trojans alike
were willing to be killed around him belongs to Achilles' happiness. After
the proper rituals had been performed, Agamemnon reports, Thetis and
her sisters rose out of the sea and frightened everyone; and the Achaeans
would have fled had not Nestor calmed them: the appearance of gods is
inseparable from a terror that drives out pity. The Muses then sang a
threnody, and everyone wept, both mortals and immortals, for seventeen
days. The Muses, it seems, did not weep. The pity they aroused and sustained contributed to Achilles' permanent glory, but it is his tomb that
makes him conspicuous both now and in the future. Achilles dies but
not his name. Hades is needed in order that Achilles may enjoy, if only
counterfactually, the reality of his name. "Though you have met with
the burial of many kings," Agamemnon tells him, "whenever young men
arrange to compete in contests, still you would have been especially
pleased in your heart had you seen the very beautiful contests silverfooted
Thetis set up for you" (24.87–92). Hades consoles in the face of the impossible. Odysseus's breach in that consolation is now being repaired.[232]

Agamemnon's long recital of Achilles' funeral is meant to throw in
relief his own inconsolability. Once the war was over his pleasure was at
an end; Zeus devised his destruction at the hands of Aegisthus and his

damned wife. There lingers in Hades the same complaint against the gods that Zeus had protested against at the beginning of the *Odyssey*, and that at least in Ithaca has been partially replaced by guilt. A perfect solution, against which no one could object, seems impossible: not all men can be held up to the standard of strict accountability. The law and Hades are for them. Achilles and Agamemnon look on in astonishment at the arrival of the suitors (24.101). Agamemnon puts to Amphimedon the same question Odysseus had put to him in Hades (11.399–403). The suitors were in a sense rustling cattle and fighting over a city and women; but the indifference to right that Agamemnon's phrasing implies is more shocking in his own case than in Odysseus's.[233] Helen does not fare well in Hades. Amphimedon's account puts Penelope squarely in the center of the conspiracy against the suitors (24.125–90). Penelope was devising their death from the moment they began to woo her. She knew, in other words, if we connect Amphimedon's conjecture with the true plot of the *Odyssey*, of the necessity that the princes of Odysseus's empire be killed if Telemachus were ever to rule. She knew besides that the beggar was her husband when she set up the contest. Amphimedon tells a neater story than Homer does. The removal of the arms and the setting up of the contest are part of the same plan; they are not, as in the *Odyssey*, coincidental through a mistake of Telemachus. Recognition is only a problem for the suitors. All of the twenty-third book could have been scrapped. In exaggerating Penelope's conscious role, Amphimedon also exaggerates the frequency with which they had thrown things at Odysseus (cf. 17.230–32),[234] and the self-evidence of the divine support Odysseus received. It is only after Amphimedon's own death that Athena took the active role he ascribes to her (22.297–309). Ghosts compare notes. Amphimedon's story is remarkably free from self-pity; his only mistake was in not being able to penetrate Odysseus's disguise. An evil god brought Odysseus home from somewhere or other (24.149). He does not admit that they were godless and Odysseus had justice on his side.[235] He implies that if they were guilty they were guilty in the eyes of Penelope qua suitors regardless of their behavior. They should have waited until Odysseus was "officially" dead (cf. 22.321–25; 23.150–51). Twenty years is close to the limit of merely human expectation; beyond that time it takes on the color of a "religious" longing (cf. 24.400–1). The one complaint Amphimedon does have is that their bodies have not yet been washed free of gore and properly mourned for, but he fully expects that as soon as they know their friends will attend to it.

On the basis of Amphimedon's inaccurate report, Agamemnon calls Odysseus happy (24.192–202). He has a wife of great virtue, with a good mind, who well remembered her husband. The fame of her virtue will never die, and the immortals will make a charming song for her. A loathsome song, however, will spread among men about his wife, and it will taint all women regardless of whether anyone is good. Agamemnon does not say who will make Clytaemestra's song (cf. 24.413), but he implies that in its disparagement of women it will overwhelm the immortals' song in praise of Penelope. The *Odyssey* does not contradict Agamemnon's prediction. As far as the *Odyssey* is concerned, Penelope's achievement is in the past; and from the first book on she is being pushed aside in favor of the son she fostered and protected. Telemachus even takes over the contest of the bow she devised (21.344–55). Her distraction of the suitors from the political issue is a given of the story, but there is no episode in which the suitors acknowledge both her charm and her distraction. Nothing corresponds to the old men on the walls of Troy speaking of Helen. The *Odyssey* seems to comprise the two songs of Agamemnon's prediction. Once he is home, Odysseus acts and speaks in the spirit of the advice Agamemnon gave to him in Hades: he seems not to have told Penelope about either Circe's wish to have him as her husband or his mother's warning that there is no embrace in Hades (23.321).

Laertes

Odysseus most distinguishes himself from Achilles by his relationship to his father. Achilles asked Odysseus whether Peleus still had honor among the Myrmidons now that he was old, and he said he wanted just a short time back on earth in order to punish those who were dishonoring him (11.494–503). Odysseus decides to tease the equally old and dishonored Laertes. Although he goes armed to the country (23.366), he gives up his armor before he goes to see his father (24.219). Laertes perhaps would have recognized an armed Odysseus at once. No one, however, has recognized him so far, and everything we have heard about Laertes makes him out to be so decrepit that it seems improbable that he alone would. It should in any case be a matter of complete indifference. We have just been given an instance of recognition after an equally long interval, but only in Hades where soul knows soul at once (cf. 11.141–44): Agamemnon recognized Amphimedon after twenty years, and Amphimedon recognized him, though they knew each other for less than a month (24.102–4, 115–22). Does Odysseus demand that at least one person know him in this way? Why should the transparency of the self be of such concern to Odysseus? The transparent self does not need any signs. It shows what it is. This is not what Odysseus realized it means to have a nature. Nature was found to be the invisible unity of mind and shape; but the transparent self is not grasped by mind, and if Hades is the region of such selves, it is shape without mind. Odysseus wants apparently for the conditions of Hades to prevail on earth. He wants, more exactly, the being of Heracles, which is "himself" (αὐτός), to be endowed with the recognizability of soul by itself (11.602). He wants to distinguish between himself as "this here such" (ὅδε τοιόσδε) and the "such" (τοῖος) of resemblance, which can be whatever Athena wishes (16.205–10).[236]

What Odysseus wants seems impossible, for it is an Odysseus without the Odysseus of the *Odyssey* (cf. 20.88–90). He seems to have forgotten that he chose self-opacity when he rejected Calypso's offer; or perhaps it would be better to say that he has come to believe his own narrative of his voyage to the Phaeacians and has dismissed Homer's account. If, moreover, the self-transparency that Odysseus demands is the kind of self-completeness that came to light as possibly Odysseus's self-understanding over against what Hades represents, then Odysseus's failure to make himself known as himself reflects the partiality of man and the irreduceability of the manifold of what is to man. Odysseus had met with great resistance to his claim from Penelope; she had refused to identify the killer with the husband. Without such an identification, however, Odysseus cannot justify the execution of the suitors. If his wife cannot know, the suitors could not either, and it would only be on the basis of the suitors' own suggestion—he is a god in disguise who punishes outrages against the nobodies—that he would be in the right. He would then be solely an agent of a divine plan, but there would be no vindication of himself. His refusal, then, to let Penelope in on the conspiracy would have been due to his desire to reserve her for the recognition. When that fails he has no recourse but to seek out Laertes. He at least must see through him.

We know quite a bit about Laertes before we ever meet him. Athena knew that he no longer comes to town but stays in the country creeping about his vineyard (1.188–93); and Odysseus hears a more elaborate version of the same report from his mother in Hades (11.187–96). Laertes' withdrawal had had nothing to do with the arrival of the suitors, but seems to have been undertaken on his own to increase his sorrowful longing for his son. Laertes had abdicated in favor of Odysseus some time before the Trojan War and after he had sacked the city of Nericus (24.377–78). His abdication gave the suitors the opportunity to take over the royal palace. Telemachus regards him as of little importance (16.137–53). When Penelope proposed that Laertes be asked to protest publicly the suitors' attempt on his grandson's life, Eurycleia dissuaded her (4.735–41, 754). He had done nothing about his desire to sleep with the young Eurycleia (1.429–33). "Odysseus" taunts him now with that failure by recounting how he once gave Odysseus four good-looking women whom Odysseus chose for himself (24.278–79). Did he expect that in this way Laertes would recognize him? That detail, boorish and cruel, seems to be of a piece with Odysseus asking, "Whose slave are you?" while declaring that he looks like a king (24.252–57; cf. 17.416, 454). Odysseus, it seems, wants to test whether Laertes really mourns for him. His standard seems to be his mother who died out of longing. Does Odysseus believe that Laertes has some lingering resentment at his loss of authority? He stops the sport only after Laertes pours ashes on his head and a black cloud of grief envelops him (24.315–17).

Odysseus aims at two things at once, which he believes to be somehow connected: he wants Laertes to know him as he is, but he does not want Laertes to know him if he does not genuinely miss him. Only if his grief is real should he recognize the real Odysseus. These are competing demands unless the standard is doglike devotion; but no human being can be like Argus, and Laertes fails the test of loyalty with knowledge. Loyalty and knowledge are as far apart from one another as the unquestioned is from the result of questioning, or as Odysseus the homeward-bound is from Odysseus the wanderer. The entire *Odyssey* seems to have strained from the start to assert their togetherness in Odysseus, who first chose memory and then professed to represent the anonymity of mind. Now that Laertes needs two signs from the past to know his son (24.331–44), whom he too never acknowledges to be the killer of the suitors (24.351–52), and Odysseus cannot expect that "I myself here"—ὅδ' αὐτὸς ἐγώ (24.321)—will suffice for recognition, Odysseus is free to submit to his fate and begin his second journey. He should now know that his destiny is to establish belief and not knowledge.

Notes

1. Cf. 5.151–52, where the nondrying of Odysseus's tears leads to the flowing away of Odysseus's life.

2. Horace, in discussing what makes for poetry, quotes one and a half lines from Ennius, through which he makes it clear that the making of gods distinguishes the poet from the versifier (*Sermones* 1.4.38–62, cf. 89). The frequency of the gods' names in Horace's own lyric poetry, as opposed to their relative rarity in the rest of his verse, is inversely related to the single instance of *natura* in the Odes (1.28.15) and its thirty-four occurrences in the rest.

3. Likewise, although Aeschylus's Clytaemestra imagines perfectly the meeting of Agamemnon and his daughter in Hades, she couples that image with her refusal to bury Agamemnon properly (*Agamemnon* 1551–59; *Choephoroe* 430–33, 439): the *Choephoroe* is the only extant tragedy in which "Hades" does not occur.

4. When Socrates asks for Ion's own reactions when he recites episodes from the *Iliad* and *Odyssey*, he mentions one terrifying event from each poem, but of pitiable events he mentions only those from the *Iliad* (*Ion* 535b1–7).

5. Cf. Plato *Republic* 620c3–d2.

6. On the first twenty-one lines, see Klaus Rüter, *Odysseeinterpretationen Hypomnemata* 19 (Göttingen: Vandenhoeck & Ruprecht, 1969), 28–52.

7. Cf. Apuleius *de deo Socratis* 24 (176–77): *ut Attius Ulixen laudavit in Philocteta suo, in eius tragoediae principio:*

Inclite, parva prodite patria,
Nomine celebri claroque potens
Pectore, Achivis classibus auctor,
Gravis Dardanis gentibus ultor,
Laertiade.

novissime patrem memorat. ceterum omnes laudes eius viri audisti. nihil inde nec Laertes sibi nec Anticlia nec Acrisius vindicat: tota, ut vides, laudis huius propria Ulixi possessio est.

153

8. Cf. Plato *Cratylus* 397c8-d6; Caesar *de bello Gallico* 6.21.2.

9. Cf. Dietrich Mülder, "Bericht über die Literatur zu Homer (Höhre Kritik) für die Jahre 1912–1919," *Jahresbericht über Fortschritte der klassischen Altertumswissenschaft* 182 (1921): 126.

10. Cf. Carl Rothe, *Die Odyssee als Dichtung und ihr Verhältnis zur Ilias* (Paderborn: Schöningh, 1914), 21.

11. Cf. Scholia DHJM^aQ on 1.33 in A.Ludwich, *Scholia in Homeri Odysseae A 1–309 auctoriora et emendatiora* (Hildesheim: Georg Olms 1966).

12. Cf. Harmut Erbse, *Untersuchungen zur Funktion der Götter im homerischen Epos* (Berlin-New York: de Gruyter, 1986), 237–44.

13. Cf. Friedrich Focke, *Die Odyssee, Tübinger Beiträge zur Altertumswissenschaft*, XXXVII (Stuttgart-Berlin: Kohlhammer, 1943), 31.

14. Cf. Plato *Laws* 682d5-e4, who adds that the young did not welcome the soldiers home in justice, and there were many deaths and much slaughter.

15. In Aeschylus's *Agamemnon*, Agamemnon, in accordance with the Chorus's advice (787–99, 807–8), proposes to remove with prudent surgery and cautery the disloyal elements of Argos (848–50); if one judges by the first stasimon (456–58), Agamemnon could never have succeeded either. For the strict application of surgery and cautery to politics, see Plato *Statesman* 293a9-c3; d4-e5.

16. Plato *Laws* 627c3–628a3.

17. 1.117, 243–44, 320–21, 397–98; cf. 15.19–23, 91; 19.533–34; 20.265.

18. Cf. Scholia HMQR at 4.167; Q at 13.387.

19. Out of the twenty-nine instances of νεμεσῶ, νεμεσ(σ)ητόν, νεμεσίζομαι, νέμεσις (righteous indignation), Homer himself uses it four times, here of Telemachus, and thrice of the suitors (17.481; 21.147, 285). Odysseus never speaks of it in his account of his adventures to the Phaeacians, but once when he is lying to Eumaeus (14.284).

20. For an analysis, see Ernst Siegmann, "Die Athene-Rede im ersten Buch der Odyssee," *Würzburger Jahrbücher für Altertumswissenschaft* N.F. 2 (1976): 21–36; Klaus Rüter, *Odysseeinterpretationen* (Göttingen: Vandenhoeck & Ruprecht, 1969), 148–201.

21. Cf. Scholium T on 1.261.

22. Cf. Scholia DE²HMA²Q on 1.255: "How would he who had turned his attention to drinking and the delight of dinner be terrifying?"

23. Of the fourteen or fifteen occasions on which Homer himself speaks of "hero," only three are his in Ithaca after Odysseus's return (18.423 [Moulius]; 22.185 [Laertes]; 24.451 [Halitherses]).

24. Cf. Harmut Erbse, *Beiträge zum Verständnis der Odyssee* (Berlin-New York: de Gruyter, 1972), 225–26.

25. Cf. Adolf Kirchhoff, *Die Homerische Odyssee* (Berlin: W. Hertz, 1879), 254–57.

26. Athena first urges Telemachus to kill the suitors if he learns that Odysseus is dead and once he has married off his mother (1.289–96); she implies as strongly as she can that he could never be king as long as the suitors are alive.

27. Eustathius suggests that the interruption of Phemius's song was a necessity of the story, for eventually he would have sung of Odysseus, and if he had said that Odysseus was dead, Penelope would have been forced to marry, but had he said that he was alive, the suitors would have left (1420,21–30); so also, succinctly, Scholia HA at 1.328.

28. In the Catalogue of Ships, Homer tells the story of how the Muse deprived Thamyras the Thracian of song; he inserts it in the account of Nestor's contingent (II.594–600).

29. None of the following—whose occurrences at Menelaus's are given in parentheses—are to be found in the third book: ἀκαχίζω, ἀργαλέος (4.397), ἀχεύω (4.100), ἄχνυμαι (4.104, 549), ἄχος (4.108), γοάω, γόος (4.102, 103, 113, 183), δύστηνος (4.182), ἐλεέω (4.364)[ἐλεαίρω once negated, 3.96], θυμαλγής, κῆδος (4.108), κλαίω (4.196, 539, 541, 544), μύρομαι, οἶκτος (or its derivatives), ὀδύρομαι (4.100, 104, 194), ὀλοφύρομαι (4.364), πένθος, στεναχίζω, στενάχω (4.516?). Insofar as there is suffering in Nestor's narration, it is more prominent in the first account (103, 104, 113, 117, 118, 134. 153, 166, 175) than in the second (262, 303, 306), where truth is stressed (254, 327, 328). None of the three words for heart (ἦτορ, κέαρ, κραδίη) occurs in the third book; at Menelaus's they occur altogether twelve times.

30. Cf. Scholium T on 9.40.

31. In the long account of his youthful exploits to Patroclus (XI.670–762), Nestor also does not quote anyone or use any similes; the closest he comes is to say that he attacked "equal to a black whirlwind" (XI.747).

32. Likewise, in Plato's *Republic*, Socrates approves of many Homeric practices that belong to the narrative—the way of medication, for example, and the preparation of food—and rarely of any speeches, and thus assigns narrative to the body and dialogue to the soul, where the morally ambiguous lies (cf. *Republic* 468c10-e3).

33. The sections of Nestor's speech are as follows: (1) 256–61, Aegisthus and Menelaus; (2) 262–63ᵃ, Achaeans at Troy; (3) 263ᵇ-75 Aegisthus; (4) 276–302, Menelaus; (5) 303–5, Aegisthus; (6) 306–12, Orestes and Menelaus.

34. The importance of the twin issues of sacrifice and burial emerges clearly in Plato's *Minos*, where the anonymous comrade objects to Socrates' definition of law—"Law wants to be the discovery of that which is"—on the grounds that different people sacrifice different kinds of animals and the Athenians have not always had the same burial practices (*Minos* 315b6-d5).

35. On Menelaus's role in the *Odyssey* see Uvo Hölscher, *Die Odyssee* (Munich: Beck, 1988), 95–100.

36. Cf. Scholium E on 3.248.

37. "Lovely" (*erateinon*) and "looks" (*eidos*) also occur here first.

38. Cf. Scholium E at 4.184.

39. Hesiod *Theogony* 98–103.

40. Cf. Jan van Leeuwen, *Odyssea* (Leyden: A. W. Sijthoff, 1917), on 4.95: "*dicit domum pristinam, dum peregre circumvagatur, direptam. a quibusnam direptam?*

fortasse a civitatis primoribus, quemadmodum Ulixis opes inter se divisuros se minati sint primores Ithacenses."

41. For a defense of this line structurally, see Calvert Watkins, "A propos de μνις," *Bulletin de la Société de Linguistique* 72 (1977): 207–8.

42. Pindar, in *Olympian* 2, seems to suggest that Zeus, in overcoming Kronos or Time (Chronos), overcame the human resentment against the irreversibility of action, whether just or unjust, by the introduction of metempsychosis (cf. 15–17 with 76); cf. Seneca *Hercules* 290–93.

43. At 4.451–53, Menelaus seems to make a pun: Proteus, he says, counted (*lekto*) the number of seals, and he was counting (*lege*) Menelaus and his three men among the creatures of the sea, and then he lay down (*lekto*) himself. Counting is impossible, he implies, if there is not rest.

44. In order to understand the issue of time in the *Oresteia* and the use Aeschylus made of the *Odyssey* in it, one must keep in mind that, once Aeschylus decided to make Agamemnon and Menelaus joint rulers in Argos, he made it impossible for the murder of Agamemnon (despite what Aegisthus claims), no less than that of Cassandra, to be anything but a last-minute arrangement, for had Menelaus returned with Agamemnon, neither could Aegisthus have usurped the throne nor could Clytaemestra have got away with the killing of one brother.

45. Euripides' Heracles was prepared to kill everyone in Thebes for their ingratitude and consequent failure to defend his family against the tyrant; Hera could prevent it only by driving him insane (*Hercules Furens* 568–72).

46. Cf. J. A. Scott, *The Unity of Homer* (Berkeley: California University Press, 1921), 256.

47. Cf. Scholia HPQT on 5.81; Jordan, *Das Kuntsgesetz Homers*, 36–37 = K. F. Ameis-C. Hentze, *Anhang zu Homers Odyssee*[4] (Leipzig: Teubner, 1890), 130.

48. Cf. Scholia HPQ on 5.220; Eustathius 1578, 7–11, on 7.224–25: "The poet shows that if one has goods of this kind one would love one's fatherland, for otherwise one's fatherland is no big deal, since, as the proverb goes, 'every country is one's homeland wherever one would fare well.' Odysseus does not mention his wife here, so that not only he may not irritate Alcinous, who will pray that Odysseus be his son-in-law, but also because this would scarcely be important for happiness, for even ordinary people have wives."

49. Aulus Gellius *Noctes Atticae* 15.21; Plato *Laws* 908a4.

50. Plato *Symposium* 221c4-d6. That Alcibiades himself quotes a line from the *Odyssey* (4.242, 271), whereby he likens Socrates implicitly to Odysseus (220c2), should not be held against him, for Plato has Socrates on one occasion liken himself to Achilles (*Apology of Socrates* 28b9-d6). There is more to Socrates than either Achilles or Odysseus can encapsulate; cf. *Theaetetus* 169a9-b4.

51. In a comparable way, in the *Iliad*, where time seems suspended from Book II through most of Book VII, the burial of the Achaean and Trojan dead brings back time (VII.421, 433, 465), and Dawn spreads over the entire earth at the beginning of Book VIII: the line is repeated just before the obsequies begin for Hector (XXIV.695).

52. The first-line numbers of Odysseus's self-addresses are: 5.298, 355, 407, 464; 13.198; 20.17.

53. At *Republic* 441b6, Socrates cites 20.17. It is one of the few lines from Homer he quotes with approval in the course of the *Republic*.

54. Cf. Franz Stürmer, *Die Rhapsodien des Odyssee* (Würzburg: Becker, 1921), 118n5.

55. It is immediately after Odysseus talks to himself in the *Iliad* that he addresses a corpse (he is the first to do so), and declares that, while the Trojan Socus will be drawn and eaten by birds, the Achaeans will give him, if he dies, the proper funeral rites (XI.455).

56. Neither Nestor nor Menelaus uses the particle of doubt που in their narrative, but Menelaus employs it twice in conversation (4.110, 181); and nowhere does either say, "I believe," ὀίω or ὀίομαι.

57. Virgil, who has Aeneas quote part of Odysseus's words as our introduction to him, has him speak of nonburial (*Aeneid* 1.94–101); he does not mention the gods. Were Aeneas in the same position as Odysseus, he would now be leaving Dido and his regret would be more immediately intelligible to us; cf. Wendell Clausen, "An Interpretation of the *Aeneid*," *Harvard Studies in Classical Philology* 69 (1964): 147n1.

58. Cf. Scholium Q on 5.333.

59. Cf. Ulrich von Wilamowitz-Moellendorf, *Homerische Untersuchungen* (Berlin: Weidmann, 1884), 136.

60. That the human may be only the bestial or the divine emerges most plainly in the opposition of Laches and Nicias in Plato's *Laches*, where, in accounting for manliness (*andreia*), Laches goes with the beasts and Nicias with the gods (cf. 196a4–7, 197a1–5); see further *Phaedrus* 230a3–6.

61. VI.138; VIII.37, 468; XVIII.292; 1.62; 5.340, 423; 19.275, 407.

62. Cf. Carl Rothe, *Die Odyssee als Dichtung*, 105.

63. Cf. Scholia HPQ at 7.16; A. Kirchhoff, *Die homerische Odyssee*, 277–78.

64. That the Corcyraean episode is meant to be linked with olden times is indicated no less by the phrase κατὰ δὴ τὸν παλαιὸν νόμον (1.24.2)—the δή has its structural counterpart at 1.128.1—than by the use here of κλέος, which occurs again in its proper sense only at 1.10.2 and catachrestically at 2.45.2.

65. Cf. Herodotus 1.24.2.

66. Cf. Scholia HA (citing Heraclides Ponticus) on 13.119; Plato *Laws* 705a4–7.

67. Cf. Carl Rothe, *Die Odyssee als Dichtung*, 109. Rothe also suggests that the Phaeacians convey Odysseus at night in order to avoid detection by Poseidon (109n1).

68. Cf. Seth Benardete, "The First Crisis in First Philosophy," *Graduate Faculty Philosophy Journal* 18 (1995): 247–48.

69. Herodotus 1.8.3–4.

70. For the difference between speech and sight, see the discussion in Athenaeus (603 E-4 B), where Ion of Chios has Sophocles remark that though the poet speaks of gold-haired Apollo, a painting would be worse if the hair were not black but gold.

71. In light of the beginning of Plato's *Sophist*, where Socrates suggests that "stranger" is not an alternative of "god," it seems that Nausicaa expresses unwittingly the issue that Athena's plan raises and Odysseus himself comes to embody.

72. Plato *Sophist* 265e2.

73. At 7.305 the PT Scholia say: "It is extraordinary (*daimoniōs*) that he includes himself in the fault."

74. Cf. Scholia HA (Heraclides Ponticus) on 13.119: "It was reasonable for the Phaeacians to be afraid of Odysseus; for when it came to war he was the most uncanny of mortals on account of both his nature and his Trojan experience."

75. Cf. Eduard Schwartz, *Die Odyssee* (Munich: M. Hueber, 1924), 193.

76. On the first and third songs of Demodocus, see E-R Schwinge, *Die Odyssee-nach den Odysseen* (Göttingen: Vandenhoeck & Ruprecht, 1993), 139–49.

77. Cf. Ameis-Hentze, *Anhang³*, vol. 2, 25.

78. As Lessing showed in his *Laokoon*, chapter 16, by reflecting on the difference between Achilles' scepter (I.234–39)—presented to us in Achilles' own words as he wields it and swears by it—and Agamemnon's, which Homer has to describe (II.101–9), and on which Agamemon supports himself.

79. Cf. Scholia EV at 8.63.

80. Cf. Eustathius 1594, 35–36. As Plato's Athenian Stranger remarks on the Ganymede myth, a divine story may merely reflect and justify a human practice (*Laws* 636c7-d4).

81. Athena gets angry at an insult when she is disguised as Mentor; she takes it out on Odysseus (22.224–35).

82. That 8.22–23 is misleading would be no more significant than the false predictions in Euripides' prologues (*Bacchae* 50–52; *Hippolytus* 42).

83. Cf. Kammer in Ameis-Hentze, *Anhang³*, vol. 2, 49.

84. In the *Agamemnon*, Aeschylus has Clytaemestra give two speeches about the fall of Troy: the first glitters; the second is gloomy (281–316, 320–50). The first leaves the Chorus amazed and eager to hear another account; the second is about the joint suffering of Trojans and Achaeans, and leads the Chorus to praise Clytaemestra for her manly moderation (351). Although Clytaemestra starts out as if she is going to balance the wailing of the Trojans with the triumphal shout of the Achaeans (324–26), she fails to do so: it is left to the Chorus to supply it (355–61).

85. Ares and Aphrodite also symbolize the Trojan War in the first stasimon of Aeschylus's *Agamemnon*, where (367–474), after the first strophic system has asserted the justice of the war's outcome, the absolute right of Aphrodite (Menelaus's experience) is followed by the absolute right of Ares (the Argives' experience): their union is to be found in the illusory image of the beautiful (*eumorphoi*, 416, 454). In *Amores* I.9, Ovid begins by connecting playfully the warrior and the lover, but as soon as he departs from a strict parallelism—the killing of unarmed men in their sleep (21–22)—he brings in the story of Rhesus from *Iliad* X, continues with Achilles and Briseis from *Iliad* I and Hector and Andromache from *Iliad*

VI, and concludes with Ares and Aphrodite from *Odyssey* 8: what was at first a bit of conversational fancy proves to be in the end a necessary union through art.

86. The equivalent within the *Iliad* to the two bursts of divine laughter is to be found in the story of Hera's attempted seduction of Zeus (XIV.153–351). She first tries to bribe Sleep with a golden chair and footstool made by Hephaestus, but only the subsequent offer of one of the Graces succeeds. She thus acknowledges that "nature" is more potent than art and unwittingly anticipates her failure to lock Zeus up in her chambers, which Hephaestus made and fitted with a secret lock that no other god could open.

87. Herodotus reports that the Massagetae, among whom women are in common though each man has one wife, worship only one god, the sun (1.216.1,4).

88. The intelligent ships of the Phaeacians live on in the two sacred ships of the Athenians, the *Paralus* and the *Salaminia*, which, according to Thucydides, saw and reported on their own (αὐτάγγελοι . . . ἰδοῦσαι . . . ἔφρασαν) the presence of the Peloponnesians near the coast of Ionia (Thucydides 3.33.2; cf. 33.1): αὐτάγγελος is a poetic word.

89. Sophocles' Oedipus makes the people of Colonus experience the Fall; he compensates for it by bringing them knowledge. The Chorus's reaction to such a gift is to express the wish never to have been born, for the price of knowledge is suffering (*Oedipus Coloneus* 1224–235).

90. Plato's Athenian Stranger uses "Rhadamanthys" to designate the time when men believed, with all the vividness of daylight (ἐναργῶς), that the gods were (*Laws* 948b3–7).

91. The Ciconian episode does not belong to Odysseus's adventures proper, not only because there is nothing fabulous about it but also because it is planned from the start and belongs as an appendix to the Trojan War; cf. P. D. Ch. Hennings, *Homers Odyssee Ein kritischer Kommentar* (Berlin: Weidmann, 1903), 273.

92. Plato *Republic* 488a1–7.

93. Cf. Scholium Q on 9.44:

Homer contradicts himself. In the *Iliad* he introduces Odysseus striking even those soldiers who were not his (II.198–99, 189); and in doing so he persuaded. Here, however, he is not even able to rule his own . . . it is characteristic of a bad general to be despised. He was, then, neither a skilled speaker (otherwise he would have persuaded) nor great in reputation, for he was afraid. So he was not good, for they elected him. We, however, say [in reply to these charges] that straight after their victory his comrades gloried in their good fortune.

94. Homer speaks of suffering six times (1.4; 5.395 [simile]; 13.90, 92 [the forgetting of suffering]; 14.32 [counterfactual]; 15.232 [Melampous]; 19.464 [Odysseus's wound]). The word characteristic of Odysseus's sufferings is *kēdos* (anxiety, grief): nineteen out of twenty-seven instances refer to Odysseus, of which the most significant is 23.306. Pain (*algos*) occurs fifty-six times, and Odysseus has only twenty-one of them. Pindar says he suspects that the story of Odysseus was more than the suffering on account of sweet-voiced Homer (*Nemean* 7.21–24).

On *pēmata paschein*, see Ameis-Hentze, *Anhang zu Homers Odyssee*⁴ (Leipzig: Teubner, 1890), vol. 1, 26–27.

95. Cf. Scholia HA at 11.51.

96. "Nibbling" (ἐρεπτόμενοι) is used elsewhere in Homer only of horses (II.776; V.196 = VIII.564), fish and eels (XXI.204), and geese (19.553).

97. Plato's *Statesman* deals with the double meaning of "lawless" (*anomos*). The *Sophist* prepares for that discussion from the very moment the Eleatic Stranger speaks of his refusal to gratify his audience as "not fitting for a stranger" or, literally "strangerless" (*axenos*) and savage (217e5–7). In the *Laws* (679e6–680a7), the Athenian Stranger, after denying that people like the Cyclopes had any need for laws (*nomoi*) or legislators, says that they lived by following habits and so-called ancestral laws (*nomoi*). In arguing for the need of the compulsory power of law, Aristotle goes so far as to describe the common neglect of education in most cities as leading to a Cyclopean way of life (κυκλωπικῶς θεμιστεύων παίδων ἠδ' ἀλόχου), since everyone is allowed to live as he wishes (*Nicomachean Ethics* 1180a26–29).

98. Cf. P.D. Ch. Hennings, *Homers Odyssee*, 279 (Jordan); F. Focke, *Die Odyssee*, 179–80.

99. Dante, *Inferno* 26.94–99. Herodotus himself records a story about Lybians, who hybristic from their youth drew lots among themselves to see for themselves the wastes of Libya (2.32.3); cf. Eduard Fraenkel, *Horace* (Oxford, 1957), 270–72 on Horace 3.53–6.

100. Herodotus 1.1–5. Herodotus's own conclusion from the Persians' vain attempt to discover right in demythologizing myth is to express his conviction that human happiness involves of necessity injustice (1.5.3–4).

101. Cf. Reinhold Merkelbach, *Untersuchungen zur Odyssee* (Munich: Beck, 1951), 158n3.

102. Cf. R. Merkelbach, *Untersuchungen zur Odyssee*, 213n2.

103. Cf. Scholia Q and V on 9.263.

104. Cf. Scholium Q at 9.218. It seems not accidental that the issue raised here by the noncoincidence of order and right shows up in Plato's *Laws* as the possible coincidence of disorder and good in the case of drinking parties (640d9–e4).

105. Herodotus 2.52.1; cf. Xenophon *Oeconomicus* viii–ix.10. The complete identification of right, order, and truth is a notable feature of Old Persian *arta* (Avestan *aša*; Sanskrit *ritá*); see Wilhelm Brandenstein-Manfred Mayrhofer, *Handbuch der Altpersischen* (Wiesbaden: Otto Harrassowitz, 1964), 97–98; cf. Herodotus 1.136.1, 137.2–138.1. Herodotus (1.96.3–97.1) has the Mede Deioces first judge "in accordance with right" (κατὰ τὸ ὀρθόν), and then have his countrymen learn that his decisions came out "in accordance with what is" (κατὰ τὸ ἐόν).

106. 14.120–28, 362–65, 378–81; compare the variant reading at 4.83; cf. Plato *Cratylus* 421b1–3. In Herodotus (1.30.2), Croesus, in his praise of Solon, couples "wisdom" and "wandering" (σοφίης εἵνεκεν τῆς σῆς καὶ πλάνης) as if he were decompounding the verb "to philosophize," which he uses immediately afterward—and nowhere else—to characterize Solon (φιλοσοφέων).

107. Cf. Scholium Q on 9.229.

108. Homer mentions the Hippemolgoe as milk-drinkers and, if ἄβιοι is not a tribal name, the most just human beings (XIII.5–6; cf. Eustathius at XIII.6). Strabo 7.3 (279), in a wide-ranging discussion of ἄβιος, remarks that one would rarely find a man who lived alone without women to be "religious."

109. Though both Odysseus and Diomedes pray to Athena before they set out on their night expedition in the *Iliad*, only Diomedes promises a sacrifice (X.277–95).

110. Plato's Athenian Stranger cites 9.112–15 as evidence for a way of life he calls "dynasty" (*Laws* 680b1-c1); and he says of those like the Cyclopes that they were too naive to suspect a falsehood, which one now knows how to do on account of wisdom (679c2–5).

111. Plato has both Alcibiades and Socrates speak of the flute tunes of Marsyas and Olympus as having the power to stir and reveal those who are in need of the gods (*Symposium* 215 c2–6; *Minos* 318b1-c1; cf. Aristotle *Politics* 1340a8–12). What Homer managed to do was to bring this irrational experience into a logos through song. This consisted, according to Plato, in the translation of *nomos* as tune into *nomos* as law.

112. It is possible that Odysseus considers the evil pains with which Polyphemus is afflicted as the punishing aspect of necessity (9.440), for the two similes he uses to describe the blinding lend an air of precision to a messy job (9.384–94).

113. Plato's *Philebus* concerns the necessary cooperation of mind and nonmind if there is to be any good.

114. This argument is strengthened if one considers it possible that Homer did not know that οὔτιν (9.366) was an older form of the accusative of οὔτις: the name must be the nominative subject of some sentence if Odysseus's trick is to work.

115. Heraclitus seems to have been the first to formulate and exploit systematically this double aspect of speech (fr.1). Plato takes it up again in the Heraclitean *Cratylus*, where Socrates starts off by arguing for the simultaneity of the diacritical and didactic functions of a name (388b10–11).

116. Herodotus expresses this thought in his book on Egypt in the following way. He says the Egyptians avoid the adoption of all foreign customs (2.91.1), and throughout the second book whatever the Egyptians say is in reported speech except when they react in horror to the foreign (2.114.2, 173.2, 181.3). Isocrates, in praising Busiris for the establishment of an unchanging order of classes in Egypt, seems to hint that that is the decent equivalent to Polycrates' praise of Busiris for his killing and eating of strangers (*Busiris* 5, 15, 31). According to Plato's Megillus, cannibalism is merely the mythological version of ancient isolation (*Laws* 680d2–3).

117. One wonders whether Homer thought there was a connection, as some linguists now believe, between ἀλέγω (to care for) and λέγω (to speak).

118. Pierre Chantraine, *Grammaire homérique* (Paris: Klincksieck, 1953), 2, 333–34.

119. There are in Odysseus's narrative seven mentions of Zeus as an agent of his experiences in the ninth book (38, 52, 67, 111, 154, 294, 551–55), and three in the twelfth (399, 415, 416); the latter seem to be due to Calypso's information.

120. Eustathius (1621, 3–8) says he distrusts his crew after the Cicones and Lotus-eaters; cf. Scholium H on 9.173.

121. Cf. Scholium T on 10.34: "Why didn't he tell them? He did not expect them to be criminally suspicious, for he had made an equal distribution of the booty from Ismaros as well as of the wild goats and flocks of Polyphemus."

122. F. Focke, *Die Odyssee*, 183, describes the crew's speech as "what can almost be called a social-revolutionary protest." Aeschylus has the Chorus of the *Agamemnon* report a not dissimilar growth of resentment in the demos of Argos (449–51, 456–57).

123. Cf. Bacchylides 5.160–64.

124. If this interpretation is along the right lines, the evidently abbreviated form of the Laestrygonian episode would not require the postulation of an earlier and fuller version; cf. Karl Meuli, *Odyssee und Argonautika* (Berlin: Weidmann, 1921), 58. One might compare the absurdly brief report that Virgil gives, as if he were his own epitomator, of Aeneas's request for and receipt of aid from the Etruscans (*Aeneid* 10.148–56).

125. After he is blinded, Polyphemus addresses the assembled Cyclopes as friends (9.408).

126. Cf. P. D. Ch. Hennings, *Homers Odyssee*, 380; F. Focke, *Die Odyssee*, 193–95.

127. The difference between Odysseus and Homer seems to be indicated by the centrality of Circe in Odysseus's account of his nine adventures and the centrality of Hades in Homer's account of Odysseus's eleven adventures (cf. Friedrich Eichorn, *Homers Odyssee. Ein Fuuhrer durch die Dichtung* [Göttingen: Vandenhoeck & Ruprecht, 1965], 64). If Hades is taken as the center, then there is a kind of matchup between the series from Lotus-eaters to Circe and the series from Sirens to Phaeacians: the first and last are two "never-never" lands, Cyclops and Calypso are connected through the notions of not seeing and not being seen, Aeolus and Sun through disturbances in the "natural" order of things, Laestrygonians and Scylla-Charybdis through cannibalism, and Circe and Sirens through two kinds of knowledge. On the other hand, there are three stories each in books 9, 10, and 12, and, as has often been remarked, two short stories are followed by one long, Cyclops, Circe, and Sun. The sequence "mind," "nature," "cosmic god," if the long stories may be so summarized, recalls Homer's proem.

128. At the beginning of the seventh book of the *Nicomachean Ethics*, Aristotle opposes bestiality to what he calls heroic virtue—Hector exemplifies it (1145a2–22)—and at 1148b15–49a20 he mentions various kinds of bestiality, among which cannibalism is prominent.

129. Plato has Protagoras deny the truth of Odysseus's experience of the Laestrygonians; he makes him say that the most unjust man, if he lives in a city, is just in comparison to savages who live apolitically (*Protagoras* 327c4–d4).

130. I owe this way of putting the problem to Jacob Stern, with whom I have often discussed the *moly*.

131. At 10.306, there is an ancient variant, "but the gods know everything," possibly based on a reminiscence of 4.379.

132. Aristarchus athetized the line on the grounds that the body alone was altered, but the soul remained unchanged; but *thelgō* (enchant) does not normally mean to alter the body, and the Scholium V glosses it at 10.291 as "to alter the mind." Scholium T at 10.305 says that for Odysseus to take the moly means he took the complete logos.

133. Cf. the Heraclitean imitation Hippocrates *de victu* I.4: "Men trust their eyes rather than understanding (*gnōmē*), though the eyes are not competent to decide even about the things seen."

134. Plato and Aristotle likewise use "heaven" for "heaven and earth"; Plato *Statesman* 269d7–8; *Epinomis* 977b2; Aristotle *de caelo* 280a21. Timaeus, who begins his account with the equivalence of "heaven" and "cosmos," concludes that it has come into being because it is visible (*Timaeus* 28b2-c2), but that is precisely what it is not (cf. *Republic* 509d1–4). It is, however, only after such an intelligible unity is established that the question of cause can be raised: as long as the eclipse of the sun is treated apart from its shining, it is impossible to find the cause of both. Socrates seems to have proposed that such unities are themselves the causes. In Homer, only the first step has been taken; perhaps he thought there could be no second.

135. Heraclitus also means that disorder ("up down" means topsy-turvy) and order are one and the same.

136. On the suffix in φύσις, Émile Benveniste, *Noms d'agent et noms d'action en indo-européen* (Paris: Adrien Maissonneuve, 1948), 80, says it is "la notion abstraite du procès conçu comme réalisation objective"; and on Homeric φύσις, he offers the following characterization (78): "constitution (accomplie), nature effective: Ce terme si important se définit bien à l'intérieur de sa catégorie comme 'l'accomplissement (effectué) d'un devenir,' et donc comme la 'nature' en tant qu'elle est réalisée, avec toutes ses propriétés."

137. Cf. Scholium T at 9.33.

138. Cf. Plato *Phaedrus* 246c5-d3.

139. In light of the sequence Laestrygonians-Circe, it is perhaps worth recalling that Horace says the story that Orpheus tamed tigers and fierce lions signifies that he terrified (*deterruit*) men into abstaining from cannibalism (*Ars Poetica* 391–93).

140. In Socrates' myth in Plato's *Phaedrus*, men can choose to be beasts, but they can only use their partial vision of the hyperuranian beings if they can speak.

141. The Cyclops episode now takes on perhaps a deeper meaning. Polyphemus stands opposed to Odysseus. Polyphemus is essentially the lawless (*athemistos*) because he violates the prohibition against cannibalism. That prohibiton expresses the boundary the law as such establishes if man is to be man. The law determines this boundary negatively. As a negative determination, the law necessarily shows up as a manifold. This lawful manifold is contained in Polyphemus's name, "He

who is with many voices." Odysseus, on the other hand, in coming forward as nothing but mind names himself "No one": as the positive determination of man, mind does not allow for a lawful voice for itself. Plato's Athenian Stranger, at any rate, when he calls upon the legislator to translate the four goods of the soul into positive enactments, finds in the laws about marriage a passable equivalent to moderation, in the laws about education an equivalent to courage, and in the laws about private property and contracts an equivalent to justice, but he cannot match up mind or wisdom with anything else than with the laws about burial (*Laws* 631c5–32c4; 828c6-d5). In the *Epinomis*, when the Athenian Stranger determines what wisdom is, he begins by denying that it was wisdom, or at least the highest wisdom, which forbade cannibalism and established lawful food (975a5-b1).

142. Aeneas discovers the golden bough prior to his descent into Orcus and breaks it off against its will and contrary to instructions (*Aeneid* 6.146–48, 210–11). If in its utter unnaturalness it is meant to match contrariwise the moly, then Virgil seems to have understood the moly along the lines we suggested: Anchises denies to the Romans preeminence in the study of nature (6.849–50). In Petronius, after Encolpius and his gang have suffered shipwreck, they come ashore near Croton, whose inhabitants, they are told, are either corpses or crows (116.9; cf. 141.2, 11). If Croton is meant to recall the Laestrygonians, and Encolpius's loss of virility before "Circe" echoes Circe's power to unman Odysseus, it is remarkable that Encolpius reflects just before his encounter with "Circe" on the guilty conscience of those who live beyond the law (125.4). His earlier reflection was on the vanity of burial (115.17–19), but his subsequent restoration to "integrity" is due to Mercury, "who is accustomed to lead away and lead back souls" (140.12): despite his strictures, Encolpius had helped to bury his enemy Lichas (115.20–116.1).

143. In Ovid's *Metamorphoses*, man is given a human shape and mind at the beginning (1.76–88), but the difference between man and woman is not established prior to the story of Deucalion and Pyrrha, both in terms of character and origin (1.322–23, 411–15). A similar distinction shows up in Plato's *Timaeus*, to say nothing of *Genesis* 1.27 and 2.7, 21–24.

144. Since Proteus is who he is when asleep—τοῖος ἐὼν οἷόν ἑ κατευνηθέντα ἴδησθε (4.421)—and that state seems to be opposed to nature as awake in the togetherness of shape and mind, the possible unmanning of Odysseus might have to do with sleep rather than sex.

145. Cf. Plato *Sophist* 222b5-c2.

146. "Elpenor" could also mean "He on whom men hope"; cf. Ferdinand Sommer, *Zur Geschichte der griechischen Nominalkomposita* (Munich: Bayerischen Akademie der Wissenschaften, 1948), 175.

147. Circe's understanding of Odysseus's suffering, which she shows here (10.456–65), seems far deeper and more extensive than anything that Athena ever expresses (cf. 1.49, 190; 13.310). It seems that she knew about the Aeolus episode if as a result she taught him a complex knot (8.447–48).

148. Herodotus 1.47–48.

149. Virgil *Aeneid* 8.730–31. The *Aeneid* was once poised, as the *Odyssey* in its

own way still is, between a Republican past, which its first readers knew was gone forever, and an Imperial future, which they are told the early death of Marcellus has already canceled.

150. Cf. Plato *Cratylus* 399d10-e3.

151. Hesiod *Works and Days* 730.

152. Cf. Plutarch *quomodo adulescens poetas audire debeat* 16 F.

153. Cf. Wilhelm Büchner, "Probleme der homerischen Nekyia," *Hermes* 72 (1937): 107-8.

154. Virgil radically alters the meaning of the Homeric underworld by representing the reunion of Dido and her husband Sychaeus (6.472-74).

155. Only at 12.10 in the *Odyssey* is "corpse" (*nekros*) put in apposition to a proper name (Elpenor); in the *Iliad* such an apposition only holds for Patroclus and Hector (XXII.386; XXIV.423; cf. XVII.127).

156. For the juxtaposition of *sēma* as tomb and sign, see Plato *Cratylus* 400c1-4.

157. Cf. Scholium V on 11.130; Eustathius (1675,32-34): "clearly in order that Poseidon may be honored on land in regions to which his name has not carried, for there is also an ambition to be honored among those to whom one is not known"; cf. Franz Dornsheiff, "Odysseus's letzte Fahrt," *Hermes* 72 (1937): 351-55.

158. There is another expression, to eat one's heart (*thumon edmenai*), that should be taken into account: Odysseus uses it both before and after the Cyclops episode of himself and his crew (9.75; 10.143, 379). It seems to mean to be indifferent to the ordinary goods of human life (cf. XXIV.128-30), and thus to be connected with the suitors' indifference, on the one hand, to the rights of another in eating Telemachus out of house and home, and, on the other, with Polyphemus's indifference to the distinctiveness of being human. That distinctiveness would consist, according to Circe, who says Odysseus sits as if he were dumb (10.378), in speech.

159. Cf. Thucydides 3.46.2.

160. Cf. Manu Leumann, *Homerische Wörter* (Basel: F. Reinhardt, 1950), 124-27.

161. This recalls Euripides' *Medea*, where the Chorus of women who do not approve of Medea's plan to kill her children allow her to go through with it in order that she may go to Athens, where a female poet may finally sing of women's sufferings and truly console them (410-45; cf. 190-204). Their own inspired anapaests are inadequate (1081-90), and Euripides is not exactly the answer to their prayers.

162. The nine groups are formed on the basis of Odysseus's use of the expression "I saw."

163. This holds regardless of whether 11.454-56 are genuine or not; in their defense, see Kjeld Matthiessen, "Probleme der Unterweltsfahrt des Odysseus," *Grazer Beiträge, Zeitschrift für die klassische Altertumswissenschaft* 15 (1988): 34-35.

164. Cf. Euripides *Bacchae* 1316-322.

165. Plato *Philebus* 39e5-6.

166. That Sisyphus is *phusis* (nature) spelled backward is hinted at in Sophocles *Philoctetes* 1310–11: τὴν φύσιν δ' ἔδειξας, ὦ τέκνον, ἐξ ἧς ἔβλαστες, οὐχὶ Σισύ-φου πατρός (i.e., Odysseus).

167. This is to take 11.613 as saying that Odysseus wishes that the artisan of the shoulder-strap, which is terrible to look upon (11.609), had made neither it nor another.

168. Cf. Wilhelm Büchner, "Probleme der homerischen Nekyia," *Hermes* 72 (1937): 116–18.

169. Horace *Ars Poetica* 148–52; Plato *Republic* 382a4-c1.

170. Eustathius says, not badly, that the Sirens represent theoretical knowledge without action (1709,13–31); cf. Cicero *de finibus* 5.49: *vidit Homerus probari fabulam non posse si cantiunculis tantus irretitus vir teneretur; scientiam pollicentur, quam non erat mirum sapientiae cupido patria esse cariorem.*

171. Julian, in urging the total abstention from fish, says that we ought not to eat what we do not sacrifice to the gods; and he goes on to distinguish, in the face of a possible objection, initiatory rites, in some of which fish are sacrificed, from sacrifices honoring the gods, in which they are not. His explanation for this restriction is that fish are not grazed and cared for by us as sheep and cattle are (*Oratio* 5 [176E-77A Spanheim]). Athenaeus 325 A-D mentions several fish sacrificed to different gods (Hecate, Apollo, Hermes); cf. also 297 D-E, 309 D-E (Antiphanes). That eels are the only fish Homer ever names (cf. D'Arcy W. Thompson, *A Glossary of Greek Fishes* (London: Oxford University Press, 1947), s.v.) might be connected with the fact that eels and nameless fishes nibble at the fat of Asteropaeus, the only corpse ever eaten in the *Iliad* (XXI.203–4).

172. One would laugh no doubt if one read in an ancient Scholium that the meaning behind the consumption of the cattle of the Sun, of which there is no generation, and which do not waste away themselves (12.130–31), was the ultimate triumph of the Olympian gods; but Pindar's *Olympian* 7 concerns the difficulty of integrating the Sun fully into the Olympian order: in his narrative, Pindar has the emergence of Athena from Zeus (mind from mind through art) precede the emergence of Rhodes from the sea (seen by the Sun while the Sun was overlooked by the gods). Ovid makes the transition from the cosmic gods to the Olympian gods through the story of Phaethon (*Metamorphoses* 1.742–2.400): Epaphus, "who in Egypt is now at last believed to be born from Jupiter" and shares a temple with him (1.748–49), casts doubt on Phaethon's parentage, and by the end of the story it is established that Apollo is the sun (2.399), and Dawn is apart from the sun (2.113). Near the beginning of Horace's *Carmen saeculare*, it is the sun that is to look on Rome with favor. Toward the end it is Apollo (12, 65): Horace manages the movement by going from celestial time in the first triad to generational in the second, to seasonal in the third, to historical in the fourth, and the cancellation of time in the fifth; in the sixth there is a report of a divine decree about the future. That the movement from cosmic gods to Olympian or their like is not inevitable, the Egyptian treatment of Amun shows: he is initially "the hidden god," and his name is derived from *imn* (to make invisible), but he is later

identified with the Sun-god Reʿ (cf. Kurt Sethe, "Amun und die Acht Urgötter von Hermopolis," *Abhandlungen der Preussischer Akademie der Wissenschaften zu Berlin, phil.-hist. Kl.*, 1929: sections 22, 178–96.

173. Cf. Richard Payne-Knight, *Carmina Homerica* (Paris: Treuttel & Wurtz, 1820), page 104 of Notae: "On Odysseus's return to his country, attractive marvels failed the poet; a way of invention unsuitable to the poet's talent ought to have been applied; the poet himself became tedious; his powers are waning; the story languishes, with a clear narrative, it is true, but overlong and frequently interrupted by speeches or rather conversations, which, though they are carefully wrought and polished, still, by the triviality of their content and very frequency, are frigid."

174. Herodotus 2.118–20.

175. Cf. David Daube, *Roman Law* (Edinburgh: Edinburgh University Press, 1969), 166–67.

176. Odysseus says twice he will speak ἀτρεκέως (accurately) when he is about to lie (14.192; 24.303). No one else, except Athena (1.179), tells anything but the truth when he uses the formula. Only once does Homer himself say of anyone that he did not tell the truth (*alēthea*); it is Odysseus (13.254; cf. 18.342).

177. Cf. Plato *Republic* 620c3-d2. The import of Pericles' praise of Athenians (Thucydides 2.41.1), that individually they could assume with grace and ease the greatest number of human types (*eidē*), is displayed in Themistocles and Alcibiades, who, unlike Pericles himself, could be and be thought to be something beside Athenians, whereas Pausanias, on the other hand, went to pieces as soon as he departed away from home from Spartan ways (cf. Thucydides 1.77.6). As Arnaldo Momigliano observed, the possibility of biography depends on the realization that the fruit may fall far from the tree (cf. Plato *Laws* 642c6-d1).

178. Ameis-Hentze, *Anhang*[3], vol. 3, 16, cites XXIII.774 for a similar juxtaposition of a "natural" and a divine explanation. This is the first time that "appears" (φαινέσκετο) in the *Odyssey* means a deceptive appearance; it is also the first time that Homer calls Odysseus ἄναξ (lord); but the line is linguistically and metrically difficult.

179. Cf. Scholium V on 13.267.

180. Thucydides 1.9.3.

181. Plato *Republic* 372c2-e2; cf. Seth Benardete, *Socrates' Second Sailing* (Chicago: University of Chicago Press, 1984), 51–53.

182. 13.190–93 are corrupt.

183. Cf. Plato *Cratylus* 413b3-c1. According to Herodotus (1.99–100), once Deïoces had gained monarchical rule, he did not allow anyone to see him, and in having eyes and ears throughout his kingdom was severe in the maintenance of right.

184. It is possible that "Dolius" covers three different people—Penelope's servant, the father of Melanthius and Melantho, and Laertes' attendant—but it seems incredible that Penelope had another Dolius in mind than the last when she proposed sending a message to Laertes (4.735–38); cf. Harmut Erbse, *Beiträge zum*

Verständnis der Odyssee, 238–40. Dolius would be, among the servants, the counterpart to Aegyptius (2.21).

185. It is in accordance with this difference that Odysseus freely borrows lines for his lie more from the second part of his story than from the first: 14.256 = 9.78, 14.293–94 = 11.294–95, 14.302–4 = 12.404, 14.305–6 = 12.415–16, 14.308–9 = 12.418–19, 14.320 = 10.542.

186. Apart from his appearance in Demodocus' songs, "Ares" occurs in the *Odyssey* only once in the mouth of Homer: he likens the bully Euryalus to him (8.115); otherwise, only Odysseus and Athena speak of Ares (11.537; 16.269; 20.50).

187. Does his confession to Amphinomus that he committed many wicked things, yielding to force and violence, apply solely to the character he has assumed, or does it refer to the Trojan War (18.139–40)?

188. Cf. Scholium Q on 13.288.

189. Aristotle *Poetics* 1455b16–23.

190. In the *Iliad*, the withdrawal of the gods is signaled at the beginning of the sixth book, and its effects are manifest throughout Books VI and VII, until Poseidon calls the gods' attention to the ungodly behavior of the Achaeans, who in building the wall and trench did not offer famous hecatombs to the gods, and whose intent is to obliterate the glory Apollo and Poseidon won in building the walls of Troy (VII.446–53).

191. Cf. F. Focke, *Die Odyssee*, 8–9.

192. Cf. Eustathius 1867,12–19.

193. 17.150–65 are athetized in the ancient vulgate; but if, with the so-called fairer editions, the athetesis of 160–61 alone is accepted, then Theoclymenus prophesies without any sign at all.

194. On the form of Eidothea, cf. Harmut Erbse, *Untersuchungen zur Funktion der Götter im homerischen Epos*, 50. Theoclymenus in Euripides' *Helen* seems to be a reflection on Homer's. His sister Theonoe, whose original name was Eido, has direct knowledge of the gods, but Theoclymenus's indirect belief, once she is persuaded to lie, becomes of necessity the standard.

195. Cf. Wilhelm Büchner, "Die Penelopeszenen in der Odyssee," *Hermes* 75 (1940): 135–36.

196. Cf. Tacitus *Germania* 9.2: *secretum illud quod sola reverentia vident [Germani]*. Ameis-Hentze, *Anhang*³, vol. 3, 47, gives a complete list (with some misprints) of Homeric examples of νοῶ with participle plus object. The implicit distinction Homer seems to invite us to make, through the speech of Theoclymenus, between prophetic and poetic language, recalls the difference, in Aeschylus's *Agamemnon*, between the lyrical visions of Cassandra (1072–177) and her unveiled and nonenigmatic speech, which begins with two images, both of which δίκην introduces (1178–83), continues with her speaking of a chorus of Furies (1186–93), who are shown in their reality in the *Eumenides*, and ends with her asking the Chorus to confirm what she says; in her appeal she uses two technical terms of the Athenian court system in almost their strictest sense (1196–197). What

Cassandra takes to be an account of the past in Argos is a future in Athens informed by the union of poetry and law. Her speech predicts Aeschylus.

197. Plato *Statesman* 266b10-d3.

198. Cf. Aristotle *Rhetoric* 1380a25-30.

199. Eustathius (1694,16–18) explains the absence of the Trojans in Hades by way of the presence of Ajax with his still-smoldering resentment: if a fellow-Achaean would not speak to him, how could the Trojans even look at him?

200. Μελειστὶ ταμεῖν (to cut limb from limb) is used twice by Odysseus (and no one else), once of Polyphemus's cannibalistic preparations, once in threatening Melantho with what Telemachus will do to her (9.291; 18.339). The threat frightened all the women since they believed he was telling the truth (18.342). Homer does not say that of any of the suitors' threats. It tells us more about the Telemachus Eumaeus only hinted at (17.188–89).

201. It would seem that Odysseus in entering the contest is imitating Menelaus, whose challenge to Paris, in the third book of the *Iliad*, silently grants that he has to prove his right to Helen; but Odysseus may just be making sure that the bow is not defective before he turns it on Antinous. The phrase "great deed" (μέγα ἔργον) occurs eight times in the *Odyssey*; on seven occasions it is in the mouth of a character and expresses disapproval or dismay (3.275; 4.663; 11.272; 12.373; 16.346; 19.92; 24.458); Homer himself uses it here (22.408). In the *Iliad*, Odysseus asks Athena to support a great deed that will be a concern to the Trojans (X.282); and in Thucydides, Nicias speaks of the Sicilian expedition as a great deed (6.8.4).

202. Nothing perhaps is more illustrative of this popular shift than that that paradigm of wickedness, Aegisthus, was so careful to keep his hands clean when it came to killing the guardian-singer of Clytaemestra (3.269–71). Odysseus, in his scrupulousness, is comparable to Aegisthus.

203. The storybook character of *tisis* shows up in Herodotus's Persian account of the cause of the enmity between Greeks and barbarians, for the Persians can balance rights only at a distance: in the first round of tit for tat, not even the Persians say the Greeks who righted the former injustice knew of it; indeed, the Persians do not even know which Greeks evened the score (1.2.1). The tragic formula *pathei mathos* may be said to express the wish that the experience of right coincide with the pattern of right.

204. That Agamemnon put a singer in charge of Clytaemestra is fully in accordance with his ignorance of rule (3.265–68).

205. Cf. Aristotle *Rhetoric* 1380b22–25, quoting 9.504. In Aeschylus's *Agamemnon*, Cassandra's words, when she asks the Chorus to bear witness that a woman will die in place of a woman and a man will fall in place of a man (1317–19), exemplify the self-deception involved if one treats pattern as punishment (cf. 1323–26); and the difference in pleasure that Clytaemestra expresses in the killing of Agamemnon and Cassandra respectively exemplifies the difference between the punishment of the ignorant victim (Agamemnon) and the self-aware Cassandra (1385–92, 1444–47). Cassandra is a slave.

206. For μοι (20.19) there is an ancient variant τοι ("yours"); the received text

assumes the identity of Odysseus with his heart despite the split between himself and his heart; cf. Ulrich von Wilamowitz-Moellendorf, *Die Heimkehr des Odysseus* (Berlin: Weidmann, 1927), 189–90.

207. Cf. Seneca *Thyestes* 245–46. Cicero discusses at length in the fourth Catilinarian the issue of punishment and necessity; he seems to favor the execution of the Catilinarians as a matter of necessity and not, as Caesar had proposed, their punishment. He points out that punishment after death is a necessary belief if execution is to be treated as punishment (4.8; cf. Plato *Republic* 610d5-e4).

208. That Odysseus has not made a complete separation of anger from reason seems to be indicated by the second simile (20.25–27), for Odysseus's prior allusion to Polyphemus's cannibalism (20.19–20) strengthens the simile's implied connection between eating and killing. Likewise, Odysseus does not know that Homer has just likened him to a bitch when he speaks of his endurance of something "bitchier" (κύντερον) than the slave girls' shamelessness. Odysseus is, to exaggerate, what he believes he experiences.

209. Cf. Ullrich Wilamowitz-Moellendorf, *Homerische Untersuchungen*, 46.

210. Observe how he alters his standard epithet πολύτλας (thirty-seven times) into πολυτλήμων when he wishes to pass for an untiring slave (18.319).

211. Cf., e.g., Herodotus 4.201; Cicero *de officiis* 1.33; Ammianus Marcellinus 28.1.29.

212. Cf. Harmut Erbse, *Beiträge zum Verständnis der Odyssee*, 140.

213. According to Plato's Socrates, when Leontius saw corpses that had been publicly executed, he could not overcome his desire to see them, and rushing up to them, he said to his eyes: "O miserable wretches, get your fill of the beautiful sight!" (*Republic* 439e6–40a3).

214. In Aeschylus's *Agamemnon*, Agamemnon begins, in what he calls his proem to the gods, with the divine support of right, which cannot be understood as allowing for two sides, in the destruction of Troy, but he ends with the Argive beast, a lion that eats raw meat and licks the blood of Priam (810–29). In Sophocles' *Philoctetes*, the Trojan War diverged from right from the moment Philoctetes was abandoned; but the purity of right, which Philoctetes seems to represent—he is destined to restore right with the killing of Paris (1425–427)—is embodied in the utterly loathsome that has over time become at one with the beasts (226); even Philoctetes believes it would be only fair for the kin of the birds and beasts he killed to eat him: "It is a beautiful thing," he tells them, "for you to sate your blood-avenging mouth in thankful pleasure on my gleaming flesh (1155–57)." Life (βίος) is a gift (βιός) and not a right.

215. Γεύομαι (to taste) is always used metaphorically in Homer (XX.258; XXI.61; 17.413; 20.181; 21.98); but the context of its use at 17.413 brings it back to its original meaning. This kind of linguistic archaeology, which is always more than linguistic, is perhaps the characteristic of ancient poetry; cf., for example, the discovery of the double meaning of *kēdos* (marriage connection and grief) at Aeschylus *Agamemnon* 699. Plato's use of Homer in the third book of the *Laws* is perhaps the most striking acknowledgment that ancient poetry is essentially archaeology.

216. Eustathius (1918,50–52) mentions this explanation in raising the question of why Odysseus did not reproach the suitors for their attempt on Telemachus's life (22.36–38).

217. Cf. John Halverson, "Social Order in the *Odyssey*," *Hermes* 113 (1985): 142.

218. Cf. Scholia EHQ on 1.389. In comparing herself to the daughter of Pandareos, who now as a nightingale laments for her son Itylus, whom she killed thoughtlessly, Penelope seems to have in mind the danger Telemachus would run if she remarried (19.518–34).

219. One may compare the killing of the magi in Herodotus (3.79.2), which precedes the discussion about the best political order (3.80–82). Of the fifty-eight occurrences of the word "priest" in Herodotus, of which the first is at 1.140.2, all but two occur before 3.38, which ends with Herodotus's citation of Pindar's "Law is king of all": 3.38 concludes that section of Herodotus's logos that had begun with the story of Gyges (1.8). The two exceptions concern the Spartan Cleomenes, who has helots whip a priest (6.81).

220. Cf. Theodor Gollwitzer, *Zur Charakteristik des Dichters der Odyssee* (Kaiserslautern: H. Kayser, 1915), 24.

221. In *Nemean* 8, Pindar connects explicitly a kingship of the kind Odysseus had before the Trojan War with the gifts of Aphrodite (6–10); later, in the same poem, he contrasts the tongue-tied Ajax with Odysseus (24–27).

222. "Ordinances" (*themistes*) seems to be corrupt; *tomouroi*, an ancient variant of unknown meaning, is probably right. Strabo (7.7.11), who discusses the reading and says it designates the priests of Zeus at Dodona, does not accept it for Homer but says *themistes* is to be taken catachrestically.

223. The Chorus of Aeschylus's *Agamemnon* begins with this problem in the parodos. In their image, the vultures who have lost their nestlings do not have to do anything but appeal to the gods to have the late-avenging Fury punish the transgressors, but the Atreidae have to avenge the injustice on their own: Zeus sends them in order that he may inflict suffering on them no less than on the Trojans (48–67). Accordingly, the Chorus in the first stasimon wants the gods to punish Agamemnon and Menelaus (461–62); the Chorus has the people's backing.

224. The possible confusion between theta and tau in the spelling of "Theodorus" is Socrates' example in Plato's *Theaetetus* of the inadequacy of "true opinion with logos" as the unique characterization of knowledge (*Theaetetus* 207e5–8a3).

225. Cf. Hubert Schraede, *Götter und Menschen Homers* (Stuttgart: Kohlhammer, 1952), 225–28.

226. Cf. P. D. Ch. Hennings, *Homers Odyssee*, 596 (Liesegang).

227. Plato *Sophist* 264b1–2.

228. In the *Eumenides*, Aeschylus seems to suggest, by the acquittal of Orestes, that the terror of guilt does not belong, except through tragedy itself, in a democracy, and only the terror of the law survives there along with its agents, the Furies (cf. 690–706).

229. Cf. Harmut Erbse, *Beiträge zum Verständnis der Odyssee*, 140.

230. Cf. Ernst Siegmann, *Homer Vorlesungen über die Odyssee* (Würzburg: Königshausen & Neumann, 1987), 103–12.

231. Plato *Republic* 386c3–7, 516c8-d7.

232. The transposition of the real into the imaginary seems to be the theme of Pindar's *Isthmian* 8, where Thetis, who was destined to give birth to a god greater than either Zeus or Poseidon, were one or the other to marry her, is to look upon the dead Achilles instead (36), but the gods grant that the Muses celebrate him at his funeral, perhaps with this very song of a frustrated fate.

233. Aeschylus's Clytaemestra, by pluralizing the name of Chryseis (*Agamemnon* 1439), implies that the killing of Iphigeneia was just a means to fulfill the real purpose of the Trojan War, the rape of women, and Cassandra was the last willing victim in that enterprise.

234. Amphimedon uses the verb "to revile" (ἐνίσσω) by way of a zeugma to cover also the blows Odysseus supposedly received (24.161). This is of some importance for understanding Plato's *Gorgias* (cf. 478e3).

235. Cf. F. Stürmer, *Die Rhapsodien des Odyssee*, 543.

236. This bears more than a casual resemblance to the issue of Plato's *Sophist*. Nominative τοῖος or τοιόσδε, when used positively of animate beings, refers to Odysseus thirteen times (1.257, 265; 4.248, 342, 345; 6.244; 7.312; 14.222; 16.205; 19.359; 20.89; 21.93; 24.379); otherwise, once of Athena in disguise (2.286), of Proteus (4.421), of Ajax and Achilles in Hades (11.499, 501, 556), of Argus (17.313), of Telemachus (19.86), and of Laertes (24.379); the feminine τοίη is used once of Athena in a dream (4.826).

Index

About the Author

Seth Benardete is professor of classics at New York University. He is the author of *The Being of the Beautiful, The Rhetoric of Morality and Philosophy, Socrates' Second Sailing,* and *The Tragedy and Comedy of Life.*